Christian Koziol

Valuation of Convertible Bonds when Investors Act Strategically

Beiträge zur betriebswirtschaftlichen Forschung

Herausgegeben von

Prof. Dr. Sönke Albers, Kiel
Prof. Dr. Bernhard Pellens, Bochum
Prof. Dr. Dieter Sadowski, Trier
Prof. Dr. Martin Weber, Mannheim

Band 110

Die „braune Reihe“, wie die „Beiträge zur betriebswirtschaftlichen Forschung“ häufig kurz genannt werden, ist eine der bekanntesten und angesehensten Buchreihen ihres Fachs. Seit 1954 erscheinen hier besonders qualifizierte, oft richtungsweisende Forschungsarbeiten (vor allem Dissertationen und Habilitationsschriften) der jeweils „neuen Generation“ der Betriebswirtschaftslehre.

Christian Koziol

Valuation of Convertible Bonds when Investors Act Strategically

With a Foreword by Prof. Dr. Dr. h.c. Wolfgang Bühler

Deutscher Universitäts-Verlag

Bibliografische Information der Deutschen Bibliothek
Die Deutsche Bibliothek verzeichnet diese Publikation in der Deutschen Nationalbibliografie; detaillierte bibliografische Daten sind im Internet über <http://dnb.ddb.de> abrufbar.

Dissertation Universität Mannheim, 2003

1. Auflage März 2004

Lektorat: Brigitte Siegel / Sabine Schöller

Der Deutsche Universitäts-Verlag ist ein Unternehmen von Springer Science + Business Media.
www.duv.de

Umschlaggestaltung: Regine Zimmer, Dipl.-Designerin, Frankfurt/Main
Gedruckt auf säurefreiem und chlorfrei gebleichtem Papier

ISBN-13: 978-3-8244-9132-2 e-ISBN-13: 978-3-322-82016-7
DOI: 10.1007/978-3-322-82016-7

Foreword

The large volume of literature on convertible bonds addresses two basic complexes of problems:

- Why and under which conditions do firms issue convertible bonds?
- What is the fair value of a convertible bond?

Christian Koziol's dissertation deals with the second problem. His dissertation differs from the predominant part of the literature in two aspects. First, he explicitly considers the strategic character of the conversion decision, as the timing and the volume of conversion affect the wealth of the stockholders and the remaining convertible bond holders. Second, he deals with a more general capital structure, where the firm has subordinated debt outstanding in addition to convertible bonds and stocks. Within this setting, he characterizes and analyzes the optimal conversion strategy and the endogenous prices of convertible bonds, stocks, and the additional debt for three cases: all convertible bonds are held by a monopolist, the convertible bond holders act competitively, and the competitive bond holders are constrained to convert their bonds in one block. The third variant is typical for the option-theoretic valuation of convertible bonds that uses the typical high contact condition for American options.

Christian Koziol's dissertation makes a number of important and far-reaching contributions to the literature. Most of these new results are driven by the fact that a (partial) conversion results in a wealth transfer from the stockholders to the holders of additional debt. Some of the most important and partly counter intuitive results are:

- In the competitive case, there exists a unique Nash equilibrium in the total conversion volume. The corresponding value of the convertible bonds can be higher but never lower as its value in the block case. This result partly contradicts and partly extends the findings by Constantinides.
- In the monopolistic case, the optimal conversion strategy need neither be a unique nor a continuous function of its determinants, e.g. the firm value, the interest rate, the dividend or the face value of the additional debt.

- In the block case, it can be optimal not to convert even if the stock price before conversion is above the face value of the convertible bond.

This dissertation proves that in the classical framework of Corporate Finance there are still many interesting, unsolved problems. Preliminary results for callable convertible bonds show that the puzzling observation of the late calls can be explained without using the assumption of asymmetric information or market frictions.

I highly recommend this outstanding dissertation to every academic student doing research in Corporate Finance.

Prof. Dr. Dr. h.c. Wolfgang Bühler

Preface

This thesis is a result of my first four years at the chair of Finance at the University of Mannheim. It was accepted as dissertation by the School of Business Administration of the University of Mannheim in June 2003.

At first, I owe a substantial debt to Professor Dr. Dr. h.c. Wolfgang Bühler who initiated and accompanied this project during the whole period of time. Thanks to numerous inspiring and valuable suggestions by him and the plenty of time he spend on this project, the thesis improved substantially. In addition, I am grateful for many discussions on finance-related topics with him that sharpened my economic intuition beyond the quantitative formalism. Professor Dr. Peter Albrecht, who was the second advisor, also deserves my gratitude. I extend my thanks to the editors Professor Dr. Sönke Albers, Professor Dr. Bernhard Pellens, Professor Dr. Dieter Sadowski, and Professor Dr. Martin Weber for accepting my dissertation in the series 'Beiträge zur betriebswirtschaftlichen Forschung'.

A further essential factor for my work was the challenging and always helpful environment at the Chair of Finance. I acknowledged many useful suggestions by my current and former colleagues Dr. Martin Bardenhewer, Martin Birn, Jens Daum, Dr. Klaus Düllmann, Christoph Engel, Christoph Heumann, Gordian Kemen, Prof. Dr. Alexander Kempf, Jens Müller-Merbach, Stephan Pabst, Antje Schirm, and Prof. Dr. Marliese Uhrig-Homburg to all kinds of questions concerning the creation of this book. Special thanks go to Peter Sauerbier for the constructive cooperation on various finance topics and many insightful discussions not only related to finance issues. I extend my gratitude to Dr. Olaf Korn and Tim Thabe who carefully read the whole first draft and provided valuable contributions.

Also deserving a special mention are my parents Marianne and Wolfgang as well as my brother Philipp. Their enormous encouragement saved me from many efforts on other issues and allowed me to focus on this work. This is the reason why I particularly dedicate this dissertation to my mother.

Last, but by no means least, I want to express my endless gratitude to my lovely wife Sabine for accompanying all phases of this work and always having an open ear for my concerns. The way how she provided me with the feeling of familiar care and security was the key to the success of this work. Nevertheless, I hope that she will consider this common time period as a such nice time as I do.

Christian Koziol

Contents

List of Figures and Tables

List of Essential Symbols

$B_t(T)$	Value of a default-free zero bond at time t with maturity T
c	Coupon of a convertible bond
$C_t(\cdot)$	Value of a call option at time t
$cov(t,T)$	Covariance of $(\ln V_T, r_T)$ under the forward measure
$D_t(V_t^-, r_t, K_t, k_t)$	Value of additional debt at time t given a current and a prior conversion volume equal to k_t and K_t
$dif_0(V_0^-, r_0)$	Value of a claim at time 0 that pays $dif_T(\mathbb{V}, V_0^-, r_T)$ at maturity T
$dif_0(V_0^-, r_0, k_0)$	Value of a claim at time 0 that pays $dif_T(V_T^-, V_0^-, r_T, k_0)$ at maturity T
$dif_T(\mathbb{V}, V_0^-, r_T)$	Difference of the value of a convertible bond and a stock at maturity in the block case given a firm value $\mathbb{V}$ and a short rate r_T at maturity and a firm value V_0^- at time $t=0$ before conversion
$dif_T(V_T^-, V_0^-, r_T, k_0)$	Difference of the value of a convertible bond and a stock at maturity in the unrestricted case given a firm value V_T^- and a short rate r_T at maturity and a firm value V_0^- and a conversion volume k_0 at time $t=0$
Div_t	Dividend payment at time t
F	Redemption value of a convertible bond
FD	Redemption value of additional debt
$f_{t,T}(x,y)$	Density function of a bivariate normal distribution
k_t	Conversion volume at time t
K_t	Aggregate conversion volume prior to time t
k_t^*	Optimal conversion volume at time t
m	Number of issued convertible bonds
M_t	Value of normalized money market account at time t
$m_r(t,T)$	Mean of r_T under the forward measure conditional to r_t
$m_V(t,T)$	Mean of $\ln V_T^-$ under the forward measure conditional to V_t and r_t

$\max S_t(\cdot - bc)$	Short form of $\lim_{\substack{V_t^- \to \overline{V}_t(bc) \\ V_t^- \geq \overline{V}_t(bc)}} S_t\left(V_t^-, r_t, 0, k_t^*\right)(\cdot) - S_t\left(V_t^-, r_t, 0, k_t^*\right)(bc)$
$\max S_t(mc - uc)$	Value of the local maximum of the difference $S_t\left(V_t^-, r_t, 0, k_t^*\right)(mc) - S_t\left(V_t^-, r_t, 0, k_t^*\right)(uc)$ in V_t^-
$\max W_t(\cdot - bc)$	Short form of $W_t\left(\overline{V}_t(bc), r_t, 0, k_t^*\right)(\cdot) - W_t\left(\overline{V}_t(bc), r_t, 0, k_t^*\right)(bc)$
$\max^{(i)} W_t(mc - uc)$	Value of the ith local maximum of the difference $W_t\left(V_t^-, r_t, 0, k_t^*\right)(mc) - W_t\left(V_t^-, r_t, 0, k_t^*\right)(uc)$ in V_t^-
$\min S_t(\cdot - bc)$	Short form of $\lim_{\substack{V_t^- \to \overline{V}_t(bc) \\ V_t^- < \overline{V}_t(bc)}} S_t\left(V_t^-, r_t, 0, k_t^*\right)(\cdot) - S_t\left(V_t^-, r_t, 0, k_t^*\right)(bc)$
$\min S_t(mc - uc)$	Value of the local minimum of the difference $S_t\left(V_t^-, r_t, 0, k_t^*\right)(mc) - S_t\left(V_t^-, r_t, 0, k_t^*\right)(uc)$ in V_t^-
n	Number of stocks outstanding before time $t = 0$
N	Number of coupon dates
$P_t(\cdot)$	Value of a put option at time t
r_t	Risk-free rate at time t
$S_t\left(V_t^-, r_t, K_t, k_t\right)$	Value of a stock at time t given a current and a prior conversion volume equal to k_t and K_t
$S_0\left(V_0^-, -\infty, k_0\right)$	Short Form of $\lim_{r_0 \to -\infty} S_0\left(V_0^-, r_0, k_0\right)$
T	Maturity of the convertible bond
t_i	Conversion date
TD	Maturity of the additional debt
V_t	Firm value at time t
$V_{t_i}^-$	Firm value at a conversion date t_i before coupon or redemption payment
$var_V(t, T)$	Variance of $\ln V_T^-$ under the forward measure
$var_r(t, T)$	Variance of r_T under the forward measure
w_t	Value of a standard Wiener process that drives the short rate
$W_t\left(V_t^-, r_t, K_t, k_t\right)$	Value of a convertible bond at time t given a current and a prior conversion volume equal to k_t and K_t
$W_{t_i}^+\left(V_{t_i}^-, r_{t_i}, K_{t_i}, k_{t_i}\right)$	Value of a convertible bond after a conversion at date t_i including the coupon or redemption payment and given a current and a prior conversion volume equal to k_{t_i} and K_{t_i}
$W_0^+\left(V_0^-, -\infty, k_0\right)$	Short Form of $\lim_{r_0 \to -\infty} W_0^+\left(V_0^-, r_0, k_0\right)$
z_t	Value of the standard Wiener process that drives the firm value
$\overline{x}$	Critical value of x that separates the complete conversion region from the non-complete conversion region

$\underline{x}$	Critical value of x that separates the conversion region from the non-conversion region in the unrestricted or monopolistic case; in the block case it indicates a stock value given no conversion equal to the convertible bond value
(bc)	Indicates block conversion
(mc)	Indicates monopolistic conversion
(uc)	Indicates unrestricted conversion
δ	Dividend rate
$\Phi(\cdot)$	Distribution function of a standard normal distribution
κ	Speed of reversion
μ	Mean of the firm value return
η	Volatility of the short rate
ρ	Correlation between w_t and z_t
σ	Volatility of the firm value return
θ	Long term mean of the short rate
τ_i	Dividend date
$\mathbb{P}_T$	Forward measure
$\mathbb{Q}$	Short rate measure
$\frac{d\mathbb{P}_T}{d\mathbb{Q}}$	Radon/Nikodym derivative
$\left(\Omega, \mathcal{F}, \{\mathcal{F}_t\}_0^T, \mathbb{Q}\right)$	Filtered probability space

Chapter 1

Introduction

A convertible bond is like a corporate bond but with the added feature of being convertible into a specified number of stocks on the notice of its holder. Therefore, convertible bonds represent a complex instrument of corporate finance, as they contain elements of two different financing instruments, namely equity and debt. If the stock price is low and a conversion is unlikely, a convertible bond has the character of a straight bond, but it behaves like stocks when a conversion is very probable.

Convertible bonds were introduced into the German market at the beginning of the 1950's. However, the popularity of these instruments in the German market has passed through cycles over the last decades. In recent years, convertible bonds have regained their popularity which is documented by several considerable issues in the last four years and a nearly doubled annual issuing volume of 1.88 billion Euros in 2000 compared to 1.11 billion Euros in 1996.

The literature on convertible bonds comprises of two major research fields. The first field addresses the question of why firms issue these hybrid financial claims. Regarding conflicts arising from moral hazard, hidden information, or other frictions, the hybrid structure of a convertible bond is a convincing argument for the use of these securities. Under certain conditions, the issue of a convertible bond is superior to a straight bond, equity, and a mixture of debt and equity.

The second field of literature concerns the valuation of these securities. The standard approach to valuing convertible bonds decomposes the convertible bond into a straight bond plus an option to convert the bond into stock. In case of European convertible bonds, Ingersoll (1977a) presents a closed-form solution for the convertible bond value, as Black/Scholes option values can be applied to price the European option embedded in the convertible bond. When dealing with American convertible bonds, the embedded option is American-style for which generally no closed-form solutions exist. Nevertheless, the fact that all outstanding American call options on stock are optimally exercised at the same date suggests that this strategy, which is called *block conversion*, is also optimal for the American options embedded in an American convertible bond. For this purpose, the typical conversion assumption in standard valuation approaches is the block conversion for which Ingersoll (1977a) and Brennan/Schwartz (1977) are the two most prominent examples.

However, there is a fundamental difference between the exercise of an American call option on stocks and the conversion of an American convertible bond. In case of a sequential strategy, which means that some but not all calls or convertible bonds are exercised at a certain date, a conversion of convertible bonds might have a side effect on the stock value, where an exercise of calls cannot in any way affect the underlying stock price. The reason for the potential side effect on the stock price evolution by a sequential conversion is that the stock after conversion is related to a firm with a different capital structure consisting of more equity and less bond obligations. Consequently, the decomposition of a convertible bond into a bond plus an American option is no justification for the easily-applicable and often used block conversion, as it is not clear whether these side effects affect the optimal conversion strategy.

Modelling the optimal conversion strategy as the result of a game among convertible bond holders, we can analyze this side effect in detail. In this game, every particular convertible bond holder intends to maximize the value of her or his portfolio by selecting a feasible conversion volume and accounting for the decisions of the other convertible bond holders. Since the conversion decisions might affect both the value of a non-converted convertible bond and a stock, the wealth of every investor, consisting of non-converted convertible bonds and stocks from conversion, is affected by the individual strategy *and* the decisions of the others. Thus, the determination of the optimal conversion volume requires the solution of a sophisticated game.

One possibility for the evaluation of this game is to assume perfect competition among convertible bond holders such that each individual investor has no price impact on the stock or the non-converted convertible bond. This conversion variant considered by Constantinides (1984) and Emanuel (1983) is denoted by *competitive* or *unrestricted conversion*. A further possibility is to assume that one investor, a monopolist, initially holds all convertible bonds. This *monopolistic conversion* is presented by Spatt/Sterbenz (1988). Under these two conversion variants, sequential conversion strategies that differ from block conversion can be optimal. Therefore, the block conversion assumption cannot be justified to explain these reasonable equilibrium conversion strategies.

However, Constantinides (1984) shows that the value of a convertible bond under block conversion is equal to the highest feasible convertible bond value resulting from a Nash equilibrium under unrestricted conversion. This finding is based on the assumption that firms have only convertible bonds and stocks but no additional debt outstanding. Only few studies consider a framework in which firms have both convertible and straight debt outstanding.[1] However, the focus of these works lies in the computational challenge to determine the endogenous asset values but not in the determination of the optimal conversion strategy in a game-theoretical framework. This has been the general literature norm since the mid 1980's.

In this dissertation, we contribute to this literature by allowing the firms issuing convertible bonds to have additional debt in their capital structure. Though at first glance the consideration of additional debt appears like a marginal extension, the consequences for the optimal conversion strategy and the related values of a convertible bond are remarkable. In the presence of additional debt, there are two groups of passive participants in this conversion game, namely stock and debt holders, who are exposed to the conversion strategy of the active participants, the convertible bond holders. As the consequences of a conversion for the debt holders differ from those for the stockholders, the convertible bond holders must account for more effects caused by their decision. In general, a conversion results in a wealth transfer from stock to debt holders, because the firm's obligations are reduced and therefore the default probability declines. As a consequence, the value of a convertible bond under unrestricted conversion does not equal the convertible bond value under block conversion anymore, unlike the framework considered by Constantinides (1984).

The primary goal of this dissertation is to analyze conversion strategies and the related values of a convertible bond and the corresponding stock. For this purpose, we consider three conversion variants: the traditional block conversion, the unrestricted conversion that corresponds to perfect competition among the convertible bond holders, and monopolistic conversion which is the strategy of one investor who controls for all convertible bonds. An additional goal is to verify whether the valuation of convertible bonds and the determination of the optimal conversion volume can be achieved by following the market view that uses the stock value rather than the firm value as a state variable.

The dissertation is organized as follows. In chapter 2, we describe the importance of the German convertible bond market and focus on the prevalent characteristics of the traded issues. Then we review the motives for the use of convertible bonds and their standard valuation approaches and question the often imposed block assumption for valuation purposes by regarding empirical conversion data. This data indicates that empirical conversions do not take place in one block which motivates the need for the consideration

---

[1] See e.g. Brennan/Schwartz (1980).

of other conversion variants that can result in a sequential conversion.

In chapter 3, we specify the model framework on the basis of the prevalent convertible bond characteristics in the German market and derive the asset values independent of the underlying conversion variant.

Chapter 4 characterizes the optimal conversion strategy and the values of both a convertible bond and a stock at maturity of the convertible bonds. Even at maturity, we can see specific characteristics of every conversion variant. The unrestricted and monopolistic conversion variants can result in a different partial conversion volume that contrasts the block conversion.

Chapter 5 provides the analogous analysis for the last conversion date before maturity. At this date the conversion decisions are driven by other factors such as for example the dividend payment. We will see that the convertible bond holders under block and monopolistic, but not under unrestricted conversion, choose a strategy that might lead to a stock value that partly decreases with the firm value. This and further, perhaps surprising, properties exclusively stem from the existence of additional debt and its effect on the conversion strategy.

A comparison between the properties of the three conversion variants is conducted in chapter 6. One of the findings is that there is a ranking for the initial convertible bond value for the three conversion variants. The value in the monopolistic case is higher than in the unrestricted case and is lowest under block conversion.

In chapter 7, we present the corresponding analysis of the optimal conversion strategy, the asset values, and the relations between the three conversion variants over time. In general, the properties at an arbitrary conversion date before maturity seem to be the same as at the premature conversion date, but the corresponding considerations become much more complicated and not all proofs can be shown for an arbitrary date. This analysis shows that the differences between the convertible bond values and between the stock values for different conversion variants can attain a remarkable size.

Chapter 8 concludes.

Chapter 2

Convertible Bonds: Markets, Motives, and Traditional Valuation

2.1 The German Convertible Bond Market

Before we analyze convertible bonds in detail, it is useful to first gain an overview of the convertible bond market and the corresponding market usance. Therefore, the main focus of this section is to consider both the development of the German convertible bond market and the prevalent characteristics of the traded bonds. For this purpose, we consider 61 convertible bonds which were issued in the German convertible bond market in the period from 1952 to 2000. The data set consists of all those convertible bonds which are contained in the "Mannheimer Anleihedatenbank"[1] which is part of the Deutsche Finanz-Datenbank.

The term convertible bond comprises all corporate bonds that have the added feature of being convertible into a specified number of stocks. Depending on the convertible bonds characteristics, the stocks received from conversion do not necessarily stem from an increase of the share capital, but a conversion might also be possible into already existing stocks. To differentiate between the consequences of a conversion on the firm's capital, we distinguish between

- *Classic Convertible Bonds* which require a conditional capital increase as stated in § 221 AktG (Deutsches Aktiengesetzbuch)
- and *Synthetic Convertible Bonds* whose conversion does not affect the firm's share capital.

---

[1] This database is the result of a project of the Deutsche Forschungsgemeinschaft (DFG). For further insights about this project see Bühler/Göppl/Möller (1993).

Classic convertible bonds according to our classification are convertible into *new stocks* of the issuing firm such that a conversion of these instruments requires an increase of the share capital of the firm. Because of this possible increase of the firm's nominal capital, an issue of this type of convertible bonds requires a conditional capital increase which has to be approved by the shareholders general meeting with a 75 percent majority of the voting rights. As a result of a possible dilution of stocks arising from an issue of convertible bonds, subscription rights for the convertible bond might be granted to the stockholders.

Synthetic convertible bonds can be settled either by a conversion into *existing stocks* or a *cash settlement payment* which depends on the current stock price. Bonds of the first type are also called *exchangeable convertible bonds.* The stocks received by conversion do not necessarily stem from the same firm that has issued the bond. For example Berliner Elektro Finance, Deutsche Finance, and Dresdner Finance issued exchangeable convertible bonds that were convertible into existing stocks of Semiconductor Industries, Allianz, and Münchner Rück, respectively. The purpose of these issues was to sell a significant position of these stocks without suffering from a negative market impact. Examples for exchangeable convertible bonds that can be converted into stocks of the same firm are the recent issues of Bayer, Henkel, Siemens, and Volkswagen. The convertible bond issued by Kamps in 2000 represents a convertible bond that is settled by a payment equal to a specified factor times the current stock price.

2.1.1 Development of the German Convertible Bond Market

Convertible bonds have been traded on the German market for many decades. Strictly speaking, the German convertible bond market, considered below, comprises of convertible bonds which were issued by German firms or their foreign subsidiaries and denominated in Deutschmark or Euro. During this time period, the popularity of these instruments has been passing through cycles.

Figure 2.1 shows the number of convertible bonds issued from 1952 to 2000. We can see that after only a few issues at the beginning of the 1950's, the interest in convertible bonds grew between the end of the 1960's and the beginning of the 1970's. At the beginning of the 1960's and from the middle of the 1970's to the middle of the 1990's only isolated convertible bond issues were placed. Since 1996, the German convertible bond market has regained its popularity in particular for synthetic bonds. A reason for the latest interest might be the market environment which was characterized by a bullish stock market and low interest rates during these years. In a bullish stock market, convertible bond issuers enjoy the good marketability of convertible bonds and investors are more willing

Figure 2.1: Number of Annual Convertible Bond Issues at the German Market

The figure shows the number of German convertible bond issues of our sample on a yearly basis for the period from 1950 to 2000. The grey and white bars distinguish between classic and synthetic convertible bonds, respectively.

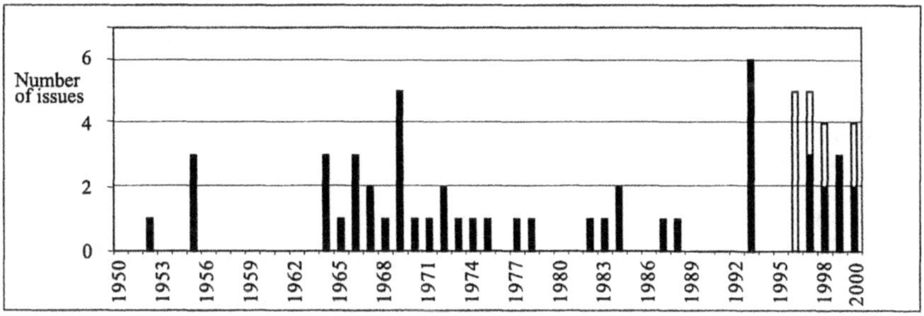

to accept higher risks by investing in convertible bonds when the risk-free alternative yields low returns.[2]

The relatively large number of German convertible bond issues in the late 1990's becomes even more striking if we consider the annual issuing volume in figure 2.2. According to figure 2.2, we can see that the issuing volume has increased over time more sharply than the number of issues. Thus, the average issuing volume must have increased over the last decades. This increase is further evidence for the rising importance that convertible bonds have gained over the years. The entire European convertible bond market and the US-American convertible bond market exhibit a similar trend. The European market capitalization of convertible bonds has tripled from 1995 to 2000, while the US-American market capitalization has approximately doubled.[3] For comparison, the growth of the market capitalization of the entire European non-government bond market for the same time period from 1995 to 2000 is only around 17 percent.[4]

2.1.2 Characteristics of German Convertible Bonds

To formulate a model framework that is capable of capturing all relevant characteristics of German convertible bonds, it is reasonable to first regard the main features of the

2 See Wolf (1999).

3 See Bohn (2001), p. 111.

4 See Bank for International Settlements (2001).

Figure 2.2: Annual Issuing Volume of Convertible Bond Issues at the German Market

The figure shows the issuing volume of German convertible bond issues of our sample on a yearly basis for the period from 1950 to 2000. The values are denominated in billion Euros. The grey and white bars distinguish between classic and synthetic convertible bonds, respectively.

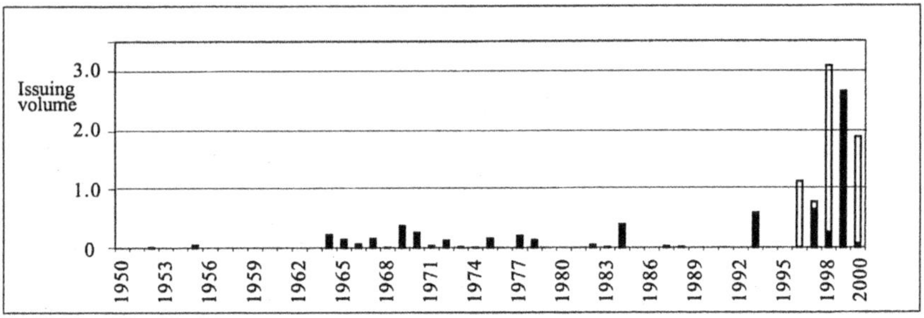

convertible bonds of our sample. Since convertible bonds are like a straight corporate bond that promises coupon and a face value payment at fixed dates plus the added feature of being convertible into stocks, we will characterize a convertible bond by the following terms: conversion conditions, issuing volume, maturity, coupon, bankruptcy rule, right to call or to put, and anti dilution clause. In what follows, we focus on classic convertible bonds and exclude synthetic ones for the reason that a conversion of classic rather than synthetic convertible bonds affects the firms share capital. These particular side effects of a conversion are an important and challenging component of the theory in the following chapters, as without the capital increase from a conversion the analysis simplifies considerably.[5]

Conversion Conditions The conversion feature, that distinguishes a convertible from a straight bond, is typically expressed by the *conversion price.* The conversion price indicates the stock price of the obtainable stock measured in units of the convertible bond's face value.[6] If an investor converts, she or he gives up a face value claim per received stock equal to the conversion price. Thus, we can interpret the conversion price as the costs per converted stock measured in units of forgone face value. In the special

---

5 Nevertheless, we can do the same theoretical analysis for synthetic convertible bonds with similar techniques as we will do for the classic convertible bonds, but the consequences are less complex and interesting.

6 See Calamos (1998), p. 25.

case that a conversion requires a conversion payment, the prorated conversion payment increases the conversion price. Though the *conversion ratio*, which states the number of stocks that are obtained by converting one convertible bond, is also an intuitive convertible bond parameter, the conversion price is generally documented in the convertible bond's prospectus. Given the conversion price, the conversion ratio of convertible bonds with no conversion payment results from the convertible bond's face value divided by the conversion price. We note that the conversion price is a specified term of a convertible bond that differs from the *conversion value*. The conversion value represents the equity portion, i.e. it equals the value that a convertible bond would be worth if it were converted into stock promptly.

If a conversion takes place, all coupon and redemption rights embedded in the bond are promptly lost and the investor receives a specific number of stocks in return. Typically, convertible bonds are convertible at any point in time during their maturity. However, they exhibit two blocking periods in which no conversion is possible in each year. The first blocking period concerns the time around the annual shareholders' general meeting. This clause is supposed to simplify the determination of the relevant number of total voting rights in the annual meeting. The second blocking period is at the end of every year. Its length ranges from two weeks to one month. Moreover, a further blocking period can be at the beginning of the convertible bond's lifetime. Firms can use this third blocking period to prevent conversions from taking place too early.

An important feature of the conversion conditions concerns the dividend rights of the stocks received from a conversion. The conversion prospectus of convertible bonds state that the stocks obtained from a conversion are entitled to the whole dividend payment for the accounting year in which the conversion is in effect. Usually, but not always, the accounting year coincides with the calendar year. Since the dividend of a certain accounting year is always paid to the stockholders in the succeeding accounting year, the stock from a conversion is qualified for dividend payments from the first year after conversion on. As a consequence, if a conversion occurs at the beginning of the year before the dividend payment, the stock that arises from a conversion will be of a certain class that does not participate in any part of the upcoming dividend payment.

Another point that the conversion conditions determine is the class of stocks that can be received by a conversion. In our data sample of German Convertible bonds, we find examples that allow for conversions into common stocks or others that allow for conversions into preferred stocks. In few examples, e.g. Klein, Schanzlin & Becker of 1983 and Fuchs Petrolub of 1997 the issues were convertible into a combination of both common and preferred stock.

Some convertible bonds require an additional payment at conversion. Primarily, the older issues are equipped with this feature. In our sample data, we can find convertible bonds that have an increasing, a decreasing, or a constant conversion payment schedule over time. As a result of a conversion payment, the conversion price of a convertible bond can vary over time, but the conversion ratio is constant in all considered examples.

Issuing Volume The issuing volume, defined as the total face value of a convertible bond issue, can vary considerably among the considered convertible bond issues. In particular, it lies between 1.4 million and 2 billion Euro found for the issues of Isar-Amperwerke of 1967 and Mannesmann of 1999, respectively. The mean and the median of the issuing volume are 224 million and 76.7 million Euro. This relation between the mean and the median indicates that there are few issues with an especially large volume. The issuing volume primarily depends on the capital demand of the corresponding firm and the marketability of the particular convertible bond issue. Evidence for the improving marketability of convertible bonds in the course of the last decades is the increase of the mean issuing volume. The mean issuing volume per decade has steadily grown from 13 million Euro in the 1950's to 345 million Euro in the 1990's with stagnation in the 1980's.

Maturity The maturity of a convertible bond denotes the length of the time period from the issue date to the redemption date. The maturities of the convertible bonds in our data sample vary from 5 to 19 years observed for the issues of e.g. Fuchs Petrolub of 1997 and Mannesmann of 1955. The mean and median maturity are 9.1 and 9 years. We find that the mean maturity of the convertible bond issues has changed over time. Convertible bonds issued in the 1950's have a long maturity of more than 15 years, but the more recent issues from the 1990's show a short maturity, of five years in most cases. The fixing of a convertible bond's maturity from the perspective of the issuer essentially depends on two points. First, the conversions occurring in the future and the related increase of the firm's equity might depend on the maturity. The shorter the maturity, the earlier the conversions might occur in many cases, as conversions are forced at maturity if the conversion value is higher than the redemption value. Second, the maturity and the related capital commitment can be selected with regard to expected re-financing terms. In this case, the maturity depends on the firm's expectations about the future evolution of the interest rate curve.

Coupon All convertible bonds in the sample have an annual coupon payment. Typically, the convertible bonds are equipped such that the coupon payment is made on January 2. In case of a conversion, the coupon right is lost and no accrued interest is due. The magnitude of the coupons ranges from one to twelve percent found for the issues of e.g. Metro in 1998 and Girmes of 1974. The mean and median magnitude of the coupon is 4.7% and 5.5%, respectively.[7] However, the coupon payment is not always constant over time. For example the Bayer convertible bonds from 1965 and 1969 have a coupon with a dividend-dependent and a fixed component.

Many firms choose the coupon such that the expected issue price of the convertible bond is slightly below par. Evidently, the more attractive the conversion feature embedded in the convertible bond, the lower the required coupon payment to obtain a given issuing value.

Bankruptcy Rule In case of an insolvency proceeding, convertible bond holders are treated as other creditors rather than like stockholders.

In our data sample, we find that German convertible bonds are generally equipped with a fairly high collateral. Special examples for a collateral are a mortgage (Hypothek) or a land charge (Grundschuld). Especially, older issues are characterized by these features. For example the convertible bond issued by Aschaffenburger Zellstoffwerke in 1955 was equipped with a Hypothek. A Grundschuld was included in the issues of Mannesmann of 1955, Eisenwerk Wülfel of 1966, Klein, Schanzlin & Becker of 1983, and Pfaff of 1984.

The widespread characteristic of the more recent convertible bonds to protect their holders is the embedded negative pledge clause. This negative pledge clause prohibits the firm to issue new debt with a better seniority than that of the convertible bond. Since the middle of the 1980's, only few issuers did not make use of the negative pledge clause. This market usance of German convertible bonds is evidence for the fairly high seniority of convertible bonds.[8]

Right to Call or to Put A call right entitles the issuer to buy back the convertible bond at a specified call price. In the German convertible bond market, only less than half of the issued convertibles have an issuer call feature. In general, a call must be notified by the issuer between 30 to 90 days prior to the effective call date. This time period between the notice and the call date is required to allow the convertible bond holders to convert before the convertible bonds are redeemed at the call date.

Similar as for a conversion, there can be a blocking period for the call right which is called a call protection. Moreover, the right to call might be in effect only if the stock value

---

7 The mean and the median relate to those convertible bonds with a fixed coupon payment.

8 Several firms issue convertible bonds via a subsidiary for tax reasons. Since in all considered cases the parent company guarantees the convertible bond, we can economically think of this structure as a direct issue from the holding company.

is sufficiently high. For example the issues by Didier of 1962, Berliner Elektro of 1996, and Dresdner Bank of 1996 require that the conversion value at the call date exceeds the conversion price of a convertible bond by more than 20%, 40%, and 30%, respectively.

The call price does not necessarily have to be equal to par over the whole maturity of the convertible bond. The issues of Hoechst from 1967 and 1970, Bayer from 1965 and 1969, and Commerzbank from 1972, for example, have a call price starting from 105% at the beginning that successively tends to par in five equidistant steps.

There are two reasons to implement such a call right. The major reason is that it gives the issuer the possibility to force a conversion. If the conversion value is higher than the call price, a call of the issuer results in a conversion of the convertible bond and in an increase of equity given that the convertible bond holders act rationally. A less important reason for the call feature is that the firm can call the convertible bond to benefit from more favorable refinancing conditions in the fixed income market. If current interest rates are very low, the firm might call the convertible bond and benefit from these interest rates by issuing a new convertible bond at more favorable conditions. There is much literature on the optimal call policy[9], how US-American convertible bond issuers call their bonds[10], and why the stock price suffers a drop caused by a call.[11]

The put right is the opposite to the call right. It entitles the convertible bond holder to sell the convertible bond at a specified price to the issuer. The put right is a very rare feature for German convertible bonds. In our sample, only Metro has implemented such a put feature in the convertible bond issue of 1998. The put terms are such that the convertible bond holders can sell their holdings after five or ten years at a put exercise price that ensures a yield to maturity equal to 3% p.a. Furthermore, some firms provide their convertible bond holders with an extraordinary put right. For example, the Mannesmann convertible bond from 1955 is putable if a convertible bond holder is not satisfied with the new conversion conditions after a certain corporate action. In addition, the more recent convertible bonds also have an extraordinary put feature in case of an insolvency proceeding.

Anti Dilution Clause An anti dilution clause is a protection of the convertible bond holders' wealth against an extraordinary stock price decline after a corporate action by

---

9 See Ingersoll (1977a), Butler (2002), and Kwok/Wu (2000).

10 See Asquith (1995), Asquith/Mullins (1991), Constantinides/Grundy (1987), Dunn/Eades (1989), Harris/Raviv (1985), Ingersoll (1977b), Jalan/Barone-Adesi (1995), King/Mauer (2000), and Mauer (1993).

11 See e.g. Bechmann (2000), Bhabra/Lee/Patel (1997), Byrd/Moore (1994,1996), Datta/Iskandar-Datta (1996), Ederington/Goh (2001), Kim/Kallberg (1998), and Mikkelson (1981).

an objective adjustment of the conversion conditions. The reasoning behind the anti dilution clause is that the value of a convertible bond is supposed to be only affected by changes of market values but not by the execution of corporate actions. Typical examples for corporate actions that affect the stock value are changes of the equity such as stock issues, issues of additional convertible bonds or warrants.

There are three different ways of how the conversion conditions are adjusted in case of an increase in share capital with subscription rights for the new shares. The first possibility is that subscription rights are also granted to the convertible bond holders on a pro rata basis. In this context, convertible bond holders are treated as if they already had converted their bonds. This adjustment was a widespread mechanism for convertible bonds issued in the 1950's and 1960's. The second possibility is to reduce the conversion price by the corresponding values of the subscription rights. In our data sample, we find this clause primarily for convertible bonds in the 1960's and 1970's. The third popular way to protect convertible bond holders from an increase of capital is to adjust the conversion price such that the new conversion price is a convex combination of the former conversion price and the issuing price of a new share.

In contrast to European call options for which an optimal anti dilution clause exists,[12] these three clauses for convertible bonds do not provide the suitable protection. In the case of the first presented adjustment, in which the subscription right is granted to the convertible bond holders promptly, the convertible bond holders might be overcompensated in case of an equity issue. The reason is that they obtain the value of the subscription rights for every stock they can receive by a conversion and not only for those stocks they in fact receive. Especially if a conversion is never optimal, the convertible bond holders' wealth is nevertheless increased by the value of the subscription rights.

In the second case, the effective number of granted subscription rights corresponds to the real conversion volume, but the convertible bond holders benefit from the value of these rights too late, namely at the conversion date rather than the date of the capital increase. Therefore, we can think of this disadvantage as the result of capital costs for the time period between the capital increase and the conversion. As a consequence, in the second case the convertible bond holders can be undercompensated.

The third mechanism provides an appropriate protection in several but not all cases. In some cases the capital increase can be in favor of the convertible bond holders, but in other cases it can be at the cost of the convertible bond holders. Whether or not convertible bond holders benefit ultimately depends on the relations between the current stock value, the issue price of a new stock, and the former conversion price.

---

12 See Merton (1973).

Some recent synthetic convertible bonds have an anti dilution clause different from those used for classic convertible bonds which provides a perfect protection.

2.2 Motives for the Use of Convertible Bonds

If a firm takes a convertible bond issue into consideration, the first step must be to evaluate the reasons for such an issue. Only after this analysis and the determination of the appropriate convertible bond features, the question about the value of this prospective convertible bond issue arises. Therefore, we first examine the question why firms issue convertible bonds and why investors buy these instruments in detail. We will find that convertible bonds represent interesting financing alternatives with numerous advantages compared to traditional financing alternatives like equity or debt issues or a combination of both. Then, in the next section we review the prevalent approaches to valuing convertible bonds.

It is an obvious reason to use convertible bonds whenever the issuer or potential investors desire a financing product with the risk/return profile of a convertible bond. However, this is only a sufficient reason and it does not necessarily require the existence of convertible bonds as long as the same payoffs can be created by other instruments. Strictly speaking, in a perfect market environment of a frictionless and complete market without any information asymmetries, there is no need for convertible bonds, as other financing alternatives are equally good. For example, if the firm wanted to issue a convertible bond, it could alternatively follow a self-financing replicating portfolio strategy by issuing equity and debt and continuously adjusting its capital structure. Therefore, there are no benefits associated with a convertible bond issue under these assumptions that cannot be achieved otherwise. In other words, there must be some frictions concerning the investors or the issuer to justify the superiority of convertible bonds compared to an equity/debt issue. Against this background, we will discuss especially those motives for convertible bonds that reveal the strict superiority relative to standard equity/debt issues and therefore require frictions.

2.2.1 Traditional Reasons

The two most prominent reasons for the use of convertible bonds are the *delayed-equity* and the *sweetened-debt* character of convertible bonds.[13] The delayed equity feature expresses

[13] See Brennan/Schwartz (1988), p. 55, Nyborg (1996), p. 182-183, Pilcher (1955), p. 59, Billingsley/Smith (1996), p. 94, Broman (1963), p. 74-75, Heubel (1983), p. 75, and Nyborg (1995), p. 358.

the possibility to raise equity with a convertible bond issue in the future. The advantage of a convertible bond in this context is that in case of a future conversion, stocks are issued with a certain premium relative to its current value. Typically, convertible bonds have a conversion value below their conversion price at the issue date. Thus, a future conversion has the character of an equity issue at a premium relative to the current conditions.[14] The sweetened-debt feature states that a bond becomes more attractive for investors by the embedded conversion right. Consequently, the firm can achieve lower coupon and/or face value payments compared to a straight bond and still obtains the same issue price as with the straight bond.

Again, we must be aware of the fact that these two reasons are no convincing arguments for the need of convertible bonds in a frictionless and complete market without information asymmetries.[15] The possibility for an increase of equity with a premium also exists without convertible bonds. A simple alternative is to issue straight debt first and to issue equity after a favorable stock value performance. Furthermore, the lower coupon and/or redemption obligations are only a result of a compensation of the investors in form of the conversion right. However, the delayed-equity and the sweetened-debt property of convertible bonds can serve as a plausible argument for convertible bonds, if we impose some reasonable frictions.

A possible friction is that firms prefer a higher price/earnings ratio independent of the real stock value. If it is the goal of a firm to raise capital via equity for a costly investment without accepting an unfavorable price/earnings ratio at the beginning, a convertible bond is a reasonable financing instrument.[16] In particular, such firms can use a convertible bond to execute an investment with high initial costs. Since conversions are not supposed to occur before the investment starts to pay off, the price/earnings ratio does not suffer from a dilution of the stock value before the earnings increase. However, the alternative to raise equity directly would depress the price/earnings ratio substantially at the beginning.

The sweetened-debt property, i.e. to make a bond more attractive for the market, is especially appreciated by highly levered firms that otherwise could not raise additional capital by straight debt. Thus, the friction is that the firm cannot sell additional straight debt even though it has a positive value. Furthermore, firms that suffer from high bankruptcy costs[17] and underpriced stocks due to information asymmetries can benefit from a con-

---

14 See Pilcher (1955), p. 62, Brigham (1966), p. 51, Fabozzi/Pollack (1987), p. 454, Ross/Westerfield (1988), p. 542, and Ross/Westerfield/Jordan (1991).

15 See Brennan/Schwartz (1988) and Lewis/Rogalski/Seward (1998b), p. 45.

16 See Pilcher (1955), p. 80, Brigham (1966), p. 51, and Fabozzi/Pollack (1987), p. 452-453.

17 Bankruptcy costs denote the current value of the proportion of the firm value that is not distributed to any shareholder when the firm goes bankrupt.

vertible bond, because the bankruptcy costs can be substantially reduced compared to a straight debt issue, on the one hand,[18] and stocks are only issued at a premium and not at the current underpriced levels, on the other hand. Moreover, the lower coupon and/or redemption payments relative to a straight bond result in a lower default probability because the danger of a failure to pay declines. As a consequence, the incentive for a costly under-investment by forgoing profitable investments to avoid a default and reduce bankruptcy costs also decreases.[19]

2.2.2 Moral Hazard Conflicts

A further important reason to use convertible bonds is to mitigate the risk incentive conflict (or also called asset substitution problem) that exists between shareholders, on the one side, and the other stakeholders of the firm, on the other side. This conflict is especially visible in a firm that has only equity and debt outstanding. In such a firm a moral hazard problem exists because a higher volatility of the firm value increases the stock value at the cost of the debt value.[20] Thus, if the managers act in favor of the stockholders, they might increase the volatility of the firm value (e.g. by substituting the firm's assets for more risky ones) even at the cost of a slight firm value reduction to maximize the stock value. As a consequence, a wealth transfer from debt holders to the stockholders is triggered, as debt holders suffer from an increase of the volatility by substituting low risky assets for high risky assets. These changes of asset values do not result from a change of the firm value but from a change in the volatility of the firm value. In a firm that has convertible bonds instead of straight debt outstanding, this moral hazard problem is less relevant. The reason is that a convertible bond consists of two components, the straight bond and the conversion right. Since the value of the bond suffers from a higher risk, but the value of the conversion option increases, a convertible bond is less sensitive for risk changes than a straight bond.[21] Therefore, it is feasible to design convertible bonds such that they are (at least) locally insensitive to risk changes.[22]

---

[18] Limratanamongkol (1999) argues that bankruptcy costs in case of a convertible bond issue are much lower than those for a straight bond issue, because in the presence of liquidation costs convertible bond holders might prevent a default by a conversion even though the firm is overindebted.

[19] Isagawa (2000) alternatively stresses the ability of convertible bonds to reduce under-investment costs same as over-investment costs in a framework with managers that have both empire-building tendencies and fears of default.

[20] See Jensen/Meckling (1976).

[21] See Ingersoll (1977a), p. 302, Spatt/Sterbenz (1993), p. 514, and Fischer/Zechner (1990).

[22] Chesney/Gibson-Asner (2001) show in a model with a default barrier for the firm value that it always exists a finite optimal volatility of the firm value that maximizes the stock value.

If firms use suchlike convertible bonds, there is no incentive for the stockholders to change the volatility of the firm value and the goal to maximize the stock value is equivalent to the reasonable goal of maximizing the firm value.[23] As a result, the described mitigation of the risk incentive conflict remarkably increases the attractiveness of these bonds for investors.[24]

The low sensitivity of convertible bonds for the volatility of the firm value allows for a further useful application of convertible bonds. This application especially concerns young firms for which no extensive data history exists. This is because the firm and the investors can agree upon the fair value of a convertible bond, even though they have diverging estimates of the volatility of the firm value.[25] Thus, this effect increases the marketability of convertible bonds.[26]

There is a similar moral hazard problem between the firm's management and its debt holders concerning the firm's dividend policy. In a standard framework in which a firm has only stocks and a bond outstanding, the cum dividend stock value increases with the dividend payment. As a consequence, the management must choose the highest possible dividend payment to maximize the value of stocks. To mitigate this dividend incentive problem, firms can use convertible bonds to reliably signal a low future dividend. We find in chapter 5 that the stock value can decrease with the dividend payment if the firm has both debt and convertible bonds outstanding. In this case, it might not be optimal for the management to pay off the highest possible dividend amount at the cost of the stock value.

---

23 See Green (1984), p. 124. However, Lewis/Rogalski/Seward (2002) find empirical evidence that the volatility of the total firm value increases following a convertible bond issue.

24 Schmitt/Spaeter (2001) relate a higher firm value risk to fewer environmental protection arrangements implemented by the firm. With a similar argumentation, they can show that with convertible bonds the firm optimally chooses a lower risk level and more pollution control. Therefore, convertible bonds can represent an instrument to increase the social welfare resulting from the lower environmental pollution.

25 See Brennan/Schwartz (1988), p. 59.

26 Welcker (1968a, 1968b) stresses the attractiveness of convertible bonds if investors have heterogeneous beliefs, i.e. investors might agree upon the expectation of the future firm value, but differ regarding the volatility of the firm value. Then, some investors might be willing to pay more for a convertible bond than other investors, where the other investors have a higher reservation price for a stock. As a consequence, the realizable proceeds from selling convertible bonds and stocks to those investors with the highest reservation prices can be higher than the proceeds from selling straight portions of the whole firm value to these investors. However, this argument requires incomplete markets.

2.2.3 Hidden Information Conflicts

In the presence of asymmetric information between management and investors, a problem of *adverse selection* hinders the raising of capital. Myers/Majluf (1984), p. 220, argue that if managers who act in favor of the stockholders have more information about the firm than investors have, a stock issue is associated with a decline of the stock price in contrast to a debt issue. The reason is that future gains and losses are shared with the new shareholders such that a positive stock value development is less favorable and a negative development is less unfavorable for the former stockholders after an equity issue. An issue of debt has the opposite effect on the stock value development due to the leverage effect. Therefore, the managers are supposed to optimally issue stocks if their private information about the future evolution of the firm value is less favorable. Dann/Mikkelson (1984), p. 171, Eckbo (1986), p. 149, and Gebhardt (2002), p. 114, find empirical evidence for the effect that stock values show an abnormal negative return at the announcement dates of a stock issue but not in case of a debt issue.[27]

Since convertible bonds are a special form of an equity issue, an issue of convertible bonds might also be interpreted as a negative signal by the market. As an increase of accounting equity after a convertible bond issue only occurs after a conversion that typically requires a positive stock value development, the signal conveyed by a convertible bond issue is less unfavorable than that from a straight issue of new stocks. Consequently, there is a less adverse effect on the stock value from a convertible bond issue. Stein (1990) argues that convertible bonds are a well-suited instrument to issue equity through the backdoor at reasonable adverse selection costs. If bankruptcy costs are also an argument against a straight bond issue, convertible bonds can be a better financing instrument than equity, debt, or a combination of both to minimize agency costs.[28]

Mikkelson/Partch (1986), p. 43, found an average abnormal stock return of −3.57% as a reaction to an equity issue announcement. As predicted by the theory, the average abnormal stock return after a convertible bond issue announcement is significantly higher at −1.97%. In a more recent study for the European market, Wachsmann (2001), p. 90,

---

[27] A model framework with asymmetric information is not required to explain the stock price reaction. In a complete market framework with additional debt a wealth transfer from stock to the debt holders can be triggered by an issue of new stocks.

[28] See also Bagella/Becchetti (1998), Brennan/Kraus (1987), and Kim (1990). In line with theory, Lewis/Rogalski/Seward (1999), p. 20, provide evidence that convertible bond issuers face relatively high debt- and equity-related financing costs, such that a standard security choice like straight debt or equity is unlikely to raise capital on the most advantageous terms. In particular, the risk incentive conflict and the asymmetric information problem play a prominent role in the way that corporate managers design convertible bonds as Lewis/Rogalski/Seward (1998a), p. 57, show.

obtains an even higher average abnormal stock return of −1.12% caused by a convertible bond issue announcement.[29]

There is another possibility to overcome information asymmetries with convertible bonds which is shown by Constantinides/Grundy (1989). If the management of a firm wants for some reasons to convey the true firm value to the market, it can do this by issuing an appropriately designed convertible bond in combination with a share repurchase program. The market participants observe that the management can only attain its goal to maximize the stock value, if the firm value pretended by the informed management is equal to the true firm value. This effect is a result of the concave/convex shape of a convertible bond as a function of the firm value. If the pretended firm value was too high or too low, the stock value at a future date would suffer, as in both cases the number of repurchased stocks would be lower than after conveying the true firm value. In the first case, the current stock price is too high to buy back the number of stocks which is possible after conveying the true firm value, but in the second case the selling price of the convertible bond is too low.

Furthermore, information asymmetries are especially in effect between entrepreneurs and their venture capitalists. Therefore, convertible bond contracts are also a popular form of deal structure for a start up financing to mitigate these asymmetries.[30] There are several studies which provide rationale for this effect. Schmidt (2003) shows the specific ability of a convertible bond contract to provide an incentive for both the entrepreneur and the venture capitalists to invest efficiently into their common project. This investment does not only concern capital expenditures but also the efforts committed by the entrepreneur and the venture capitalists. In this context a convertible bond contract is superior to equity, debt, or a combination of both.[31]

Bascha/Walz (2000) illustrate the selection function of convertible bonds to overcome information asymmetries. They argue that entrepreneurs with good projects are willing to accept higher face values than entrepreneurs with less good projects.[32]

Moreover, convertible bond contracts are well-suited to implement an efficient exit rule of the contract between the entrepreneurs and the venture capitalists after carrying this

---

29 See also Abhyankar/Dunning (1999), Brennan/Her (1995), Fields/Mais (1991), Bhabra/Patel (1996), Wolve/Daliakopoulos (1999), Kim/Stulz (1992), Herzog (1992), and Davidson/Glascock/Schwarz (1995).

30 See Gompers (1997).

31 See also D'Souza (2000).

32 See also Bell (2000), p. 194-195.

project to a success.[33] Bascha/Walz (2001) show that the ex-ante agreed optimal exit policy can be achieved.

2.2.4 Additional Reasons

There are several additional reasons which support the use of convertible bonds. Transaction costs associated with an issue of securities are one possibility, since the issuing costs of a convertible bond are close to those of a straight bond issue, but they are remarkably lower than those of an issue of new shares.[34] Therefore, convertible bonds can serve as an instrument to raise equity at relatively low issue costs.[35]

Mayers (1998) shows how to minimize issuing costs via convertible bonds if a firm fears over-investment costs. In this theoretical framework, the structure of a convertible bond is such that conversions primarily occur in case of a favorable firm performance that is a result of further profitable investment opportunities available for the firm. Thereby, a conversion is associated with saved redemptions of the convertible bond which can be used for these value-adding investments. Thus, the firm raises the whole capital for both an initial and valuable future projects by a singular convertible bond issue that only causes issuing costs once. Since the bond is redeemed in the absence of valuable future projects, over-investment costs do not incur.

Furthermore, an outstanding convertible bond issue can protect a firm against a hostile takeover when the takeover price is paid in cash. The idea behind this argument is that the success of a takeover offer made to current stockholders requires an offer price considerably above the stock price before the takeover offer announcement. In realistic cases, the offered price is supposed to be such that a conversion together with an acceptance of the offer would be optimal for the convertible bond holders which would result in a higher number of outstanding stocks. Therefore, the price required to take over the firm can be substantially higher if the firm has convertible bonds outstanding. This higher price complicates a successful takeover, since a higher capital demand in cash is required for the execution.[36] This effect is particularly important, if the bidding company is constrained in raising cash for this plan.

---

33 See Bascha (1998).

34 According to Long/Sefcik (1990), p. 31, the average issue costs of a convertible bond are 3.4%. However, the corresponding costs of a straight bond and stock issue are at about 1% and between 4 and 15%, respectively, as shown by Baskin (1989), p. 27.

35 See Pilcher, p. 85.

36 See Emanuel (1983), p. 221.

Furthermore, the issue of convertible bonds can be seen as a hidden dividend payment to the stockholders.[37] The reason for this view is that a convertible bond issue equips stockholders with subscription rights. These valuable subscription rights can be liquidated on the capital market. This argument is especially relevant if the firm's capital is bonded in illiquid investments such that an alternative cash dividend is impossible.

In addition, convertible bonds address more investors than e.g. stocks do. The reason is that certain groups of institutional investors are not allowed to invest in stocks but in convertible bonds.[38] Thus, convertible bonds are a reasonable instrument to benefit from a positive stock performance without holding stock. Similarly, convertible bonds address a new potential of stockholders who would otherwise not invest in stocks directly. Therefore, the capital market for common funds is broadened by a convertible bond issue.[39] This is due to the fact that convertible bond holders usually have other demands as stockholders and they show other characteristics.

2.3 Valuation of Convertible Bonds

In the literature, we can find three prevalent types of approaches to valuing convertible bonds. The first type which we call the non-market based approach, was established before the development of the risk-neutral valuation in a Black/Scholes framework. It provides the expectation about the future convertible bond value which might act as a decision helper to find the current convertible bond price, because market values primarily depend on the expectation of future values. This approach already contains the basic ideas for the following two approaches. These two approaches differ in terms of how they treat a default. The structural approach describes the value of a convertible bond (particularly in case of bankruptcy) as a function of the value of a certain underlying. Assuming a standard Black/Scholes framework for the underlying asset and a risk-free rate, we can determine the value of a convertible bond by replicating it with holdings of the underlying and the risk-free asset. The third type comprises reduced form models. Following this idea, the value of a convertible bond is represented by a claim that suffers from credit risk. The value of the credit-risky claim is given by a reduced-form model typically used to describe prices of defaultable bonds. In some approaches, a second component representing the conversion right is separately considered. This second component can be priced by applying standard option-pricing techniques.

37 See Pilcher (1955), p. 90.

38 See Brigham (1966), p. 51, and Bohn (2002), p. 112.

39 See Pilcher (1955), p. 83.

For all these valuation approaches, two points are of major importance. First, we must decide for a certain variable to be the underlying for the valuation. Second, we must impose an appropriate assumption about the conversion behavior of the convertible bond holders.

In general, there are two quantities which can serve as a reasonable state variable to price convertible bonds. These are the firm value and the stock value of the corresponding firm. The advantage of the choice of the firm value as the state variable is that it allows for an intuitive decomposition into the proportions held by every stakeholder of the firm at certain dates. However, the advantage of the stock value over the firm value is the empirical observability. In general, at least the value of a frequently traded stock can be directly obtained from the market. Conversely, the firm value is generally not observable. This effect is because the firm value represents the value held by all the stakeholders. However, certain positions such as accruals or bank loans are not traded on capital markets and therefore no observable market prices exist for these claims.

Moreover, all approaches must implicitly or explicitly impose assumptions on the conversion strategy followed by the convertible bond holders. We often find a block assumption, i.e. all outstanding convertible bonds are converted at the same time or not at all, in the non-market based and structural approaches. The reduced form models do not make any explicit but implicit conversion assumptions. Alternatively, some authors regard more sophisticated conversion variants in a game-theoretical framework that are supposed to map the conversion decision of a particular investor in a better way.

2.3.1 Non-Market Based Approach

Two non-market based approaches to valuing convertible bonds are presented by Welcker (1968a, 1968b) and Poensgen (1965). These approaches suggest that investors base their pricing decision of any asset on the expectation of the future value of the corresponding asset.[40] Welcker considers a firm that has exclusively two kinds of assets, namely stocks and convertible bonds, outstanding. The number of outstanding stocks and the number of initially outstanding convertible bonds is denoted by n and m, respectively. Either all the convertible bonds are converted into the m new stocks at maturity or the firm must redeem them at a face value equal to F per convertible bond. This framework does not allow for any further conversion possibilities and abstracts from possible coupon and

---

[40] See Welcker (1968a), p. 19. In this age in which these two approaches were developed, standard no-arbitrage option-pricing techniques were not established. To gain an intuitive quantity that is relevant for the current market value of convertible bonds, the authors consider the current expectation of the convertible bond value at maturity.

dividend payments. At maturity T the firm is liquidated, where the liquidation value is denoted by V_T. If the liquidation value is not sufficient to redeem the m convertible bonds, because V_T is below $m \cdot F$, the value V_T is distributed among the convertible bond holders according to their holdings. If the firm is able to satisfy the convertible bond holders' claim, the convertible bond holders can choose between the redemption value or the liquidation value divided by the number of outstanding shares in case of a conversion. If and only if the prorated liquidation value $\frac{V_T}{n+m}$ is above F, a conversion is optimal. In the first case, the convertible bond value equals its conversion value $\frac{V_T}{n+m}$ at maturity and is F in the second case. Therefore, the expected future convertible bond value EWO is given by[41]

$$\begin{aligned} EWO &= \int_0^{m \cdot F} \frac{V_T}{m} \cdot f(V_T)\, dV_T + \int_{m \cdot F}^{(n+m) \cdot F} F \cdot f(V_T)\, dV_T \\ &+ \int_{(n+m) \cdot F}^{\infty} \frac{V_T}{n+m} \cdot f(V_T)\, dV_T, \end{aligned}$$

where $f(V_T)$ denotes the density function of the liquidation value. We can interpret these three terms as the expectation of the convertible bond value in case of bankruptcy, redemption, and conversion, respectively.

Poensgen (1965), p. 80, takes the market view to determine the expectation of the convertible bond value. He characterizes the value of a convertible bond by other asset values which investors can better judge. For this purpose, he uses the value of a stock S after conversion and the value of an otherwise identical bond Y without any conversion rights.[42] At maturity, the value of the bond Y either equals the redemption value F of a convertible bond, or it is even lower in case of default. In case of default, the stock value is zero. Whenever, the stock value S after conversion at maturity exceeds the value of the straight bond, a conversion is optimal. Hence, a conversion is optimal if and only if S is higher than the redemption value F. We can think of a conversion as the exercise of the right of the convertible bond holders to receive stocks by giving up their bonds Y. Therefore, the convertible bond value at maturity is either equal to Y or is even higher namely equal to S if the stock value exceeds Y and the convertible bond holders exercise their conversion option. These considerations result in the following representation for

---

41 This representation corresponds to that given by Welcker (1968a), p. 19. The required arrangements of terms is presented by Welcker (1968a), p. 16.

42 We note that Y is not a bond whose market prices can be observed in the market. It is rather the value of a straight bond issued by a fictive firm with identical assets as the considered firm. In general, such a firm does not exist, but investors might have a more precise idea about the distribution of this traditional instrument (even though it is issued by a fictive firm) than about the more complex convertible bond (issued by a real firm).

the expectation of a convertible bond[43]

$$EWO = \int_0^F Yg(Y)\,dY + \int_0^F \int_Y^\infty (S - Y) \cdot h(S,Y)\,dSdY, \tag{2.1}$$

with $g(Y)$ as the density function of the straight bond value at maturity and $h(S,Y)$ as the common density function of the stock value S after conversion and the straight bond Y at maturity. Equation (2.1) represents the expectation EWO by two components, namely the expectation of the value of the straight bond and the expectation of the value of the option to receive a stock by giving up the bond.

These non-market based approaches do not represent the state of the art, as they are incapable of providing a theory for a unique current market value of convertible bonds. However, they contain the basic principles for the following two valuation types. The Welcker approach corresponds to the structural models and the Poensgen idea is similar to that in the reduced-form types.

2.3.2 Structural Models

The two most prominent examples for the valuation of convertible bonds are presented by Ingersoll (1977a) and Brennan/Schwartz (1977). According to our classification, they belong to the class of structural models. This is the case as the underlying state variable in these two approaches is the firm value that uniquely determines the payoff of the convertible bond at certain dates. To have a consistent notation, we again regard a firm with n outstanding stocks and m convertible bonds having a conversion ratio equal to one. In these models, the firm is not liquidated at maturity as in the Welcker framework. However, in the absence of any liquidation and bankruptcy costs, the firm value V_T, which is the relevant underlying in the Brennan/Schwartz and Ingersoll model, is identical to the liquidation value.

Under these specific assumptions, the value of a convertible bond at maturity obtained by Ingersoll (1977a) and Brennan/Schwartz (1977) must be the same as that used by Welcker (1968a, 1968b) to determine the expectation. Therefore, the value of a convertible bond $W(T)$ at maturity can be represented as follows:

$$W(T) = \min\left(F, \frac{V_T}{m}\right) + \max\left(\frac{V_T}{n+m} - F, 0\right) \tag{2.2}$$

If the convertible bond can be converted only at maturity, we can apply closed-form solutions. This is because both terms in (2.2) can be represented as European options. The first one equals the value of a default-free zero bond minus a European put option

[43] See also Uhlir (1976), p. 13-14.

written on a proportion of the firm value $\frac{1}{m}V_T$ with strike price F. Analogously, the second term corresponds to a European call option written on a different proportion of the firm value $\frac{V_T}{n+m}$, but with the same strike price and maturity as the put option. Assuming a Black/Scholes market model with a firm value V_t that follows a geometric Brownian motion, we obtain the convertible bond value from the corresponding Black/Scholes option values.

These approaches presented so far disregard the possibility of a premature conversion. As Poensgen (1965), p. 79-80, indicates, the value of a convertible bond can be even higher than that from these approaches, as the value of a convertible bond might additionally benefit from a premature conversion.

Brennan/Schwartz (1977, 1980) take into account the possibility to convert prematurely. They impose the block conversion assumption which states that all convertible bonds are converted at the same time or not at all. The conversion strategy considered above that only allows for a conversion at maturity is also a special case of a block conversion, but now the bonds can be converted prematurely. The optimal conversion strategy arises from a comparison of the non-converted convertible bond value $W^+(t)$ and the conversion value $\frac{V_t}{n+m}$ which is the total firm value divided by the number of outstanding claims. Analogously as at maturity, a conversion occurs if and only if the conversion value is higher. This conversion strategy results in the following conversion condition:

$$W(t) = \max\left(W^+(t), \frac{V_t}{n+m}\right) \tag{2.3}$$

If the firm pays dividends, a premature conversion can be optimal. Then, no closed-form solutions will exist and the value of a convertible bond must be determined numerically. Brennan/Schwartz (1977) present a numerical method to determine $W(t)$. The imposed assumptions allow Brennan/Schwartz to use the partial differential equation from Black/Scholes (1973) with the convertible bond value in place of the call value. For all non-dividend dates, the partial differential equation is given by

$$\frac{1}{2}\sigma^2 V^2 W_{VV} + rVW_V - rW + W_t = 0, \tag{2.4}$$

where r is the risk-free rate, σ the volatility of the firm value return, and the subscript denotes partial differentiation. By applying a finite difference approach subject to the initial and the free boundary condition (2.2) and (2.3), Brennan/Schwartz (1977) obtain the value for the convertible bond $W(t)$ as long as the firm pays discrete dividends.[44] As alternatives or extensions, continuous dividend payments, coupon payments, and call

[44] Zhu/Sun (1999) present another numerical method that is especially well-suited for the pricing of convertible bonds.

features of the convertible bonds can be considered in a similar way, too.[45] Analogous approaches to valuing convertible bonds are Kruschwitz/Schöbel (1985), Reiß/Schöbel (1999), and Swoboda/Kamschal (1979), etc.[46]

2.3.3 Reduced-Form Models

Reduced-form models for valuing convertible bonds are especially popular for practitioners because they primarily focus on observable market values. For this purpose, the value of a convertible bond is seen as a credit-risky claim that is additionally affected by the conversion value. To account for the uncertainty of the value of the conversion right, these approaches consider the pre-default stock value S after a potential conversion as the state variable rather than the firm value. Thus, the conversion conditions analogous to (2.2) and (2.3) for the value of a non-defaulted convertible bond are

$$W(T) = \max(F, S(T)), \tag{2.5}$$
$$W(t) = \max\left(W^{+}(t), S(t)\right).$$

To capture the default risk of convertible bonds in a commonly accepted way, standard reduced-form models are applied to include this source of risk. Examples for the application of reduced-form models to valuing convertible securities can be found in Goldman Sachs (1994), Tsiveriotis/Fernandes (1998), Takahashi/Kobayashi/Nakagawa (2001), Hung/Wang (2002), and Koziol/Sauerbier (2003).

Next, we sketch the valuation principle proposed by Takahashi/Kobayashi/Nakagawa (2001). The main parameter that drives the default event is the hazard rate, $\lambda(S,t)$ which depends on S, the stock value of a non-defaulted firm after conversion and time t. Since a higher stock value reduces the danger of a default, the hazard rate $\lambda(S,t)$ is supposed to decrease with S. The value of a stock S of the non-defaulted firm after a conversion follows a geometric Brownian motion with a volatility of stock value return σ_S. In addition to the hazard rate, we need the fractional loss rate of market value at default, $L_B(S,t)$, to price an asset. Defining the risk-adjusted discount rate as

$$R_B(t) := r + L_B(S,t)\,\lambda(S,t),$$

we can price every asset as shown by Duffie/Singleton (1999). The value of a non-defaulted straight bond is equal to the expectation of promised payments discounted by the con-

[45] See Brennan/Schwartz (1980).

[46] The ability of the structural approaches to explain market prices of convertible bonds is analyzed by various studies e.g. King (1986), Carayannopoulos (1996), Ammann/Kind/Wilde (2001, 2003), and Bohn (2001). In general, these models tend to overprice convertible bonds especially if their conversion value lies deeply below their face value.

tinuously compounding rate $R_B(t)$ under a risk-neutral measure. Under this risk-neutral measure the corresponding expected instantaneous returns of the pre-default values of a convertible bond and a stock are

$$\begin{aligned} R_W(t) &= r + L(S,t)\,\lambda(S,t), \\ R_S(t) &= r + \lambda(S,t), \end{aligned}$$

where the expected loss rate of a convertible bond is denoted by $L(S,t)$. The expected loss rate of a stock at default equals one to ensure that the stock value is zero after a default.

If a non-defaulted convertible bond is delta hedged, the gain from this portfolio over an instant of time is certain and equal to $\left(-\left(r+\lambda(S,t)\right)SW_S + \left(r + L(S,t)\cdot\lambda(S,t)\right)W\right)dt$ if no default occurs during this time span. Following Ito's Lemma, this increment of the portfolio value reads $\left(\frac{1}{2}\sigma_S^2 S^2 W_{SS} + W_t\right)dt$. Otherwise in the case of a default, this portfolio suffers a loss equal to $W\cdot L(S,t) - SW_S$. Since the risk-neutral default probability for this time span equals $\lambda(S,t)\,dt$, we can verify that the expected gain from this portfolio is — conform with the risk-neutral valuation — as high as the risk-free interest on the portfolio value, $(W - SW_S)\cdot r dt$. However, we are primarily interested in the pre-default value of a convertible bond W. For this purpose, we can relate the certain gain if no default occurs to the increment of the portfolio derived by Ito' s formula to obtain a partial differential equation that corresponds to (2.4). For all non-dividend dates, we can write:

$$\frac{1}{2}\sigma_S^2 S^2 W_{SS} + \left(r+\lambda(S,t)\right)SW_S - \left(r + L(S,t)\cdot\lambda(S,t)\right)W + W_t = 0 \tag{2.6}$$

This equation allows us to solve for $W(t)$ by any numerical method using backward induction in a discretized setting. The finite difference approach proposed by Brennan/Schwartz (1977), for example, is a well-suited procedure to solve for the corresponding partial differential equation (2.6). Now the challenge in pricing a convertible bond lies in the determination of an appropriate risk-neutral measure that particularly requires knowledge of the hazard rate $\lambda(S,t)$ and the specification of the fractional loss rate $L(S,t)$ of the convertible bond.

Other reduced-form models of valuing convertible bonds consider a system of two coupled partial differential equations.[47] Therefore, the convertible bond is decomposed into two components. The components are constructed such that the value of the first one bears credit risk and of the second one only stock value risk. Each particular partial differential equation describes one of these two components. To price the credit-risky position, a

[47] See Goldman Sachs (1994) or Tsiveriotis/Fernandes (1998).

standard reduced-form model is applied. Using analogous boundary conditions to (2.5), the convertible bond value is a solution of these partial differential equations. As in the structural models, these numerical procedures also allow for the consideration of continuous dividend payments, coupon payments, and call features of the convertible bond.

2.3.4 Discussion of Conversion Assumptions

The special interest of this dissertation concerns the optimal conversion strategy. Thus, we analyze in detail the imposed conversion assumptions of the valuation approaches introduced above.

Though Welcker, Poensgen, and Ingersoll regard convertible bonds which are only converted at maturity, there must nevertheless be an assumption about the conversion strategy. All these authors do not explicitly discuss the conversion strategy followed by the investors. According to these approaches, a conversion occurs, if the stock value after conversion, which is the firm value divided by the number of afterwards outstanding stocks or S respectively, is above the redemption value F. This behavior implies a unique conversion decision for all outstanding convertible bonds (block conversion). At first glance, this assumption seems to be the only rational possibility. In chapter 4, we will find that the relation between the stock and the convertible bond value at maturity can deviate from that pattern, even though investors follow a rational conversion strategy.

The structural approaches that allow for a premature conversion also assume block conversion. Constantinides (1984) relaxes this assumption and considers a continuum of competitive investors in an equilibrium framework. The individual strategy of an individual investor is assumed to have no price impact. Each of the investors follows a personal optimal conversion strategy. The aggregate optimal conversion volume at each conversion date results from a Nash equilibrium of a game among convertible bond holders. This conversion variant of unrestricted conversion will be discussed in detail in chapter 3.

Constantinides shows that under these assumptions Nash equilibria that determine the conversion volume exist. In certain cases, sequential strategies can represent an equilibrium strategy due to the dynamic structure of the game. This strategy means that at a conversion date a few, but not all, convertible bonds might be optimally converted and no investor has an incentive to deviate from her or his conversion strategy. Therefore, the unrestricted conversion in equilibrium can result in a conversion strategy different from the block strategy. However, in the framework from Constantinides the values of a convertible bond and a stock under unrestricted conversion are the same as in the block case.

The idea of the proof of the equality between asset values is as follows. From the conversion condition in the block case (2.3), we know that a conversion occurs if the stock value after conversion, $\frac{V_t}{n+m}$, is equal or higher than $W^+(t)$. Then, $W(t)$ is equal to the conversion value $\frac{V_t}{n+m}$ in the block case. In the unrestricted case, a sequential conversion, that is not feasible in the block case, requires the stock value to be as high as the value of the convertible bond. Otherwise, this conversion volume cannot represent an equilibrium, since investors would have an incentive to deviate from their strategy. As a consequence of the indifference between the stock and convertible bond value in case of a sequential conversion the values of both instruments, the stock and the convertible bond, must equal the firm value divided by the total number of outstanding claims, $\frac{V_t}{n+m}$. Thus, the value of a convertible bond is either equal to $W^+(t)$ in the case of no conversion or $\frac{V_t}{n+m}$ if a sequential conversion occurs. Evidently, every convertible bond holder has an incentive not to convert if and only if $W^+(t)$ is higher than $\frac{V_t}{n+m}$. Therefore, Constantinides argues that an equilibrium strategy exists such that the conversion dates in the block case and those in case of perfect competition are the same. In particular, a conversion under both conversion variants occurs if the value of $W^+(t)$ hits or exceeds the conversion value $\frac{V_t}{n+m}$. Since the conversion value $\frac{V_t}{n+m}$ in the block case is the same as the conversion value $\frac{V_t}{n+m}$ for the perfect competition case, even if a sequential conversion is optimal, the values of the convertible bonds for the two different conversion variants coincide. Accordingly, the stock values must also coincide. Hence, these considerations by Constantinides justify the simpler block conversion for valuation purposes under perfect competition in this special framework without any additional stakeholders. In particular, things will substantially differ if the firm has additional debt outstanding. We will analyze these effects in chapters 4 and 5.

The assumed conversion policy of the reduced-form approaches documented in (2.5) can be seen as the outcome of a block conversion. According to the findings of Constantinides presented above, these asset values for block conversion are the same as those that arise from perfect competition among convertible bond holders. Therefore, the assumed conversion behavior is also consistent with a perfect competition among the convertible bond holders. However, if the firm has additional debt outstanding, stock value jumps can occur if a convertible bond is converted in one block. Therefore, block conversion is not necessarily consistent with the conversion assumption of the reduced-form models for levered firms. We will analyze the important role of additional debt in chapters 4 and 5.

Table 2.1: Empirical Conversion Volume

The table shows the annual conversion volume of eight convertible bond issues from the German market over the time to maturity reported in years. The conversion volume is denominated in percent of the outstanding issuing volume at the beginning of every particular period. A dash indicates that a conversion was not feasible for this particular time to maturity.

		Time to Maturity									
		9	8	7	6	5	4	3	2	1	0
bond number	1	42.92	23.63	0.81	0.73	18.81	3.22	0.06	0	34.28	96.12
	2	—	70.43	4.15	0.23	1.81	54.25	23.81	14.97	15.94	89.45
	3	—	30.19	62.81	15.43	13.45	76.44	14.93	0.96	2.30	75.27
	4	—	70.43	4.15	0.23	1.81	54.25	23.81	14.97	15.93	89.45
	5	—	—	5.85	2.30	1.44	1.44	0.33	2.89	12.31	1.55
	6	—	—	—	—	10.42	14.64	1.77	1.46	0.49	75.22
	7	—	0	0	0	0.04	0.00	0	0	0	0
	8	—	—	0	0	0	0	0	0	0	0

2.4 Analysis of Observed Conversion Volume

The consideration of the standard valuation approaches in the previous section has shown that the complexity of the convertible bond valuation declines substantially if one of the following two conditions holds. The first condition is that all the convertible bonds are either converted at maturity or not at all. The second condition allows for a conversion at an arbitrary date but requires that the convertible bonds are converted in one block. The advantage in the first case is that we can apply the closed-form solutions for European convertible bonds. In the second case, the block conversion assumption is especially well-suited for valuation purposes even if a premature conversion is possible. This is due to the simple form of the premature conversion condition. If other more complex conversion variants are assumed, the prior conversion volume might be needed as a further state variable. Now, our objective is to examine whether the data of empirical convertible bond conversions in the German market provides evidence for one or both of the hypotheses that conversions occur at maturity only or in one block.

Table 2.1 shows the annual conversion volume of eight convertible bond issues in the German market. Including the possibility of a premature conversion, we have 65 conversion periods, in total. The conversion volume is denominated in percent of the issue that was still outstanding at the beginning of the particular period. Therefore, the reported conversion volume can lie between zero and 100 percent in every period. The grounding for this denomination is that after a large conversion in the first periods, the absolute conversion volume must be low afterwards and does not exhibit such a high explanatory power to visualize whether a block conversion has occurred afterwards or not. To gain this data, two data sources were accessible to us. First, a bank provided us with client's individual conversion orders and other internal documents from which the conversion volume is apparent. However, a complete data set for a certain issue was only available if this bank acted as central office. The fact that banks are only obliged to deposit these documents for ten years explains the low number of convertible bonds with available conversion data. The second source is the Hoppenstedt stock guide which reports all annual changes of firm's capital structure broken down by their origin. From these changes, we could obtain the conversion volume of few further issues of firms which only had one particular issue outstanding. Otherwise, the capital increase might stem from conversions of different issues. Furthermore, the Hoppenstedt stock guide allowed us to perform consistency checks with the bank data.

First, we evaluate the hypothesis that conversions only occur at maturity. If we are to take this term literally, we must immediately reject this hypothesis, since there are convertible bonds that violate this condition. However, it might be too rash if we reject this hypothesis only because some conversions occur before maturity. It could be that very few investors who do not understand convertible bonds in detail convert without being aware of the consequences. For us a conversion volume up to 5% is a very tolerant level to estimate it as unconscious conversion. Conversely, if the premature conversion volume is above 5%, it must have the character of a systematic conversion that contradicts the hypothesis that conversions occur at maturity only. Table 2.1 shows that in 24 out of 57 cases the annual conversion volume before maturity lies above five percent. These observations are a strong contradiction of the hypothesis that premature conversions do not occur even if we allow for a tolerant level of non-rational conversions. In particular, given that any systematic conversions occur at maturity, we observe on average 4.6 premature periods with a systematic conversion above five percent. This relation indicates that if the conversion value of the convertible bond is high, which is documented by systematic conversions at maturity, there is also a considerable number of premature conversion periods.

Next, we examine the second hypothesis that convertible bonds are converted in one block or not at all. Again, a literally application of the block conversion results in a rejection of the block hypothesis, because each empirical conversion is below 100 percent. Similar as before, we want to prevent an early rejection which only results from a few unconsciously acting investors. We find that conversions of more than five percent represent a considerable conversion volume that can no longer be explained by an unconscious behavior of investors. Correspondingly, we argue that conversions below the symmetric rate of 95 percent cannot be interpreted as a complete conversion. We can see that in 27 out of 65 cases the annual conversion volume is in between five and 95 percent. These observations are strong evidence to reject the block assumption empirically even if we allow for some non-rational conversions. Nevertheless, we find a conversion behavior consistent with block conversion in 16 periods which are all characterized by a conversion volume identical to zero. On the contrary, if a systematic conversion above five percent occurs, in 27 out of 29 cases we observe no conversion above 95 percent. Therefore, in our data sample conversions primarily occur as non-complete conversions.

As a consequence of the rejection of the hypotheses that conversions do not occur before maturity and only take place in one block, we can see that the empirical conversion strategy followed by the convertible bond holders is much more sophisticated than assumed in most valuation approaches.

The goal of this work is to allow for a non-block conversion in the context of convertible bond pricing. At first glance, it seems necessary to impose frictions such as e.g. investor-specific transaction costs to explain an endogenous sequential conversion.[48] However, we do not need to apply any frictions. As seen in Constantinides (1984), a sequential conversion can result from equilibria under perfect competition among convertible bond holders. Moreover, we regard other reasonable conversion variants that can imply a sequential conversion without assuming any frictions.

---

[48] See e.g. Stanton (1995). In this model, a similar framework with mortgage holders facing heterogenous transaction costs is adapted to the pricing of mortgage backed securities.

Chapter 3

General Framework for the Analysis of Convertible Bonds

To achieve our goal of valuing convertible bonds with a special focus on the conversion behavior, we now describe the considered model framework. Since convertible bonds have numerous complex characteristics, as presented in the previous chapter, we must select the components of the model set up carefully. Our purpose is to build a framework that accounts for all major parameters, on the one hand, but that also abstracts from minor ones obstructing the view on the essential points, on the other hand. Therefore, we regard a typical firm with convertible bonds outstanding, which also has stocks and debt in its capital structure. The reason to deal with both stock and debt is that a conversion might have a different effect on the stock value than on the debt value. Thus, the conversion strategy and the values of both convertible bonds and stocks may show fundamentally different properties caused by the existence of additional debt.

As a convertible bond is a hybrid security consisting of a bond component and an equity component, there are two major sources of uncertainty borne by a convertible bond. If the conversion value is remarkably above the conversion price, i.e. the conversion probability is high, the value of a convertible bond is essentially driven by the firm value. In this case, the firm value risk is the dominant source of uncertainty. On the other hand, if the stock value is such that a conversion is most unlikely, the convertible bond behaves like a straight bond. At this point, the relevant source of risk is interest rate uncertainty. As there are two major sources of uncertainty that play a more or less important role for the convertible bond value, we take them both into account by modelling the firm value process and the process of the interest rate in a commonly accepted way. In the following section, we will describe the model framework in detail.

3.1 Model Framework

Cash Flow Structure

For the following analysis, we consider a firm having m convertible bonds, n stocks, and additional debt outstanding. In line with the typical characteristics of a *convertible bond* presented in section 2.1.2, we can characterize a convertible by its *maturity date* T upon which a promised *face value* F is due and a set of N *coupon dates* t_i

$$t_1 < t_2 < ... < t_N < T$$

upon which a *coupon payment* c is due. Strictly speaking, F is the face value of the convertible bond that also includes potential accrued interest. Although a convertible bond can have an arbitrary conversion ratio, we assume a conversion ratio of one, implying that one convertible bond can be converted into one stock. This simplification allows us to save one variable to characterize a convertible bond without loss of generality. If a given convertible bond has a conversion ratio equal to γ, it follows from a replication argumentation that the value of this convertible bond is equal to the value of γ convertibles that have a conversion ratio of one and a corresponding prorated coupon, c/γ, and redemption value, F/γ.

All the *stocks*, even those created by a conversion, are equipped with identical rights. Therefore, the *total dividend* Div_t at time t is distributed among the old and new stockholders on a pro rata basis. We allow for one dividend payment in every time span between two consecutive coupon dates and a further one in the period between the last coupon date and the convertible's maturity. As a consequence, we obtain the following sequence of *dividend dates* τ_i:

$$t_1 < \tau_1 < t_2 < ... < \tau_{N-1} < t_N < \tau_N < T$$

The magnitude of the total dividend Div_{τ_i} at every dividend date τ_i is proportional to the *firm value* V_{τ_i}. This specification bases on the idea that high profits of the firm are documented by both a high firm value and a high dividend payment. Hence, a higher firm value implies a higher dividend payment. Defining δ as the proportion of the firm value used for the dividend payment, we can represent Div_{τ_i} as follows:

$$Div_{\tau_i} = \delta \cdot V_{\tau_i},\ i = 1, ..., N$$

The *dividend rate* δ is a positive real number which does not depend on the dividend date τ_i. Moreover, the dividend policy given by δ is known with certainty.

The consideration of the same number of dividend and coupon dates is consistent with the empirical characteristics of German convertible bonds. In general, one dividend and one coupon payment are made each year. For the majority of the convertible bonds considered in section 2.1.2, the coupon date is January 2nd. We recall from section 2.1.2 that a conversion in the preceding year is required to participate in the current dividend payment. As a consequence, no convertible bond holder can receive a coupon and a dividend payment in the same year with one convertible bond. Translating this condition into our notation, it means that after a convertible bond has paid a coupon at time t_i, it can thereafter only be converted into a stock without a dividend right at τ_i. It follows from standard considerations in Ingersoll (1977a) that a conversion can only be optimal at those dates at which a dividend claim for the convertible bond holders would expire without a conversion.[1] Therefore, the optimal conversion date is the end of every year.

As a result of these considerations, we impose the assumption that the premature conversion dates coincide with the coupon dates. In addition, we allow for a conversion at maturity of the convertible bond. If a conversion takes place at a coupon date t_i, the convertible bond will immediately loose any coupon or redemption payment claims, i.e. the holder of one convertible bond gets one stock but no coupon payment when she or he converts at time t_i. Different coupon and conversion dates could be considered by determining the present value of the succeeding coupon payment at every conversion date.[2] However, this specification would require a more sophisticated analysis[3] which does not provide any further insights about convertible bonds. As stated above, a conversion undertaken at other dates than at the end of every year or at maturity does not come into question even though it would be feasible. Hence, in our model we can account for the empirically involved right to convert a convertible at any time by allowing the conversion to take place once a year at time t_i.

At every coupon date t_i and at maturity T, the total *conversion volume* at this date is denoted by k_t. It must be between zero and the number of outstanding convertibles $m - K_t$, where $K_t := \sum_{t_i<t} k_{t_i}$ denotes the *aggregate conversion volume* until time t. The aggregate conversion volume enables us to quantify the dividend per share $\frac{\delta V_{\tau_i}}{n+K_{\tau_i}}$ at time τ_i which is the total dividend divided by the number of outstanding shares.

The third outstanding security of the firm is *straight debt* in the form of a zero bond maturing at time TD after the convertible bond. The promised *debt face value* is FD.

1 We will show that this property also holds in our more general model with other conversion variants.

2 As every convertible bond has an institutional blocking period at the end of every year between two weeks to at most one month in which no conversion is allowed, the optimal conversion date is in general between 15 to 31 days before the coupon date of January 2nd.

3 In case of different coupon and conversion dates, the value of the coupon payment at a conversion date is not the discounted coupon payment but it is rather the value of an option. Strictly speaking, the coupon payoff is c or even lower equal to the prorated firm value if the firm defaults.

We are aware of the fact that firms can generally have a more sophisticated debt structure. Nevertheless, this widespread assumption of modeling outstanding debt by a particular zero bond is made, because the debt value shows all relevant aspects of more sophisticated debt structures.

Bankruptcy Rule

Due to the outstanding obligations of the considered firm, a default has to be taken into account. Thus at this point, we have to specify how a default is triggered and which bankruptcy rule is applied. In line with Merton (1974), we allow for bankruptcy if and only if the firm value is not sufficient to meet the current obligation. Strictly speaking, when the coupon payment $c \cdot (m - K_{t_i} - k_{t_i})$ at time t_i, the redemption payment of the convertible bond $F \cdot (m - K_T - k_T)$ at time T, or the debt face value FD at time TD are below the firm value, bankruptcy occurs. Then, the firm is liquidated at its current value and the proceeds are distributed among the corresponding claim holders. To have a clear bankruptcy rule consistent with the empirical characteristics of German convertible bonds, we assume that the claim of the convertible bond holders is senior to that of the other debt holders. Therefore, the proceeds from liquidation at a conversion date are distributed exclusively among the convertible bond holders. Only at time TD can debt holders get a liquidation payment. The fact that this sharing rule in case of bankruptcy is consistent with the empirical characteristics of convertible bonds is because German convertible bonds are usually equipped with a negative pledge clause as shown in section 2.1.2. With this negative pledge clause, firms with an outstanding convertible bond are only allowed to issue debt with a non-higher seniority than that of the convertible bond. Thus, equipping the debt issued after the convertible bond with a lower seniority is one way to satisfy the negative pledge clause. For this reason, we can think of the debt in our model as a straight bond issued after the convertible bond regarding the negative pledge clause. Of course, other assumptions concerning the liquidation rule, e.g. a lower or the same priority, are also possible. However, independent of the bankruptcy rule, the main properties of the asset values are the same and do not result in remarkably different findings.[4] These arguments justify the assumption of this easily-applicable bankruptcy rule. Moreover, the focus of the following analysis lies on the conversion of the convertible bonds which typically takes place when the bond is distant from a default and therefore the liquidation rule plays a minor role. This is also a reason to justify the implicitly

---

4 Strictly speaking, the main properties for the analysis in chapter 5 are that the debt value increases with the conversion volume as the convertible bond value in the unrestricted case does. If the convertible bond has e.g. a lower or the same priority as the additional debt, these properties are still valid and can be even more striking. However, these bankruptcy rules would require a detailed discussion to specify the liquidation payments in case of default properly.

imposed assumptions for abstraction from liquidation costs and from a default occurring at non-coupon or -redemption dates caused by a possible failure of the firm to pay or an overindebtedness.[5]

This description of a convertible bond contains all typical and important features. According to the previous chapter, we have seen that convertible bonds could also be equipped with conversion payments, call or put rights, variable coupon payments, and might be convertible into both common and preferred stock. However, these features are exceptions in the German market. Since these features do not seem to affect the core of our analysis, the optimal conversion policy, we decide to defer from these characteristics. If required, they could be incorporated in our framework and the following analysis.

Refinancing of Payments

The fact that the considered firm has to make coupon, dividend, and redemption payments poses the question regarding the financing of these payments. At this point, we impose the assumption that the required payoffs result from a sale of a proportion of the firm's assets at their fair value. Consequently, the firm value process might show a jump at every coupon, dividend, or redemption date. Alternatively, we could deal with a constant investment program of the firm such that the capital demand is financed by new issues of further securities.

In the case of equity issues, the value of additional debt is hardly affected by the conversion decision and therefore the interesting wealth transfer between debt and stockholders caused by a conversion almost vanishes such that the effects are nearly the same as in the much simpler case without additional debt. The main challenge in this case is to apply anti dilution clauses in every payment date which result in a fairly (but not perfectly) protection of the convertible bond value as we have seen in section 2.1.2.

Another possibility to finance the payments of the firm is the issue of further debt. If the further-issued debt is subordinated to the initially outstanding additional debt, the effects are similar to those of an equity issue, where a conversion hardly affects the position of the debt holders. In the case that the issued debt is senior to the formerly outstanding debt, the number of different debt claims outstanding increases with every payment date. The important wealth transfer between stock and debt holders caused by a conversion is still in effect, but then much more relations between stockholders and holders of the different types of debt must be taken into account, even though the aggregate value of all these

---

[5] More advanced approaches allowing for an exogenous premature default at non-coupon dates are in Black/Cox (1976), Geske (1977), Kim/Ramaswamy/Sundaresan (1993), and Longstaff/Schwartz (1995). Alternatively, models with an endogenous default are presented by Leland (1994,1998), Leland/Toft (1996), Mella-Barral (1999), Fan/Sundaresan (2000), and Uhrig-Homburg (2001).

debt claims shows similar properties as one large bond outstanding. In the case of a debt issue with the same seniority, the outstanding amount of debt is a random variable that increases in every payment date. Due to this increase, the effects caused from additional debt become even more striking than with the sale-of-asset assumption, because there is a higher amount of outstanding debt under the debt-issuing assumption.

Since all these refinancing alternatives either result in an uninteresting or very complex analysis that does not reveal further important insights, we do not proceed with these alternatives, but assume the sale of assets for the financing of any payments. In particular, we impose the scale-reduction assumption implying that the composition of the firm's investment program remains unchanged.

Sources of Uncertainty

The firm value process at any non-coupon, non-dividend, and non-redemption date follows a geometric Brownian motion. This standard assumption is one possibility to satisfy the scale-reduction assumption in a coupon, dividend, or redemption date. Thus, the increment of the firm value is given by

$$dV_t = \mu \cdot V_t \cdot dt + \sigma \cdot V_t \cdot dz_t \;\; (t \neq t_i, \tau_i, T, TD,\; i = 1, ..., N)\,, \tag{3.1}$$

where μ and $\sigma > 0$ respectively denote the mean and the standard deviation of the instantaneous firm value return and z_t is the value of a standard Wiener process. For every coupon, dividend, or redemption date, we have to distinguish between the firm value before and after the payment. We define the firm value V_t, at such a date t, as the firm value after the corresponding payment. The firm value before the payment results from the (existing) left-sided limit $\lim_{\substack{u \to t \\ u<t}} V_u$ of the firm value at a particular payment date t and is abbreviated by V_t^- in the following examination. The relations between the firm values before and after the payment at every coupon, dividend, and redemption date are as follows:

$$\begin{aligned} V_{t_i} &= \max\left\{V_{t_i}^- - (m - K_{t_i} - k_{t_i}) \cdot c, 0\right\}, \; i = 1, ..., N \\ V_{\tau_i} &= V_{\tau_i}^- \cdot (1 - \delta)\,, \; i = 1, ..., N \\ V_T &= \max\left\{V_T^- - (m - K_T - k_T) \cdot F, 0\right\} \\ V_{TD} &= \max\left\{V_{TD}^- - FD, 0\right\} \end{aligned} \tag{3.2}$$

A firm value equal to zero can only result from a default at $t = t_i, T$, or TD. We note that the definition of the firm value evolution (3.1) accounts for the fact that only after a default occurring at $t = t_i, T$, or TD the future firm value also equals zero. This specification is consistent with the assumption of a liquidation at the default date.

The stocks and the additional debt are traded continuously on arbitrage-free, competitive, complete, and frictionless markets. In addition, we assume that a corresponding unlevered firm with an identical investment program as the considered firm with outstanding convertible bonds exists. The shares of this unlevered firm are also traded on this market. Thus, V_t can be treated as a traded asset.

Moreover, a competitive, complete, and frictionless market for default-free zero bonds of every maturity exists. The uncertainty in this market is represented by a term structure model of the Vasicek (1977) type. The well-known evolution of the *short rate* r_t is given by

$$dr_t = \kappa \cdot (\theta' - r_t) \cdot dt + \eta \cdot dw_t. \tag{3.3}$$

$\kappa > 0$ denotes the *speed of the reversion* of r_t towards its *long term mean* θ' and η is a *volatility parameter.* The value of the standard Wiener process w_t is related to the value of the Wiener process z_t of the firm value process by the *correlation* ρ:

$$\rho \cdot dt = dz_t \cdot dw_t$$

These two markets form a market model such that every derivative written on the firm value V_t and the short rate r_t can be replicated by a dynamic strategy. The replication can be achieved by a portfolio consisting of traded shares V_t of the corresponding unlevered firm and zero bonds with an appropriate maturity.

Conversion Variants

Following the work of Emanuel (1983), Constantinides (1984), and Spatt/Sterbenz (1988), there are three plausible conversion variants to deal with: *block conversion*, *unrestricted conversion*, and *monopolistic conversion.* In the block case, all m convertible bonds have to be converted in one block, i.e. at the same point of time. The objective of this conversion strategy is to maximize the value obtained with the m convertible bonds subject to the block condition $k_t \cdot K_t = 0$ at every conversion date t.

In the unrestricted case, the convertible bonds are held by numerous investors represented by a continuum $\mathbb{I} = [0, 1]$.[6] Among these investors perfect competition exists, which means that they cannot cooperate and no individual investor has an impact on the aggregate conversion volume or the asset prices. The initial holding rate of every convertible bond holder $i \in \mathbb{I}$ is denoted by m^i where the volume of the holdings $m = \int_{\mathbb{I}} m^s ds$ results from the integral over the holding rates of all investors. The relative holding rate m^i/m has the character of a density function, i.e. the volume of holdings of every particular investor is zero but the aggregation over the relative holdings of all convertible bond holders equals one. The conversion volume k_t aggregated over all investors $i \in \mathbb{I}$ at time t results from the conversion decisions of every individual investor k_t^i, $0 \leq k_t^i \leq m^i$, at this time. Integrating

6 See Constantinides/Rosenthal (1984) and Schmeidler (1973).

over the conversion decisions of all the investors yields the aggregate conversion volume $k_t = \int_{\mathbb{I}} k_t^s ds$. We can see from this representation that the conversion decision k_t^i of one particular investor i does not affect the aggregate conversion volume, because m^i/m and therefore k_t^i/k_t have the character of a density function. The optimal conversion volume results from Nash equilibria of a game among these investors in which every convertible bond holder aims to maximize the value obtained with her or his convertible bonds.

In the monopolistic case, all outstanding convertible bonds are held by one investor, the monopolist. It is the goal of the monopolist to choose a feasible conversion strategy $0 \leq k_t \leq m - K_t$ at every conversion date that maximizes her or his wealth. This wealth not only consists of the still outstanding convertible bonds but also of the stocks received by a prior conversion of the already converted bonds. Thus, in the beginning the monopolist only cares for the convertible bond value but after a conversion the monopolist becomes a stockholder who additionally holds the outstanding convertible bonds.

According to section 2.3, the block assumption is widespread for the valuation of convertible bonds. Its advantage is the simple applicability. However, the block assumption prohibits a sequential conversion that might be an equilibrium strategy. In the unrestricted case, the assumed perfect competition among the convertible bond holders appears to be a fairly appropriate assumption to model real convertible bond holdings. In general, we can suppose that there is a large number of convertible bond investors so that no individual convertible bond holder has any price impact. However, the theoretical determination of the optimal conversion strategy results from complex game-theoretical considerations. The monopolistic conversion is the complement of the unrestricted conversion. In the monopolistic case, one investor completely controls the conversion decision, but in the unrestricted case a perfect competition exists among the investors. The monopolistic case serves as a limiting case because the monopolistic strategy is the strategy that yields the highest possible value obtained with the initially outstanding convertibles. As in the unrestricted case, the theoretical determination of the optimal conversion strategy requires sophisticated computations relative to the block conversion.[7]

---

[7] At this point, we could also regard other conversion variants such as e.g. an oligopol in which a limited number of investors holds the outstanding convertible bonds. Nevertheless, we focus on the three conversion variants described above as many other variants like the oligopol have the character of a mixture between the monopolistic and the unrestricted case.

3.2 Asset Pricing in the Presence of Interest Rate and Firm Value Uncertainty

In this section, we derive the values of financial claims X_t that depend on both the short rate and the firm value. The firm value and the short rate process satisfy the specifications imposed in the previous section. In this section, we abstract from coupon- or dividend payments. Thus, the dynamics of the firm value given in (3.1) hold for the complete life time of the claim and V_t is not subject to any jumps. These preconsiderations will enable us to state the values of the convertible bond, the stock, and the debt in section 3.3.

By the assumption of complete markets without arbitrage opportunities, we know that there exists a unique equivalent martingale measure such that the value of these financial claims is also unique. One possibility to obtain their value is to employ the risk-neutral valuation. Thus, the first task is to specify the corresponding risk-neutral measure. First, we regard the short rate measure $\mathbb{Q}$ under that the value of every traded asset divided by the value of the normalized money market account $M_t = e^{\int_0^t r_s ds}$ is a martingale. M_t is a feasible numeraire as the money market account is a traded asset and therefore every payoff X_T at time T can be replicated by a self-financing portfolio consisting of holdings of traded assets.[8] Assuming a constant market price of interest rate risk, we can apply the Cameron/Martin/Girsanov theorem in a standard way to write the processes (3.1) and (3.3)

$$\begin{aligned} dV_t &= r_t \cdot V_t + \sigma \cdot V_t \cdot dz'_t, \\ dr_t &= \kappa \cdot (\theta - r_t) \cdot dt + \eta \cdot dw'_t \end{aligned}$$

where z'_t and w'_t stand for the values of standard Wiener processes under the measure $\mathbb{Q}$ with correlation ρ. We note that θ is a real number denoting the risk-neutral long-term mean of the short rate r_t. It is well-known that the value of the self-financing and replicating portfolio of X_T is given by the following risk-neutral pricing formula:

$$X_t = M_t \cdot \mathbb{E}_t^{\mathbb{Q}}\left(X_T / M_T\right),$$

where $\mathbb{E}_t^{\mathbb{Q}}(\cdot)$ is a short form for the expectation $\mathbb{E}^{\mathbb{Q}}(\cdot \mid \mathcal{F}_t)$ under the measure $\mathbb{Q}$ conditional to $\mathcal{F}_t$ which is a σ algebra in the considered filtered probability space $\left(\Omega, \mathcal{F}, \{\mathcal{F}_t\}_0^T, \mathbb{Q}\right)$. For $X_T \equiv 1$, we obtain the value of the default-free zero bond $B_t(T)$ with maturity T which will play a certain role in what follows. According to Vasicek (1977), the value of

8 See Baxter/Rennie (1996), p. 137-139.

a zero bond with remaining time to maturity $T-t$ amounts to

$$\begin{aligned} B_t(T) &= M_t \cdot \mathbb{E}_t^{\mathbb{Q}}(1/M_T) \\ &= e^{A_t^{(1)}(T) - r_t \cdot A_t^{(2)}(T)}, \end{aligned} \tag{3.4}$$

where

$$\begin{aligned} A_t^{(1)}(T) &= \left(\frac{\eta^2}{2\kappa^2} - \theta\right)(T-t) + \left(\theta - \frac{\eta^2}{\kappa^2}\right)\frac{1-e^{-\kappa(T-t)}}{\kappa} \\ &\quad + \left(\frac{\eta^2}{4\kappa^3}\right)\left(1 - e^{-2\kappa(T-t)}\right), \\ A_t^{(2)}(T) &= \frac{1-e^{-\kappa(T-t)}}{\kappa}. \end{aligned}$$

The valuation of a financial claim X_T depending on both r_T and V_T requires to determine the expectation of the product of two correlated random variables namely X_T and $1/M_T$. To avoid this complex representation, we introduce the risk-neutral forward measure $\mathbb{P}_T$. Under the forward measure $\mathbb{P}_T$ the values of all traded assets divided by the corresponding zero bond value $B_t(T)$ are martingales. Choosing the traded asset $B_t(T)$ as the numeraire, we can represent the value X_t of any financial claim in a more convenient manner:

$$X_t = B_t(T) \cdot \mathbb{E}_t^{\mathbb{P}_T}(X_T) \tag{3.5}$$

To determine X_t, we need to take the expectation with respect to the measure $\mathbb{P}_T$ of the claim X_T according to pricing rule (3.5). We can change the measure from $\mathbb{Q}$ to $\mathbb{P}_T$ by employing the Radon/Nikodym derivative[9]

$$\frac{d\mathbb{P}_T}{d\mathbb{Q}} = \frac{1}{B_t(T) \cdot M_T}.$$

It follows that $B_t(T) \cdot \mathbb{E}_t^{\mathbb{P}_T}(X_T)$ is equal to $M_t \cdot \mathbb{E}_t^{\mathbb{Q}}(X_T/M_T)$ as $\mathbb{E}_t^{\mathbb{P}_T}(X_T)$ is identical to $\left(\mathbb{E}_t^{\mathbb{Q}}\left(\frac{d\mathbb{P}_T}{d\mathbb{Q}}\right)\right)^{-1} \cdot \mathbb{E}_t^{\mathbb{Q}}\left(X_T \frac{d\mathbb{P}_T}{d\mathbb{Q}}\right) = \frac{M_t \cdot B_t(T)}{B_t(T)} \cdot \frac{1}{B_t(T)} \mathbb{E}_t^{\mathbb{Q}}(X_T/M_T)$.

Following the Cameron/Martin/Girsanov theorem, the processes for the firm value and the short rate read[10]

$$\begin{aligned} dV_t &= \left(r_t - \frac{1-e^{-\kappa(T-t)}}{\kappa}\eta\rho\sigma\right) \cdot V_t dt + \sigma \cdot V_t \cdot dz_t'', \\ dr_t &= \left(\kappa(\theta - r_t) - \eta^2 \cdot \frac{1-e^{-\kappa(T-t)}}{\kappa}\right) dt + \eta \cdot dw_t'', \end{aligned}$$

9 See Baxter/Rennie (1996), p. 191.

10 We can apply this theorem according to Baxter/Rennie (1996), p. 74, by using the following representation $\frac{d\mathbb{P}_T}{d\mathbb{Q}} = \frac{1}{B_t(T) \cdot M_T} = \frac{1}{B_t(T)} e^{-\int_t^T r_s ds} = e^{-\frac{1}{2}\eta^2 \int_t^T B(s,T)^2 ds - \eta \int_t^T B(s,T) dz_s'}$ which results from Fubini's theorem. The processes for the firm value and the short rate correspond to those in Longstaff/Schwartz (1995), p. 816, who derive them in a different way.

where z_t'' and w_t'' are the values of standard Wiener processes under the measure $\mathbb{P}_T$ with instantaneous correlation ρ. To evaluate the expectation in pricing rule (3.5), we can make use of the fact that both $\ln V_T$ and r_T conditional to V_t and r_t are normally distributed under $\mathbb{P}_T$. Their conditional mean and variance under $\mathbb{P}_T$ are as follows

$$\begin{aligned} \ln V_T|\, V_t, r_t &\sim N\left(m_V(t,T), var_V(t,T)\right), \\ r_T|\, r_t &\sim N\left(m_r(t,T), var_r(t,T)\right), \end{aligned}$$

where

$$\begin{aligned} m_V(t,T) &= \ln V_t + \left(\theta - \left(\frac{\eta}{\kappa}\right)^2 - \frac{\eta\rho\sigma}{\kappa} - \frac{1}{2}\sigma^2\right)(T-t) \\ &\quad + \left(r_t - \theta + \left(\frac{\eta}{\kappa}\right)^2 + \frac{\eta^2}{2\kappa}\frac{1-e^{-\kappa(T-t)}}{\kappa} + \frac{\eta\rho\sigma}{\kappa}\right)\frac{1-e^{-\kappa(T-t)}}{\kappa}, \\ var_V(t,T) &= \left(\frac{\eta^2}{\kappa^2} + \sigma^2 + 2\frac{\eta\sigma\rho}{\kappa}\right)(T-t) \\ &\quad - \left(\frac{2\eta^2}{\kappa^2} + 2\frac{\eta\sigma\rho}{\kappa}\right)\frac{1-e^{-\kappa(T-t)}}{\kappa} + \eta^2\frac{1-e^{-2\kappa(T-t)}}{2\kappa^3}, \\ m_r(t,T) &= (r_t - \theta)\cdot e^{-\kappa(T-t)} + \theta - \frac{\eta^2}{2}\left(\frac{1-e^{-\kappa(T-t)}}{\kappa}\right)^2, \\ var_r(t,T) &= \frac{\eta^2}{2\kappa}\cdot\left(1-e^{-2\kappa(T-t)}\right). \end{aligned} \tag{3.6}$$

The conditional covariance of $(\ln V_T, r_T)$ is given by:

$$\begin{aligned} cov(t,T) &= Cov_t^{\mathbb{P}_T}(\ln V_T, r_T) \\ &= \eta\frac{1-e^{-\kappa(T-t)}}{\kappa}\left(\frac{\eta}{2}\frac{1-e^{-\kappa(T-t)}}{\kappa} + \sigma\rho\right) \end{aligned}$$

Let X_t be the value of a financial claim which pays $X_T = X_T(V_T, r_T)$ that depends on V_T and r_T at time T. At any other point in time τ $(0 \le \tau < T)$ X_τ pays nothing. The value of X_t can be obtained by the evaluation of the following integral:

$$\begin{aligned} X_t &= B_t(T)\cdot \mathbb{E}_t^{\mathbb{P}_T}\left(X_T(V_T, r_T)\right) \\ &= B_t(T)\cdot\int_{-\infty}^{\infty}\int_{-\infty}^{\infty} X_T(e^x, y)\cdot f_{t,T}(x,y)\,dxdy, \end{aligned}$$

where $f_{t,T}(x,y)$ denotes the density function of a bivariate normal distribution with mean $\begin{pmatrix} m_V(t,T) \\ m_r(t,T) \end{pmatrix}$ and covariance matrix $\begin{pmatrix} var_V(t,T) & cov(t,T) \\ cov(t,T) & var_r(t,T) \end{pmatrix}$ conditional to (V_t, r_t).

In particular, the values of a *European call* and *put option* on the firm value V_t will play a certain role for the following examination. The corresponding call value $C_t(V_t)$ of an option with strike price E and time to maturity $T-t$ can be obtained by[11]

$$\begin{aligned} C_t(V_t) &= B_t(T) \cdot \int_{-\infty}^{\infty} \int_{\ln E}^{\infty} X_T(e^x, y) \cdot f_{t,T}(x,y)\, dx dy \\ &= V_t \cdot \Phi(d_1) - E \cdot B_t(T) \cdot \Phi(d_2), \end{aligned} \tag{3.7}$$

where

$$\begin{aligned} d_1 &= \frac{m_V(t,T) - \ln E + var_V(t,T)}{\sqrt{var_V(t,T)}}, \\ d_2 &= \frac{m_V(t,T) - \ln E}{\sqrt{var_V(t,T)}}. \end{aligned}$$

$\Phi(\cdot)$ stands for the standard normal distribution function. Accordingly, the value of an European put option $P_t(V_t)$ with identical terms as the call option results in

$$P_t(V_t) = -V_t \cdot \Phi(-d_1) + E \cdot B_t(T) \cdot \Phi(-d_2).$$

3.3 Basic Relations between Asset Values

In this section, we discuss the basic relations between the three considered values of a convertible bond, a stock, and debt. In addition, we show how to determine their values. For this purpose, we revert to the pricing rule and the option values introduced in the previous section.

The total firm value V_t at an arbitrary time t before the maturity of the convertible bond is given by:

$$V_t = (n + K_t) \cdot S_t + (m - K_t) \cdot W_t + D_t, \qquad (t < T), \tag{3.8}$$

where S_t denotes the value of one share, W_t stands for the value (dirty price) of one convertible bond, and D_t is the total value of the additional debt. We note that at a conversion date $t = t_i$ or $t = T$, these asset values denote the corresponding values before a conversion of k_t convertible bonds. According to (3.2), the firm value can have drops at these dates due to coupon or redemption payments. Moreover, the firm value is discontinuous in every dividend date.

These asset values are functions of the firm value V_t, the short rate r_t, the prior conversion volume K_t, and the succeeding conversion strategy $k^*_{t_i}(\cdot)$,..., $k^*_T(\cdot)$ for all $i = 1, ..., N$ with $t_i \geq t$. In principle, the optimal conversion strategy $k^*_t(\cdot)$ at time t could also depend on the whole firm value path until the particular conversion date, the short rate level path, and the prior path of conversions. Due to the Markov property of V_t and r_t, the optimal

[11] Compare Shimko/Tejima/van Deventer (1993), p. 60-61.

conversion strategy at time t can be characterized by the firm value immediately before conversion V_t^-, the short rate r_t, and the volume of prior conversion K_t. For the ease of notation, the dependencies of $k_{t_i}^*\left(V_{t_i}^-, r_{t_i}, K_{t_i}\right)$ and $k_T^*\left(V_T^-, r_T, K_T\right)$ respectively are not explicitly taken into account.

Analysis of the Continuity of the Vales of a Convertible Bond, a Stock, and Debt in Time t at a Conversion Date

The values of a stock and debt, $S_t\left(V_t^-, r_t, K_t, k_t^*\right)$ and $D_t\left(V_t^-, r_t, K_t, k_t^*\right)$, are continuous in time t in every conversion, coupon, and redemption date, even though the firm value V_t might drop. The reason is that in the absence of arbitrage previsible jumps of every (particularly) traded asset can only occur from payments of this asset. As a consequence, the debt value is always continuous in time t and the stock value only exhibits drops due to dividend payments but is otherwise continuous in time t.

To evaluate the continuity of the convertible bond value, we must distinguish between the value $W_t\left(V_t^-, r_t, K_t, k_t\right)$ before and $W_t^+\left(V_t^-, r_t, K_t, k_t\right)$ after conversion including the coupon or redemption payment, respectively. The value after conversion at time t can be interpreted as a non-converted convertible bond $W_t^+\left(V_t^-, r_t, K_t, k_t\right)$ which is defined for all $k_t \in [0, m - K_t)$. In the case of an exogenous complete conversion, we consider $W_t^+\left(V_t^-, r_t, K_t, k_t\right)$ as the last marginal convertible bond that is not converted such that $W_t^+\left(V_t^-, r_t, K_t, m - K_t\right)$ is a short form of $\lim_{\substack{x \to m-K_t \\ x<m-K_t}} W_t^+\left(V_t^-, r_t, K_t, x\right)$. If the *optimal* conversion volume k_t^* is below $m - K_t$, there are still convertible bonds outstanding after conversion and we can interpret $W_t^+\left(V_t^-, r_t, K_t, k_t^*\right)$ as the market value of a convertible bond after conversion. Otherwise, it is not reasonable to speak from the convertible bond value after conversion if there are no convertible bonds outstanding.

We can see from the identity (3.8) that in every coupon or redemption date after the coupon or redemption payment

$$\begin{aligned} V_t = {} & (m - K_t - k_t) \cdot \left(W_t^+\left(V_t^-, r_t, K_t, k_t\right) - \text{coupon or redemp. paym.}\right) \\ & + (n + K_t + k_t) \cdot S_t\left(V_t^-, r_t, K_t, k_t\right) + D_t\left(V_t^-, r_t, K_t, k_t\right) \end{aligned}$$

holds. Regarding the corresponding identity before conversion and the relation $V_t^- = V_t + (m - K_t - k_t) \cdot (\text{coupon or redemp. paym.})$, it follows that the value of a convertible bond before conversion is a convex combination of the value of a non-converted convertible bond and the conversion value:

$$W_t\left(V_t^-, r_t, K_t, k_t\right) = \frac{m - K_t - k_t}{m - K_t} W_t^+\left(V_t^-, r_t, K_t, k_t\right) + \frac{k_t}{m - K_t} S_t\left(V_t^-, r_t, K_t, k_t\right) \quad (3.9)$$

Of course, the value of a convertible bond is discontinuous in a coupon date due to the coupon payment. However, the value of a convertible bond before conversion, $W_t\left(V_t^-, r_t, K_t, k_t^*\right)$, can differ from the value after conversion, $W_t^+\left(V_t^-, r_t, K_t, k_t^*\right)$

(including coupon or redemption payments). The reason for a non-zero difference $W_t^+\left(V_t^-, r_t, K_t, k_t^*\right) - W_t\left(V_t^-, r_t, K_t, k_t^*\right)$, which is consistent with our no-arbitrage assumption, will become clear when we examine the optimal conversion strategies. As a result of this effect, we must consider both $W_t^+\left(V_t^-, r_t, K_t, k_t^*\right)$ and $W_t\left(V_t^-, r_t, K_t, k_t^*\right)$ separately.

Representation of the Vales of a Convertible Bond, a Stock, and Debt at Maturity T

At maturity of the convertible bond and during the time period before the maturity of the additional debt, the firm value evolution depends on the fact whether or not default occurs at time T:

$$V_t = \begin{cases} 0, & \text{if } V_T^- < (m - K_T - k_T) \cdot F \\ (n + K_T + k_T) \cdot S_t + D_t, & \text{otherwise} \end{cases} \tag{3.10}$$
$$(T \leq t \leq TD)$$

In the further examination, which focuses on the conversion strategy, it is sufficient to regard the asset values at a conversion date and at maturity of the additional debt. For all other dates, the asset values result from the expectation of the values at the succeeding considered date multiplied by the corresponding zero bond value. At the last point of time, the asset values of both additional debt and total equity result from the values of options in a well-known manner. For this purpose, we require the value of a sold European put option $P_t(V_t)$ with strike price FD and time to maturity $TD - t$ and the value of a bought call option $C_t(V_t)$ with the same strike price and maturity. Following Merton (1974), the corresponding values of debt and total equity for any exogenous conversion strategy K_T, k_T at time T read

$$D_T = D_T\left(V_T^-, r_T, K_T, k_T\right) = B_T(TD) \cdot FD - P_T(V_T), \tag{3.11}$$
$$(n + K_T + k_T) \cdot S_T = (n + K_T + k_T) \cdot S_T\left(V_T^-, r_T, K_T, k_T\right)$$
$$= C_T(V_T).$$

Thus, the value of one stock is

$$S_T\left(V_T^-, r_T, K_T, k_T\right) = \frac{C_T(V_T)}{n + K_T + k_T}. \tag{3.12}$$

A closed-form solution for these option values was given at the end of section 3.2. Due to $V_T = \max\left(0, V_T^- - (m - K_T - k_T) \cdot F\right)$, the values of both debt and equity depend on the prior K_T and the current conversion volume k_T, respectively. The total value of the convertible bonds for this strategy before conversion at time T given no default amounts to

$$(m - K_T) \cdot W_T\left(V_T^-, r_T, K_T, k_T\right) = (m - K_T - k_T) \cdot F + k_T \cdot S_T.$$

Accordingly in this case, the value of one convertible bond before conversion is given by

$$W_T\left(V_T^-, r_T, K_T, k_T\right) = \frac{(m - K_T - k_T) \cdot F + k_T \cdot S_T\left(V_T^-, r_T, K_T, k_T\right)}{m - K_T}.$$

In the case of bankruptcy at the convertible bond's maturity, the total convertible bond value before conversion satisfies

$$(m - K_T) \cdot W_T\left(V_T^-, r_T, K_T, k_T\right) = V_T^-$$

and the value of one convertible bond is

$$W_T\left(V_T^-, r_T, K_T, k_T\right) = \frac{V_T^-}{m - K_T}$$

by the assumption about the priority of convertible bonds over additional debt, while the values of the additional debt and the equity are worthless.

At this point, we must distinguish $W_T^+\left(V_T^-, r_T, K_T, k_T\right)$, the value of a non-converted convertible bond at time T although a conversion of k_T occurs, from the value of a convertible bond W_T immediately before conversion. Evidently, W_T^+ might differ from W_T the value obtained with one convertible bond at maturity. For W_T^+, we get

$$W_T^+\left(V_T^-, r_T, K_T, k_T\right) = \min\left(\frac{V_T^-}{m - K_T - k_T}, F\right).$$

Representation of the Vales of a Convertible Bond, a Stock, and Debt before T

Due to the considerations in the previous section, we can determine the values of a stock and debt at a conversion date $t_i < T$ from the discounted expectation of the asset values at the succeeding conversion date t_{i+1} regarding the optimal succeeding conversion strategy $k_{t_{i+1}}^*(\cdot)$ and adding the value of the dividend payment if necessary. This idea leads us to the following representations for the values of the additional debt and a stock at an arbitrary conversion date t_i prior to maturity $T =: t_{N+1}$:

$$D_{t_i}\left(V_{t_i}^-, r_{t_i}, K_{t_i}, k_{t_i}\right) = B_{t_i}(t_{i+1}) \cdot \mathbb{E}_{t_i}^{\mathbb{P}_{t_{i+1}}}\left(D_{t_{i+1}}\left(V_{t_{i+1}}^-, r_{t_{i+1}}, K_{t_i} + k_{t_i}, k_{t_{i+1}}^*(\cdot)\right)\right), \quad (3.13)$$

$$S_{t_i}\left(V_{t_i}^-, r_{t_i}, K_{t_i}, k_{t_i}\right) = B_{t_i}(t_{i+1}) \cdot \mathbb{E}_{t_i}^{\mathbb{P}_{t_{i+1}}}\left(S_{t_{i+1}}\left(V_{t_{i+1}}^-, r_{t_{i+1}}, K_{t_i} + k_{t_i}, k_{t_{i+1}}^*(\cdot)\right)\right) + \frac{\delta V_{t_i}}{n + K_{t_i} + k_{t_i}} \quad (3.14)$$

The value at time t_i of the total dividend payment at the next dividend date is δV_{t_i}, even though the payment is due at a later date τ_i. This is because the total dividend payment is a fixed proportion of the firm value $\delta V_{t_i} = B_{t_i}(\tau_i) \cdot \mathbb{E}_{t_i}^{\mathbb{P}_{\tau_i}}(\delta V_{\tau_i})$, where V_{t_i} is the firm value after the coupon payment given by $V_{t_i} = \max\left(V_{t_i}^- - (m - K_{t_i} - k_{t_i}) \cdot c, 0\right)$. The notations $D_{t_i}\left(V_{t_i}^-, r_{t_i}, K_{t_i}, k_{t_i}\right)$ and $S_{t_i}\left(V_{t_i}^-, r_{t_i}, K_{t_i}, k_{t_i}\right)$ indicate that these values depend on the conversion volume k_{t_i} at time t_i but the succeeding conversion strategy $k_t^*(\cdot)$ for all $t > t_i$ is the optimal one.[12] This notation will be convenient for the determination of the optimal conversion volume $k_{t_i}^*$ presented in the following chapters, since we will derive the optimal conversion volume by backward induction assuming that the conversion volume is also optimal at the succeeding conversion dates.

When dealing with the value of the convertible bond, we distinguish between the value of a convertible bond before conversion $W_{t_i}\left(V_{t_i}^-, r_{t_i}, K_{t_i}, k_{t_i}\right)$ and the value of a non-converted convertible bond $W_{t_i}^+\left(V_{t_i}^-, r_{t_i}, K_{t_i}, k_{t_i}\right)$. It follows from (3.8) that the value of a convertible bond before conversion at time t_i results in

$$\begin{aligned} & W_{t_i}\left(V_{t_i}^-, r_{t_i}, K_{t_i}, k_{t_i}\right) \\ = \; & \frac{V_{t_i}^- - (n + K_{t_i}) \cdot S_{t_i}\left(V_{t_i}^-, r_{t_i}, K_{t_i}, k_{t_i}\right) - D_{t_i}\left(V_{t_i}^-, r_{t_i}, K_{t_i}, k_{t_i}\right)}{m - K_{t_i}}. \end{aligned} \tag{3.15}$$

The value of a non-converted convertible bond can be written as follows using (3.9) and (3.15):

$$\begin{aligned} & W_{t_i}^+\left(V_{t_i}^-, r_{t_i}, K_{t_i}, k_{t_i}\right) \\ = \; & \frac{V_{t_i}^- - (n + K_{t_i} + k_{t_i}) \cdot S_{t_i}\left(V_{t_i}^-, r_{t_i}, K_{t_i}, k_{t_i}\right) - D_{t_i}\left(V_{t_i}^-, r_{t_i}, K_{t_i}, k_{t_i}\right)}{m - K_{t_i} - k_{t_i}}. \end{aligned}$$

We can interpret $W_{t_i}^+\left(V_{t_i}^-, r_{t_i}, K_{t_i}, k_{t_i}\right)$ as the present value of the prorated total convertible bond value at the succeeding conversion date t_{i+1} plus the value of the current coupon payment. Thus, we can alternatively rewrite $W_{t_i}^+\left(V_{t_i}^-, r_{t_i}, K_{t_i}, k_{t_i}\right)$ as

$$\begin{aligned} W_{t_i}^+\left(V_{t_i}^-, r_{t_i}, K_{t_i}, k_{t_i}\right) &= \min\left(c, \frac{V_{t_i}^-}{m - K_{t_i} - k_{t_i}}\right) \\ &+ B_{t_i}(t_{i+1}) \cdot \mathbb{E}_{t_i}^{\mathbb{P}_{t_{i+1}}}\left(W_{t_{i+1}}\left(V_{t_{i+1}}^-, r_{t_{i+1}}, K_{t_i} + k_{t_i}, k_{t_{i+1}}^*(\cdot)\right)\right). \end{aligned} \tag{3.16}$$

For the evaluation of all the expectations, we note that the coupon and the dividend payment have to be taken into account to compute the expectations under the measure $\mathbb{P}_{t_{i+1}}$. Given $V_{t_i}^-$ the mean of $\ln V_{t_{i+1}}^-$ under the measure $\mathbb{P}_{t_{i+1}}$ can be obtained from (3.6) as

$$\begin{aligned} & \ln\left(\left(V_{t_i}^- - (m - K_{t_i} - k_{t_i}) \cdot c\right) \cdot (1 - \delta)\right) + \left(\theta - \left(\frac{\eta}{\kappa}\right)^2 - \frac{\eta\rho\sigma}{\kappa} - \frac{1}{2}\sigma^2\right)(t_{i+1} - t_i) \\ + & \left(r_{t_i} - \theta + \left(\frac{\eta}{\kappa}\right)^2 + \frac{\eta^2}{2\kappa}\frac{1 - e^{-\kappa(t_{i+1} - t_i)}}{\kappa} + \frac{\eta\rho\sigma}{\kappa}\right)\frac{1 - e^{-\kappa(t_{i+1} - t_i)}}{\kappa} \end{aligned}$$

---

12 To ensure that the expectation required for the asset values exists, we must assume that the optimal conversion strategy $k_{t_{i+1}}^*(\cdot)$ for all $t_{i+1} > t_i$ is an integrable function. We will see in the following chapters that this technical assumption holds.

as long as the coupon payment $(m - K_{t_i} - k_{t_i}) \cdot c$ at time t_i is below the firm value $V_{t_i}^-$. This representation corresponds to $m_V(t_i, t_{i+1})$ using the ex-dividend and coupon firm value $\left(V_{t_i}^- - (m - k_{t_i} - K_{t_i}) \cdot c\right) \cdot (1 - \delta)$ at time t_i. Otherwise, the firm defaults at time t_i and $V_{t_{i+1}} \equiv 0$ a.s.

Chapter 4

Optimal Conversion Strategies and Valuation of Convertible Bonds at Maturity

In this chapter, we examine the optimal conversion strategies *at maturity* of the convertible bond for the three conversion variants introduced in section 3.1: block conversion, unrestricted conversion, and monopolistic conversion. Additionally, we determine the related values of both the convertible bond and the stock resulting from the corresponding conversion strategy. In the succeeding chapter, we conduct the analogous analysis for a premature conversion date. The reason why we analyze both cases at maturity and prior to maturity is that the conversion decisions at maturity and at a prior conversion date are driven by different determinants. At maturity T, the fact that a later conversion is no longer possible might force a conversion in several cases. Prior to maturity, the investors have to weigh up the advantages of a prompt and a deferred conversion. The analysis is conducted by the following three steps.

In the first step, we examine the effect of the underlying on the conversion strategy and the asset values. In principle, there are two asset values that come into question to represent the underlying, as we have seen in section 2.3. The first one is the firm value V_t. This choice is the general view taken by structural models in which the outstanding securities of the firm, convertible bonds, stocks, and debt can be seen as derivatives written on the firm value. The second possibility in characterizing the underlying comes from the market side. As the firm value is generally not observable, it is in line with the market view to base the conversion decision and the valuation of a convertible bond on the observable stock value. Thus, the stock value is also a feasible underlying. In our analysis, we consider both the effect caused by the firm and the stock value. Due to the existence of additional debt, we find striking differences depending on the choice of the underlying.

In the second step, we look at the impact of the current short rate r_t on the conversion strategy and the asset values. As convertible bonds have a certain interest rate exposure, it is essential to analyze this effect in detail due to the presence of interest rate uncertainty taken into account by our model.

In the third step, we account for other parameters that play a certain role which are not straightforward. In particular, the considered parameters are the dividend rate δ and the debt face value FD. Since there is no dividend payment at maturity, the impact of the dividend rate is only relevant for the analysis at a premature conversion date. The importance of δ stems from the fact that the incentive for a premature conversion might depend on the dividend rate. The face value FD measures the role of the additional debt. For the following examination, we assume that a variation of FD does not result from an issue or a repurchase of debt, which might impact the firm value. Rather, we regard the differences to an otherwise identical firm with a different debt face value by a variation of FD. Thus, we vary FD for a fixed firm value V_t^- and short rate r_t. If not otherwise stated, we refer to the case that $FD > 0$ and $\delta < 1$ holds, i.e. the firm has a positive amount of debt outstanding and a total liquidation does not occur at the dividend date. The special cases $FD = 0$ and $\delta = 1$ are discussed separately.

After examining the effects of all the other parameters, we find that a variation of further parameters is either analogous to a variation of one of the considered parameters or does not provide remarkable insights. To avoid an analysis of redundant parameters, we will not explicitly account for the other parameters.[1]

The following analysis for the block case presents results of Crouhy/Galai (1994), which were originally derived for warrants, in a modified form. The findings in the block, unrestricted, and monopolistic case contain the results of Bühler/Koziol (2001, 2002) as special cases.

4.1 Block Conversion

1a) Conversion Strategy and the Values of a Convertible Bond and Stock as a Function of the Firm Value

[1] The effects caused by other parameters like the volatility σ were already examined by Ingersoll (1977a). It turns out that the volatility can increase or decrease the conversion volume as well as the asset values. In this context, it is important whether the convertible bond behaves like equity or straight debt. In the first case the convertible value increases with σ, while it decreases in the second one. Similarly, we could analyze a variation of the coupon c. However, it is easy to see that the coupon affects the conversion volume in the opposite direction as the dividend payment.

Conversion Strategy

In the block conversion case, the conversion volume at time T is restricted to two possibilities $k_T = 0$ and $k_T = m$. Thus, the question of the *optimal conversion decision* k_T^* at time T only arises if $K_T = 0$ is presumed. A conversion of all the m outstanding convertible bonds is optimal, if for the stock value $S_T\left(V_T^-, r_T, 0, m\right)$ *after conversion*

$$S_T\left(V_T^-, r_T, 0, m\right) > F$$

holds. As described in chapter 3, we can represent the stock value by the value of a call option written on $V_T = \max\left(V_T^- - (m - K_T - k_T) \cdot F, 0\right)$ with strike price FD. Therefore, it follows from the monotonicity property of the call value in V_T that a unique critical value $\overline{V}_T$ exists which satisfies

$$S_T\left(\overline{V}_T, r_T, 0, m\right) = F$$

and accordingly

$$C_T\left(\overline{V}_T\right) = (n+m) \cdot S_T\left(\overline{V}_T, r_T, 0, m\right) = (n+m) \cdot F. \tag{4.1}$$

Since after a complete conversion $V_T = V_T^-$ holds, $\overline{V}_T$ is the critical firm value *before* and *after conversion*. Therefore, a complete conversion occurs for $V_T^- > \overline{V}_T$ and no conversion for $V_T^- < \overline{V}_T$.

In the case of bankruptcy in which the value of a non-converted convertible bond $W_T^+\left(V_T^-, r_T, 0, 0\right) = \min\left(\frac{V_T^-}{m}, F\right)$ is smaller than F, $W_T^+\left(V_T^-, r_T, 0, 0\right)$ equals $\frac{V_T^-}{m}$ and is obviously higher than its conversion value $S_T\left(V_T^-, r_T, 0, m\right) = \frac{V_T^-}{n+m}$. Hence, no conversion is optimal if default can be triggered by the convertible bond holders.

In the case of $V_T^- = \overline{V}_T$, both conversion volumes $k_T^* = 0$ and $k_T^* = m$ are optimal, i.e. the value obtained with a converted or a non-converted convertible bond equals the redemption value F. To avoid a separate examination of this special case in detail, we presume a complete conversion in this case of indifference.

It follows immediately from the properties of the value of the European call option that k_T^* increases with V_T^-.[2] This property means that k_T^* in the block case does not change or shows an upward jump at $\overline{V}_T$ from zero to m as illustrated in figure 4.1.

Values of the Convertible Bond and the Stock

For the analysis of the convertible bond *value* at maturity in the block case, it is reasonable to consider the convertible bond value $W_T\left(V_T^-, r_T, 0, k_T^*\right)$ before conversion rather than

[2] By an increase, we always mean the weak monotonicity rather than the strict one. If a function f is increasing, $f(x_1) \leq f(x_2)$ holds for all $x_1 < x_2$. The strict monotonicity requires $f(x_1) < f(x_2)$ for all $x_1 < x_2$.

the value of a non-converted convertible bond $W_T^+(V_T^-, r_T, 0, k_T^*)$. This is because there are no non-converted convertible bonds after a conversion and $W_T^+(V_T^-, r_T, 0, k_T^*)$ is not reasonably defined, but $W_T(V_T^-, r_T, 0, k_T^*)$ exists for all conversion strategies. The value of a convertible bond before conversion at time T resulting from the optimal block conversion strategy is as follows:

$$W_T(V_T^-, r_T, 0, k_T^*) = \begin{cases} \frac{V_T^-}{m}, & \text{for } V_T^- < m \cdot F \\ F, & \text{for } m \cdot F \leq V_T^- < \overline{V}_T \\ S_T(V_T^-, r_T, 0, m), & \text{for } V_T^- \geq \overline{V}_T \end{cases}$$

The convertible bond value $W_T(V_T^-, r_T, 0, k_T^*)$ as we can see in figure 4.1 is a continuous and increasing function of the firm value V_T^-, even though the block strategy k_T^* might show jumps in V_T^-. Moreover, given no conversion at maturity, $k_T^* = 0$, the value of a convertible bond after the conversion decision $W_T^+(V_T^-, r_T, 0, k_T^*)$ is the same as before the conversion decision $W_T(V_T^-, r_T, 0, k_T^*)$ because in this case both $W_T^+(V_T^-, r_T, 0, k_T^*)$ and $W_T(V_T^-, r_T, 0, k_T^*)$ denote the value of a non-converted convertible bond.

For the *stock value*, we obtain:

$$S_T(V_T^-, r_T, 0, k_T^*) = \begin{cases} 0, & \text{for } V_T^- < m \cdot F \\ S_T(V_T^-, r_T, 0, 0), & \text{for } m \cdot F \leq V_T^- < \overline{V}_T \\ S_T(V_T^-, r_T, 0, m), & \text{for } V_T^- \geq \overline{V}_T \end{cases}$$

$S_T(V_T^-, r_T, 0, k_T^*)$ is a continuous and strictly increasing function of the firm value V_T^- as long as the firm does not default at time T and the conversion volume does not change with V_T^-. In the case of a default, the stock value is worthless. These properties of the stock value are a result of the representations of $S_T(V_T^-, r_T, 0, 0)$ and $S_T(V_T^-, r_T, 0, m)$ as a call option given in equation (3.12).

The question whether $S_T(V_T^-, r_T, 0, k_T^*)$ is also continuous at $\overline{V}_T$ can be illustrated by regarding the impact of a conversion on the debt value. From the perspective of the debt holders, a conversion is always preferred relative to no conversion. The reason is that after a conversion the firm value is not reduced by the redemption payment of the convertible bond and thus the firm value at the debt's maturity TD is higher. This effect yields a higher debt value at time T if a conversion takes place. The increase is caused by a wealth transfer to the debt holders from the other two groups of shareholders. Referring again to the stock value, these considerations about the debt value indicate that no conversion can be in favor of the stockholders because the wealth transfer to the debt holders is prevented. Hence, our intuition tells us that for firm values V_T^- in a neighborhood of $\overline{V}_T$ for which no conversion is optimal, the stock values $S_T(V_T^-, r_T, 0, k_T^*)$ must lie above $S_T(\overline{V}_T, r_T, 0, m) = F$. At $\overline{V}_T$, the stock value $S_T(V_T^-, r_T, 0, k_T^*)$ drops to F.

In fact, there is a second critical firm value $\underline{V}_T < \overline{V}_T$, at which the stock value is also equal to the redemption value F of the convertible bond. This second critical firm value at $\underline{V}_T$ is associated with *no conversion* $k_T^* = 0$. It can be implicitly defined by the relation

$$S_T\left(\underline{V}_T, r_T, 0, 0\right) = F$$

or

$$C_T\left(\underline{V}_T - m \cdot F\right) = n \cdot S_T\left(\underline{V}_T, r_T, 0, 0\right) = n \cdot F. \tag{4.2}$$

The equation has a unique solution as the call value C_T is strictly increasing in V_T. The fact that the critical firm value $\underline{V}_T$ is below $\overline{V}_T$, follows from a representation arising from equations (4.1) and (4.2)

$$C_T\left(\overline{V}_T\right) = (n+m) \cdot F = C_T\left(\underline{V}_T - m \cdot F\right) + m \cdot F. \tag{4.3}$$

As the delta of a call option is below one in our framework, equation (4.3) can only be satisfied if $\underline{V}_T$ is below $\overline{V}_T$. Due to the strict monotonicity of $S_T\left(V_T^-, r_T, 0, k_T^*\right)$ for $V_T^- \neq \overline{V}_T$, the stock value $S_T\left(V_T^-, r_T, 0, k_T^*\right)$ exceeds the redemption value of a convertible bond for firm values $\underline{V}_T < V_T^- < \overline{V}_T$. However, for these firm values, it is not optimal to convert, as the related stock value *after conversion* would lie below F. These considerations and the condition $S_T\left(\overline{V}_T, r_T, 0, m\right) = F$ indicate why the stock value shows a downward jump at $\overline{V}_T$ as presented in figure 4.1.[3] We summarize the properties of the optimal block conversion strategy and those of the related values of a convertible bond and a stock in the first result.

Result 1 *The optimal conversion volume k_T^* of the convertible bond at maturity T increases with the firm value V_T^-. The optimal block conversion strategy at maturity has the structure $k_T^* = 0$ for $V_T^- < \overline{V}_T$ and $k_T^* = m$ for $V_T^- \geq \overline{V}_T$. The value of a convertible bond $W_T\left(V_T^-, r_T, 0, k_T^*\right)$ at maturity T before conversion continuously increases with V_T^-. The stock value $S_T\left(V_T^-, r_T, 0, k_T^*\right)$ at maturity T continuously increases with the firm value V_T^- for $V_T^- < \overline{V}_T$ and for $V_T^- > \overline{V}_T$. At the critical firm value $\overline{V}_T$, the stock value decreases discontinuously. Therefore, the stock value can lie above the redemption value of a convertible bond and no conversion is advantageous.*

1b) Conversion Strategy and the Value of a Convertible Bond as a Function of the Stock Value

In this subsection, we take the market view and follow the goal of characterizing the optimal conversion volume k_T^* and the endogenous value of a convertible bond before

---

3 The parameter values for the short rate process, κ, θ, and η, are obtained by Koziol/Sauerbier (2002). They use data about the spot rate curves of the German Bundesanleihen from the beginning of 2000 to the end of 2001 to estimate these parameters.

Figure 4.1: Optimal Conversion Strategy and Values of a Convertible Bond and a Stock at Maturity under Block Conversion

The left diagram shows the optimal conversion volume k_T^* in the block case at maturity as a function of the firm value V_T^-. The right diagram shows the related values of a convertible bond $W_T\left(V_T^-, r_T, 0, k_T^*\right)$ and a stock $S_T\left(V_T^-, r_T, 0, k_T^*\right)$. The parameter values are $n = 100$, $m = 100$, $F = 100$, $FD = 50{,}000$, $TD - T = 1$, $r_T = 0.05$, $\sigma = 0.5$, $\eta = 0.01097$, $\rho = -0.1$, $\kappa = 0.16643$, $\theta = 0.0639$. The critical firm values $\underline{V}_T$ and $\overline{V}_T$ result in 58,547.8 and 62,635.5, respectively.

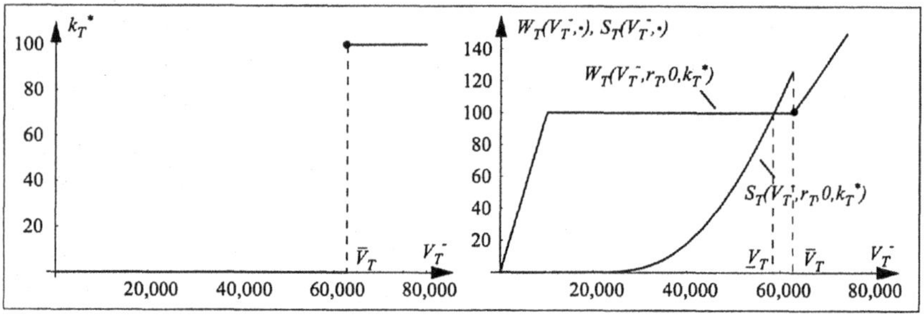

conversion $W_T\left(V_T^-, r_T, 0, k_T^*\right)$ as a function of the stock value $S_T\left(V_T^-, r_T, 0, k_T^*\right)$.

Analogous to our considerations in subsection 1a) using the firm value V_T^- as the relevant underlying, we can determine k_T^* and $W_T\left(V_T^-, r_T, 0, k_T^*\right)$ depending on $S_T\left(V_T^-, r_T, 0, k_T^*\right)$. For this purpose, we can still use our firm value model by regarding the combinations $\left(k_T^*, S_T\left(V_T^-, r_T, 0, k_T^*\right)\right)$ and $\left(W_T\left(V_T^-, r_T, 0, k_T^*\right), S_T\left(V_T^-, r_T, 0, k_T^*\right)\right)$ for all non-negative firm values V_T^-.

A particular example of the optimal conversion volume k_T^* and the convertible bond value $W_T\left(V_T^-, r_T, 0, k_T^*\right)$ as a function of the endogenous stock value $S_T\left(V_T^-, r_T, 0, k_T^*\right)$ is given in figure 4.2. This figure shows that both the *conversion strategy* k_T^* and the *value* of a *convertible bond* $W_T\left(V_T^-, r_T, 0, k_T^*\right)$ are not uniquely defined by $S_T\left(V_T^-, r_T, 0, k_T^*\right)$ for stock values between $S_T\left(\underline{V}_T, r_T, 0, k_T^*\right) = F$ and $S_T\left(\overline{V}, r_T, 0, 0\right) = 125.5$. The reason for this non-uniqueness is the downward jump of the stock value $S_T\left(V_T^-, r_T, 0, k_T^*\right)$ in V_T^- illustrated in figure 4.1. As a consequence, the same stock value can be related to a complete conversion $k_T^* = m$ and to no conversion $k_T^* = 0$. This non-uniqueness also holds for the value of a convertible bond. The stock value related to a complete conversion results from a higher firm value and therefore the corresponding convertible bond value is higher than that of the same stock value in the case of no conversion.

A second non-uniqueness of the convertible bond value occurs for a stock value equal to

Figure 4.2: Optimal Conversion Strategy and Value of a Convertible Bond at Maturity under Block Conversion

The left diagram shows the optimal conversion volume k_T^* in the block case at maturity as a function of the stock value $S_T\left(V_T^-, r_T, 0, k_T^*\right)$. The right diagram shows the related value of a convertible bond $W_T\left(V_T^-, r_T, 0, k_T^*\right)$. The parameter values are $n = 100$, $m = 100$, $F = 100$, $FD = 50{,}000$, $TD - T = 1$, $r_T = 0.05$, $\sigma = 0.5$, $\eta = 0.01097$, $\rho = -0.1$, $\kappa = 0.16643$, $\theta = 0.0639$.

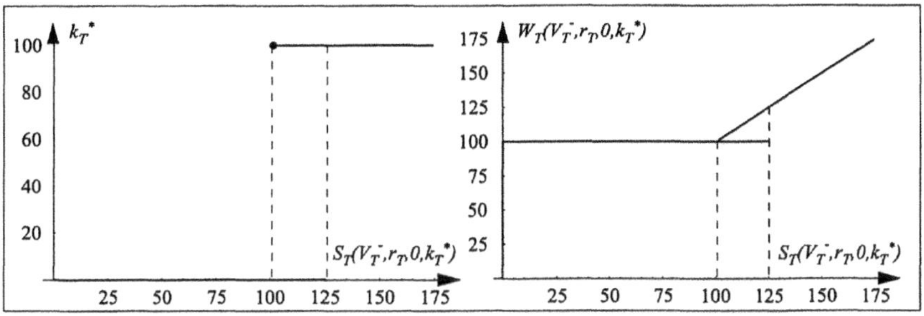

zero, i.e. in case of bankruptcy. In this case, the convertible bond value can attain every value between zero and F depending on the firm value. The findings of this subsection are presented in the next result.

Result 2 *The conversion strategy k_T^* and the convertible bond value $W_T\left(V_T^-, r_T, 0, k_T^*\right)$ are uniquely defined for stock values in the intervals $(0, F)$ and $\left(S_T\left(\overline{V}_T, r_T, 0, 0\right), \infty\right)$. In the first interval, no conversion is the unique strategy, in the second one, a complete conversion is optimal and the convertible bond value equals the stock value. For a given stock value in the interval $\left(F, S_T\left(\overline{V}, r_T, 0, 0\right)\right)$, both conversion strategies $k_T^* = 0$ and $k_T^* = m$ can be optimal depending on the firm value. Accordingly, two different convertible bond values are related to every stock value in this interval $\left(F, S_T\left(\overline{V}_T, r_T, 0, 0\right)\right)$. In addition, the value of a convertible bond is not unique if bankruptcy occurs, i.e. if $S_T\left(V_T^-, r_T, 0, k_T^*\right) = 0$.*

This result shows that this approach to discussing and representing the conversion strategy k_T^* and the convertible bond value $W_T\left(V_T^-, r_T, 0, k_T^*\right)$ under block conversion as a function of the stock value cannot be justified.

2) Conversion Strategy and the Values of a Convertible Bond and Stock as a Function of the Short Rate

In the next step, we regard the effect caused by the second major factor of a convertible bond, the short rate r_T. We note that in the Vasicek term structure model employed in this framework the short rate r_T at maturity T affects the spot rates $-\ln B_T(\tau)/(\tau - T)$ of every maturity $\tau - T > 0$. Thus, an increase of r_T leads to two changes. First, the spot rates $-\ln B_T(\tau)/(\tau - T)$ for every maturity increase. Second, the shape of the interest rate curve changes. These two effects follow immediately from the representation of the zero bond value (3.4).

Conversion Strategy

To evaluate the effect of the short rate r_T on the *conversion volume* k_T^*, we regard the value of a convertible bond $W_T(V_T^-, r_T, 0, 0)$ given no conversion and the conversion value which is equal to the stock value $W_T(V_T^-, r_T, 0, m) = S_T(V_T^-, r_T, 0, m)$. Again, the optimal conversion strategy states that a conversion is optimal if and only if the stock value after a conversion $S_T(V_T^-, r_T, 0, m)$ is at least as high as the convertible bond value $W_T(V_T^-, r_T, 0, 0)$, if not converted. This value either equals the redemption value F or the prorated firm value in case of default. Thus, if no conversion is optimal, the convertible bond value does not depend on the short rate r_T.

On the contrary, the conversion value $S_T(V_T^-, r_T, 0, m)$ is continuously and strictly increasing with r_T. This effect results from the call option property of the stock value and the call option value (3.7).

Thus, one critical short rate $\bar{r}_T$ at most exists for which the convertible bond value without a conversion $W_T(V_T^-, r_T, 0, 0)$ equals the conversion value $S_T(V_T^-, r_T, 0, m)$. As a consequence, no conversion is optimal for short rates r_T below $\bar{r}_T$ and a complete conversion occurs otherwise. It is not clear whether there exists always a critical short rate $\bar{r}_T$. To address this question, we determine conversion values $S_T(V_T^-, r_T, 0, m)$ for the limiting cases that r_T goes to plus and minus infinity. In case that r_T tends to infinity, $S_T(V_T^-, r_T, 0, m)$ approaches $\frac{V_T^-}{n+m}$ as the debt value $D_T(V_T^-, r_T, 0, m)$ converges to zero. In the opposite case that r_T goes to minus infinity, $S_T(V_T^-, r_T, 0, m)$ converges to zero. Thus, $S_T(V_T^-, r_T, 0, m)$ is a continuous strictly increasing function of r_T covering the interval $\left(0, \frac{V_T^-}{n+m}\right)$. As a consequence, if $F \geq \frac{V_T^-}{n+m}$ holds, independent of r_T it is optimal not to convert as the conversion value $S_T(V_T^-, r_T, 0, m)$ is always lower than the value F of a non-converted convertible bond. Otherwise, if the firm value is high enough (or F small enough) such that F lies in the interval $\left(0, \frac{V_T^-}{n+m}\right)$, a unique critical short rate $\bar{r}_T$ exists that satisfies the condition $S_T(V_T^-, \bar{r}_T, 0, m) = W_T(V_T^-, \bar{r}_T, 0, 0) = F$.

Values of the Convertible Bond and the Stock

If no critical short rate $\overline{r}_T$ exists, no conversion occurs and $W_T\left(V_T^-, r_T, 0, k_T^*\right) = W_T\left(V_T^-, r_T, 0, 0\right)$ does not depend on r_T. If $\overline{r}_T$ exists, the optimal conversion strategy leads to a *convertible bond value* $W_T\left(V_T^-, r_T, 0, k_T^*\right)$ independent of r_T for short rates r_T below $\overline{r}_T$. For short rates above $\overline{r}_T$, the convertible bond value $W_T\left(V_T^-, r_T, 0, k_T^*\right)$ equals the conversion value and increases continuously and strictly with r_T towards $\frac{V_T^-}{n+m}$. We note that $W_T\left(V_T^-, r_T, 0, k_T^*\right)$ is always continuous as $W_T\left(V_T^-, r_T, 0, 0\right) = F = S_T\left(V_T^-, r_T, 0, m\right)$ for $r_T = \overline{r}_T$ holds by definition.

As the *stock value* $S_T\left(V_T^-, r_T, 0, k_T^*\right)$ can be represented by call option values, $S_T\left(V_T^-, r_T, 0, k_T^*\right)$ increases with r_T as long as the optimal conversion volume k_T^* is not affected by r_T. At the critical short rate $\overline{r}_T$, at which a conversion is triggered, the stock value $S_T\left(V_T^-, r_T, 0, k_T^*\right)$ exhibits a downward jump due to a wealth transfer to the debt holders. This effect is identical to that discussed in subsection 1a) for a variation of the firm value. Again, for interest rates r_T in a neighborhood of $\underline{r}_T$, the stock value $S_T\left(V_T^-, r_T, 0, k_T^*\right) = S_T\left(V_T^-, r_T, 0, 0\right)$ can be above F and it is not optimal to convert the bond. This property is due to the fact that a conversion would result in a conversion value of $S_T\left(V_T^-, r_T, 0, m\right)$ being lower than F. This finding allows us to define a second critical short rate $\underline{r}_T$ for which the stock value $S_T\left(V_T^-, r_T, 0, k_T^*\right)$ is also equal to F but no conversion occurs. Thus, the stock value $S_T\left(V_T^-, r_T, 0, k_T^*\right)$ is above F for short rates between $\underline{r}_T$ and $\overline{r}_T$ and no conversion is optimal.

These effects associated with a variation of the short rate r_T are illustrated in figure 4.3 for a particular example and are summarized in the next result.

Result 3 *The optimal conversion volume k_T^* of the convertible bond at maturity T increases with the short rate r_T. The optimal block conversion strategy at maturity shows the structure $k_T^* = 0$ for $r_T < \overline{r}_T$ and $k_T^* = m$ for $r_T \geq \overline{r}_T$ if the firm value V_T^- is above $(n+m) \cdot F$. Otherwise, no critical short rate exists and independent of r_T the convertible bond will not be converted. The value of a convertible bond $W_T\left(V_T^-, r_T, 0, k_T^*\right)$ before conversion at maturity T continuously increases with r_T. The stock value $S_T\left(V_T^-, r_T, 0, k_T^*\right)$ at maturity T continuously increases with the short rate r_T for $r_T < \overline{r}_T$ and for $r_T > \overline{r}_T$. At the critical short rate $\overline{r}_T$, the stock value decreases by a jump.*

The economic intuition behind this result is as follows. If the firm value V_T^- is independent of the interest rates r_T, a higher short rate generally results in a lower debt value in favor of a higher stock value. Thus, as long as the optimal conversion volume is not affected by the short rate, a wealth transfer from the debt holders to the stockholders is triggered by a higher short rate. The convertible bond holders are not affected by a change of

Figure 4.3: Optimal Conversion Strategy and Values of a Convertible Bond and a Stock at Maturity under Block Conversion

The left diagram shows the optimal conversion volume k_T^* in the block case at maturity as a function of the short rate r_T. The right diagram shows the related values of a convertible bond $W_T\left(V_T^-, r_T, 0, k_T^*\right)$ and a stock $S_T\left(V_T^-, r_T, 0, k_T^*\right)$. The parameter values are $n = 100$, $m = 100$, $F = 100$, $FD = 50,000$, $TD - T = 1$, $V_T^- = 60,000$, $\sigma = 0.5$, $\eta = 0.01097$, $\rho = -0.1$, $\kappa = 0.16643$, $\theta = 0.0639$. *The critical short rates $\underline{r}_T$ and $\overline{r}_T$ result in* 0.002034 *and* 0.12898, *respectively.*

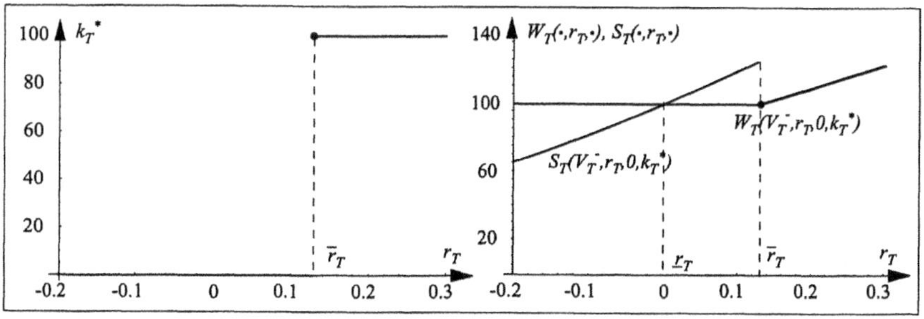

the short rate, if it is not optimal to convert. However, if a conversion is optimal, the convertible bond holders become stockholders and benefit from a higher short rate as do the stockholders.

3) Conversion Strategy and the Values of a Convertible Bond and Stock as a Function of the Amount of Additional Debt

In the third step, we examine — in principle — the conversion strategy and the values of a convertible bond and a stock as a function of two parameters, the dividend rate, δ, and the debt face value FD. As the last dividend payment in our model takes place at a point in time before T, this parameter does not influence the conversion strategy or the convertible bond value, and it is sufficient for us to vary the debt face value FD.

To conduct this analysis, we can — analogous to subsection 2) — compare the change of the value of a non-converted convertible bond $W_T\left(V_T^-, r_T, 0, 0\right) = \max\left(\frac{V_T^-}{m}, F\right)$ with that of the conversion value $S_T\left(V_T^-, r_T, 0, m\right) = \frac{V_T^- - D_T\left(V_T^-, r_T, 0, m\right)}{n+m}$ caused by a variation of FD. According to these representations, $W_T\left(V_T^-, r_T, 0, 0\right)$ is independent of FD, but a variation of FD only affects the stock value $S_T\left(V_T^-, r_T, 0, m\right)$ by a different debt value $D_T\left(V_T^-, r_T, 0, m\right)$. Since the debt value covers the same interval for face values FD from zero to infinity as for short rates r_T from minus infinity to plus infinity, we can trace back the optimal conversion strategy as a function of the debt face value to the results obtained for a variation of the short rate. We only have to note that a higher short rate decreases the debt value, where a higher debt face value affects the debt value in the opposite direction.

As a result of this analogy, no conversion occurs for every debt face value FD, if and only if $F \geq \frac{V_T^-}{n+m}$. Otherwise, there are two critical debt face values $\underline{FD}$ and $\overline{FD}$ that correspond to $\underline{r}_T$ and $\overline{r}_T$. The first critical debt face value $\underline{FD}$ is associated with a stock value in the case of no conversion equal to F, where $\overline{FD}$ is the critical value that triggers a complete conversion for lower FD. Contrary to the considerations of the firm value V_T^- and the short rate r_T, $\underline{FD}$ lies above $\overline{FD}$.

In an analogous way, we find that the *convertible bond value* $W_T\left(V_T^-, r_T, 0, k_T^*\right)$ is a continuous and decreasing function of FD, because in case of no conversion $W_T\left(V_T^-, r_T, 0, 0\right)$ is independent of FD and otherwise $W_T\left(V_T^-, r_T, 0, m\right) = S_T\left(V_T^-, r_T, 0, m\right)$ decreases with FD as the stock value. Accordingly, the *stock value* $S_T\left(V_T^-, r_T, 0, k_T^*\right)$ is also continuously decreasing with FD as long as the conversion strategy k_T^* is not affected. If k_T^* shows a downward jump in FD, the stock value $S_T\left(V_T^-, r_T, 0, k_T^*\right)$ benefits from the higher debt face value FD and exhibits an upward jump. This is due to the fact that a higher FD prevents a wealth transfer to the debt holders in this case. Thus, a higher FD can result in a higher stock value $S_T\left(V_T^-, r_T, 0, k_T^*\right)$ and for debt face values FD between $\overline{FD}$ and $\underline{FD}$ the stock value $S_T\left(V_T^-, r_T, 0, k_T^*\right)$ exceeds the redemption value F of the convertible bond. These considerations provide us with the next result.

Result 4 *The optimal conversion volume k_T^* of the convertible bond at maturity T decreases with the debt face value FD. If the firm value V_T^- is below $(n+m) \cdot F$, no conversion is optimal for all FD. The value of a convertible bond $W_T\left(V_T^-, r_T, 0, k_T^*\right)$ before conversion at maturity T continuously decreases with FD. The stock value $S_T\left(V_T^-, r_T, 0, k_T^*\right)$ at maturity T either continuously decreases with the debt face value FD or shows an upward jump.*

The results obtained from the analysis of the conversion strategy k_T^* in the block case at maturity and the related values $W_T\left(V_T^-, r_T, 0, k_T^*\right)$ and $S_T\left(V_T^-, r_T, 0, k_T^*\right)$ fairly coincide with our intuition. The better the standing of the firm documented by a higher firm or stock value, the higher the conversion volume and the higher the values of a convertible bond and a stock in general. The same effect is associated with an increase of the short rate. In general, the debt holders suffer from higher short rates. Therefore, the convertible bond and the stockholders benefit at the cost of the debt holders in this case. The opposite effect results from an increase of the debt face value FD because a higher FD is associated with a more valuable claim of the debt holders.

However, at first glance there are a few surprising properties of the stock value. The stock value can drop in the firm value and the short rate and jump upward with the debt face value. These findings indicate that in some cases a lower firm value or short rate or a higher debt face value is in favor of the stockholders. The reason for this possibly unexpected behavior of the stock value is that a lower firm value or short rate or a higher debt face value can prevent a conversion, which triggers a wealth transfer from the stockholders to the debt holders.

These jumps of the stock value result in the non-uniqueness of the conversion volume and the value of a convertible bond as a function of the stock value. Therefore, conversion decisions cannot necessarily be made on the basis of an information set that consists of the stock price alone.

4.2 Unrestricted Conversion

1a) Conversion Strategy and the Values of a Convertible Bond and Stock as a Function of the Firm Value

Conversion Strategy

In section 3.1, we have characterized in detail the unrestricted conversion variant. Following the intuition behind this characterization, we can think of the unrestricted conversion as a game among a huge number of anonymous convertible bond holders in which every individual investor seeks to maximize the value obtained with her or his convertible bond holdings. In this game, an individual convertible bond holder has no impact on the aggregate conversion volume k_T. However, the aggregation of the conversion decisions of all the investors determines the total conversion volume that is denoted by k_T. The absence of an individual investor's ability to impact the aggregate conversion volume also results in the fact that she or he cannot affect any asset values either, because there is no possibility for her or him to influence any asset values by the individual conversion decision.

Following Constantinides/Rosenthal (1984), we can characterize the optimal conversion strategies by Nash equilibria resulting from an anonymous, non-atomic game.[4] According to a result by Schmeidler (1973), it follows that in this conversion game a Nash equilibrium in pure strategies exists. [5]

---

[4] See Blonski (1999).

[5] See Schmeidler (1973), p. 296.

Intuitively, an equilibrium strategy in the case of unrestricted conversion can be characterized as follows. Consider an individual convertible bond holder. Due to her or his inability to impact k_T, she or he has to compare the values of both a stock $S_T\left(V_T^-, r_T, K_T, k_T\right)$ and a non-converted convertible bond $W_T^+\left(V_T^-, r_T, K_T, k_T\right)$ conditional to any given aggregate conversion volume of k_T convertible bonds. The optimal conversion decision of a particular investor is to convert her or his entire holdings if $S_T\left(V_T^-, r_T, K_T, k_T\right) > W_T^+\left(V_T^-, r_T, K_T, k_T\right)$. If $S_T\left(V_T^-, r_T, K_T, k_T\right) < W_T^+\left(V_T^-, r_T, K_T, k_T\right)$, no conversion is optimal. In the case of $S_T\left(V_T^-, r_T, K_T, k_T\right) = W_T^+\left(V_T^-, r_T, K_T, k_T\right)$, the investor is indifferent and her or his optimal conversion decision is not uniquely determined.

On the aggregate level, a complete conversion $k_T^* = m - K_T$ is optimal, if $S_T\left(V_T^-, r_T, K_T, k_T\right) > W_T^+\left(V_T^-, r_T, K_T, k_T\right)$ holds for all $k_T \in [0, m-K_T]$. In this case, every investor converts her or his entire holdings resulting in a conversion of $k_T^* = m - K_T$. In the opposite case in which $S_T\left(V_T^-, r_T, K_T, k_T\right) < W_T^+\left(V_T^-, r_T, K_T, k_T\right)$ holds for all $k_T \in [0, m - K_T]$, the aggregate conversion volume k_T^* equals zero, as no investor has an incentive to convert.

If $S_T\left(V_T^-, r_T, K_T, k_T\right) = W_T^+\left(V_T^-, r_T, K_T, k_T\right)$ is satisfied for a certain conversion volume $k_T \in [0, m - K_T]$, the strategy k_T represents an aggregate equilibrium conversion volume. This effect results from the fact that given this aggregate conversion volume k_T, every particular investor can optimally choose an arbitrary conversion volume. Thus, an aggregate conversion volume equal to k_T is a consistent equilibrium because no investor would benefit from a deviation of her or his strategy. Conversely, a conversion volume $k_T \in (0, m - K_T)$ cannot represent an equilibrium strategy if $S_T\left(V_T^-, r_T, K_T, k_T\right)$ does not equal $W_T^+\left(V_T^-, r_T, K_T, k_T\right)$. In this case, every particular investor either has an incentive to convert everything, $S_T\left(V_T^-, r_T, K_T, k_T\right) > W_T^+\left(V_T^-, r_T, K_T, k_T\right)$, or not to convert at all. This would lead to a conversion volume of zero or $m - K_T$ and $k_T \in (0, m - K_T)$ cannot be an equilibrium.

We now characterize the *optimal conversion volume* k_T^* as a function of the firm value V_T^- using the representations of the conversion value $S_T\left(V_T^-, r_T, K_T, k_T\right)$ and the value of a non-converted convertible bond $W_T^+\left(V_T^-, r_T, K_T, k_T\right)$ given in section 3.3. For this purpose, we define two critical firm values $\underline{V}_T(K_T)$ and $\overline{V}_T$ in an analogous way to the block case. $\underline{V}_T(K_T)$ stands for the firm value before conversion that leads to a stock value $S_T(\underline{V}_T(K_T), r_T, K_T, 0)$ equal to F if no conversion takes place at time T. $\overline{V}_T$ denotes the firm value for which the stock value $S_T\left(\overline{V}_T, r_T, K_T, m - K_T\right)$ equals F after a complete conversion of all the outstanding convertible bonds. Hence, $\underline{V}_T(K_T)$ and $\overline{V}_T$

are implicitly defined by the following relations

$$\begin{aligned} S_T\left(\underline{V}_T\left(K_T\right), r_T, K_T, 0\right) &= F \\ &= \frac{1}{n+K_T} C_T\left(\underline{V}_T\left(K_T\right) - \left(m-K_T\right)\cdot F\right), \\ S_T\left(\overline{V}_T, r_T, K_T, m-K_T\right) &= F \\ &= \frac{1}{n+m} C_T\left(\overline{V}_T\right). \end{aligned} \tag{4.4}$$

The same arguments as in the block case tells us that $\underline{V}_T(K_T)$ always lies below $\overline{V}_T$. We note that $\underline{V}_T(K_T)$ converges to $\overline{V}_T$, when K_T tends to m.

For firm values V_T^- above $\overline{V}_T$, the marginal conversion value $S_T\left(V_T^-, r_T, K_T, k_T\right) = \frac{V_T^- - (m-K_T-k_T)\cdot F - D_T\left(V_T^-, r_T, K_T, k_T\right)}{n+K_T+k_T}$ is above the value of a non-converted convertible bond $W_T^+\left(V_T^-, r_T, K_T, k_T\right) = \min\left(\frac{V_T^-}{m-K_T-k_T}, F\right)$ for all $k_T \in [0, m-K_T]$. This property can be understood as follows. If $k_T = m-K_T$ attains the highest feasible value for the conversion volume, $S_T\left(V_T^-, r_T, K_T, m-K_T\right)$ is higher than F due to $V_T^- > \overline{V}_T$. In case that k_T is lower than $m-K_T$, $S_T\left(V_T^-, r_T, K_T, k_T\right)$ is higher than for $k_T = m-K_T$. The reason is that the stock value is a decreasing function in the conversion volume for those firm values, because the wealth transfer from the stockholders to the debt holders is reduced by a lower conversion volume.

Applying the same argumentation, we find that $S_T\left(V_T^-, r_T, K_T, k_T\right)$ is always below $W_T^+\left(V_T^-, r_T, K_T, k_T\right)$ for all $k_T \in [0, m-K_T]$ when the firm value V_T^- is below $\underline{V}_T(K_T)$.

For firm values V_T^- in the interval $\left(\underline{V}_T(K_T), \overline{V}_T\right)$, there exists a unique interior solution k_T^* of the condition

$$\begin{aligned} S_T\left(V_T^-, r_T, K_T, k_T^*\right) &= \frac{V_T^- - (m-K_T-k_T^*)\cdot F - D_T\left(V_T^-, r_T, K_T, k_T^*\right)}{n+K_T+k_T^*} \\ &= W_T^+\left(V_T^-, r_T, K_T, k_T^*\right) = F \end{aligned}$$

and equivalently

$$S_T\left(V_T^-, r_T, K_T, k_T^*\right) = \frac{V_T^- - D_T\left(V_T^-, r_T, K_T, k_T^*\right)}{n+m} = F. \tag{4.5}$$

The existence and the uniqueness of the solution k_T^* follows from the condition $S_T\left(V_T^-, r_T, K_T, 0\right) \geq F \geq S_T\left(V_T^-, r_T, K_T, m-K_T\right)$ together with the property that $S_T\left(V_T^-, r_T, K_T, k_T\right)$ strictly and continuously decreases with k_T for those firm values.

These considerations lead us to the following representation of the aggregate conversion volume k_T^* in equilibrium at time T:

$$k_T^* = \begin{cases} 0, & \text{for } V_T^- < \underline{V}_T(K_T) \\ x, & \text{with } S_T\left(V_T^-, r_T, K_T, x\right) = F \text{ for } \underline{V}_T(K_T) \leq V_T^- \leq \overline{V}_T \\ m-K_T, & \text{for } V_T^- > \overline{V}_T \end{cases}$$

k_T^* is continuous and strictly increasing with $V_T^- \in \left(\underline{V}_T(K_T), \overline{V}_T\right)$. The reason for this property is that for a firm value V_T^- of the interval $\left(\underline{V}_T(K_T), \overline{V}_T\right)$, an increase of V_T^- results in a strictly higher stock value $S_T\left(V_T^-, r_T, K_T, k_T\right)$ for a fixed conversion strategy. Therefore, a strictly higher conversion volume k_T^* is required to satisfy the conversion condition (4.5). Figure 4.4 shows k_T^* as a function of the firm value for a particular example.

Figure 4.4: Optimal Conversion Strategy and Values of a Convertible Bond and a Stock at Maturity under Unrestricted Conversion

The left diagram shows the optimal conversion volume k_T^* in the unrestricted case at maturity as a function of the firm value V_T^-. The right diagram shows the related values of a convertible bond $W_T\left(V_T^-, r_T, 0, k_T^*\right)$ and a stock $S_T\left(V_T^-, r_T, 0, k_T^*\right)$. The parameter values are $n = 100$, $m = 100$, $F = 100$, $FD = 50{,}000$, $TD - T = 1$, $r_T = 0.05$, $\sigma = 0.5$, $\eta = 0.01097$, $\rho = -0.1$, $\kappa = 0.16643$, $\theta = 0.0639$. The critical firm values $\underline{V}(0)$ and $\overline{V}_T$ result in $58{,}547.8$ and $62{,}635.5$, respectively.

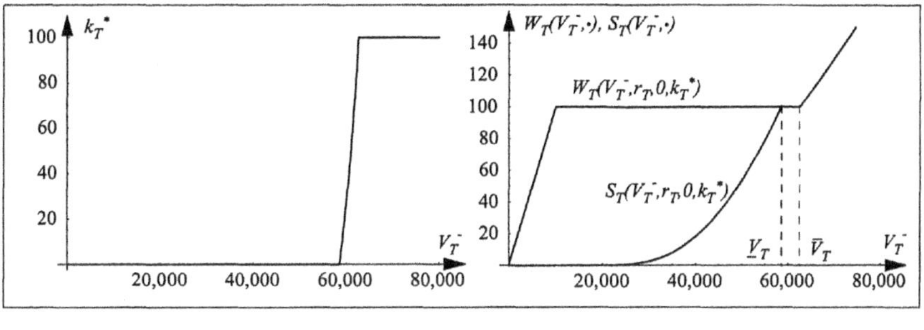

The slope of this curve for the firm value range $\left(\underline{V}_T(K_T), \overline{V}_T\right)$ can be implicity determined by the condition that the endogenous stock value $S_T\left(V_T^-, r_T, K_T, k_T^*\right)$ regarding the optimal conversion strategy is equal to F when the firm value changes. As $S_T\left(V_T^-, r_T, K_T, k_T\right)$ is a differentiable function in all arguments, the differentiability of k_T^* follows from the implicit function theorem and we can write

$$\frac{\partial S_T\left(V_T^-, r_T, K_T, k_T^*\right)}{\partial V_T^-} = \left.\frac{\partial S_T\left(V_T^-, r_T, K_T, k_T\right)}{\partial V_T^-}\right|_{k_T=k_T^*}$$

$$+ \left.\frac{\partial S_T\left(V_T^-, r_T, K_T, k_T\right)}{\partial k_T}\right|_{k_T=k_T^*} \cdot \frac{\partial k_T^*}{\partial V_T^-} = 0.$$

Rearranging terms and substituting the stock value by equation (3.12), we obtain

$$\frac{\partial k_T^*}{\partial V_T^-} = - \frac{\left.\frac{\partial S_T\left(V_T^-, r_T, K_T, k_T\right)}{\partial V_T^-}\right|_{k_T = k_T^*}}{\left.\frac{\partial S_T\left(V_T^-, r_T, K_T, k_T\right)}{\partial k_T}\right|_{k_T = k_T^*}}.$$

Values of the Convertible Bond and the Stock

In principle, when discussing the *value* of the *convertible bond*, we should differentiate between the value before and after conversion. However, it is sufficient to regard only the value $W_T\left(V_T^-, r_T, K_T, k_T^*\right)$ before conversion at maturity as this value is always as high as the value of a non-converted convertible $W_T^+\left(V_T^-, r_T, K_T, k_T^*\right)$ for $k_T^* < m - K_T$. This result is a direct consequence of the optimal conversion condition in the unrestricted case. In the case of an optimal complete conversion $k_T^* = m - K_T$, $W_T^+\left(V_T^-, r_T, K_T, k_T^*\right)$ is no reasonable asset value as no investor obtains $W_T^+\left(V_T^-, r_T, K_T, k_T^*\right)$ with a convertible bond when she or he optimally converts.

From the results of the optimal conversion strategy k_T^*, it follows that the value of $W_T\left(V_T^-, r_T, K_T, k_T^*\right)$ behaves differently in three ranges of the firm value V_T^-. In the first range, $[0, (m - K_T) \cdot F]$, bankruptcy occurs. In this case, $W_T\left(V_T^-, r_T, K_T, k_T^*\right)$ continuously and strictly increases with V_T^- as the firm value is distributed among the convertible bond holders on a pro rata basis. The second range, $\left((m - K_T) \cdot F, \overline{V}_T\right)$, represents the case that no complete conversion is optimal and $W_T\left(V_T^-, r_T, K_T, k_T^*\right)$ equals its redemption value. We note that even in the case of a partial conversion, the value of a convertible bond coincides with the redemption value F. Thus, a convertible bond value higher than F requires a complete conversion. For firm values $V_T^- \geq \overline{V}_T$ of the third range, a complete conversion is optimal resulting in a continuously and strictly increasing convertible bond value equal to the stock value. Therefore, $W_T\left(V_T^-, r_T, K_T, k_T^*\right)$ is given by:

$$W_T\left(V_T^-, r_T, K_T, k_T^*\right) = \begin{cases} \frac{V_T^-}{m - K_T}, & \text{for } V_T^- < (m - K_T) \cdot F \\ F, & \text{for } (m - K_T) \cdot F \leq V_T^- < \overline{V}_T \\ S_T\left(V_T^-, r_T, K_T, k_T^*\right), & \text{for } V_T^- \geq \overline{V}_T \end{cases}$$

This representation reveals that $W_T\left(V_T^-, r_T, K_T, k_T^*\right)$ is a continuous and increasing function of the firm value V_T^-.

To characterize the *stock value* $S_T\left(V_T^-, r_T, K_T, k_T^*\right)$, we have to differentiate between four intervals. In the first interval, $[0, (m - K_T) \cdot F]$, the firm goes bankrupt and $S_T\left(V_T^-, r_T, K_T, k_T^*\right)$ equals zero. In the second interval, $\left((m - K_T) \cdot F, \underline{V}_T(K_T)\right]$, the conversion volume is zero and the stock value equals the call value $\frac{1}{n + K_T} C_T\left(V_T^- - (m - K_T) \cdot F\right)$. In the interval $\left(\underline{V}_T(K_T), \overline{V}_T\right)$, a partial conversion occurs and therefore the stock value $S_T\left(V_T^-, r_T, K_T, k_T^*\right)$ equals the redemption value F of the convertible bond. For higher firm values, a complete conversion is optimal and the stock value can be represented by the call value $\frac{1}{n+m}C_T\left(V_T^-\right)$. Thus, the stock value $S_T\left(V_T^-, r_T, K_T, k_T^*\right)$ can be rewritten as:

$$S_T\left(V_T^-, r_T, K_T, k_T^*\right) = \begin{cases} 0, & \text{for } V_T^- < (m-K_T)\cdot F \\ \frac{V_T^- -(m-K_T)\cdot F - D_T\left(V_T^-, r_T, K_T, 0\right)}{n+K_T}, & \text{for } (m-K_T)\cdot F \leq V_T^- \\ & < \underline{V}_T(K_T) \\ F, & \text{for } \underline{V}_T(K_T) \leq V_T^- \leq \overline{V}_T \\ \frac{V_T^- - D_T\left(V_T^-, r_T, K_T, m-K_T\right)}{n+m}, & \text{for } V_T^- > \overline{V}_T \end{cases}$$

The values of $W_T\left(V_T^-, r_T, K_T, k_T^*\right)$ and $S_T\left(V_T^-, r_T, K_T, k_T^*\right)$ are illustrated in figure 4.4.

As a result for the conversion strategy and the values of a convertible bond and a stock, we get the following properties.

Result 5 *The optimal unrestricted conversion volume k_T^* at maturity T is unique in V_T^- and continuously increases with the firm value V_T^-. It has the structure $k_T^* = 0$ for $V_T^- \leq \underline{V}_T(K_T)$ and $k_T^* = m - (K_T)$ for $V_T^- \geq \overline{V}_T$. For firm values $V_T^- \in \left(\underline{V}_T(K_T), \overline{V}_T\right)$, a partial conversion is the unique optimal strategy. The value of a convertible bond $W_T\left(V_T^-, r_T, K_T, k_T^*\right)$ before conversion at maturity T and the value of a stock $S_T\left(V_T^-, r_T, K_T, k_T^*\right)$ continuously increase with V_T^-. Moreover, the stock value equals the convertible bond's redemption value F for all firm values $V_T^- \in \left[\underline{V}_T(K_T), \overline{V}_T\right]$. Thus, the stock value cannot lie above the face value of a convertible bond if no complete conversion is advantageous.*

1b) Conversion Strategy and the Value of a Convertible Bond as a Function of the Stock Value

Next, we regard the optimal conversion volume k_T^* and the value of a convertible bond $W_T\left(V_T^-, r_T, K_T, k_T^*\right)$ as a function of the *stock value* $S_T\left(V_T^-, r_T, K_T, k_T^*\right)$. As in the block case, we can obtain these relations within our firm value framework by determining the combinations $\left(S_T\left(V_T^-, r_T, K_T, k_T^*\right), k_T^*\right)$ and $\left(S_T\left(V_T^-, r_T, K_T, k_T^*\right), W_T\left(V_T^-, r_T, K_T, k_T^*\right)\right)$ for every firm value V_T^-. Figure 4.5 illustrates these relations for a particular example.

This figure shows that in contrast to the block case the optimal *conversion volume* k_T^* is uniquely determined by the stock value for all $S_T\left(V_T^-, r_T, K_T, k_T^*\right) \neq F$. For the stock value $S_T\left(V_T^-, r_T, K_T, k_T^*\right) = F$, k_T^* can attain every value between zero and $m - K_T$. The exact fixing of k_T^* is only feasible if the value of V_T^- lies between $\underline{V}_T(K_T)$ and $\overline{V}_T$ is known.

The *value* of a *convertible bond* $W_T\left(V_T^-, r_T, K_T, k_T^*\right)$ before conversion at maturity is constant and equal to F, if for the stock value $0 < S_T\left(V_T^-, r_T, K_T, k_T^*\right) < F$ holds. In

Figure 4.5: Optimal Conversion Strategy and Value of a Convertible Bond at Maturity under Unrestricted Conversion

The left diagram shows the optimal conversion volume k_T^* in the unrestricted case at maturity as a function of the stock value $S_T\left(V_T^-, r_T, 0, k_T^*\right)$. The right diagram shows the related value of a convertible bond $W_T\left(V_T^-, r_T, 0, k_T^*\right)$. The parameter values are $n = 100$, $m = 100$, $F = 100$, $FD = 50{,}000$, $TD - T = 1$, $r_T = 0.05$, $\sigma = 0.5$, $\eta = 0.01097$, $\rho = -0.1$, $\kappa = 0.16643$, $\theta = 0.0639$.

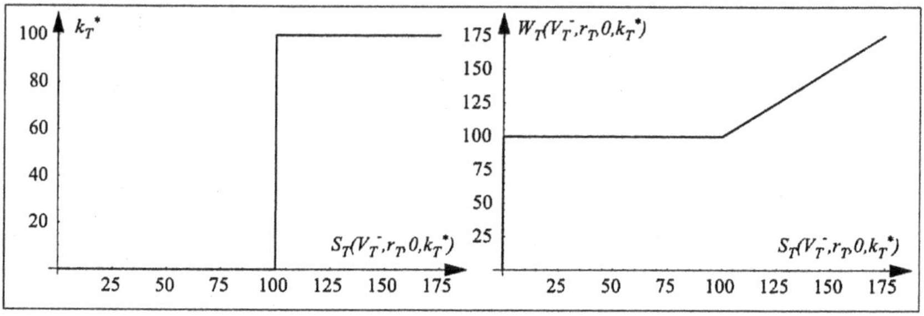

this case, no conversion occurs. For stock values $S_T\left(V_T^-, r_T, K_T, k_T^*\right) > F$, a complete conversion is optimal and $W_T\left(V_T^-, r_T, K_T, k_T^*\right)$ equals the stock value $S_T\left(V_T^-, r_T, K_T, k_T^*\right)$. The stock value $S_T\left(V_T^-, r_T, K_T, k_T^*\right) = F$ is also associated with a convertible bond value equal to F, even though the aggregate conversion volume can attain any arbitrary value between zero and $m - K_T$. In the case of bankruptcy $S_T\left(V_T^-, r_T, K_T, k_T^*\right)$ is zero and the convertible bond value — analogous to the block case — can attain every value between zero and F depending on the firm value. We summarize these findings in the next result.

Result 6 *The optimal aggregate conversion strategy k_T^* as a function of the stock value $S_T\left(V_T^-, r_T, K_T, k_T^*\right)$ shows the structure $k_T^* = 0$ for $S_T\left(V_T^-, r_T, K_T, k_T^*\right) < F$ and $k_T^* = m - K_T$ for $S_T\left(V_T^-, r_T, K_T, k_T^*\right) > F$. For $S_T^* = F$, the conversion volume k_T^* can obtain every value between zero and $m - K_T$. The value of the convertible bond is uniquely defined by the stock value except for $S_T\left(V_T^-, r_T, K_T, k_T^*\right) = 0$.*

2) Conversion Strategy and the Values of a Convertible Bond and Stock as a Function of the Short Rate

Conversion Strategy

The effect of the short rate r_T on the optimal conversion strategy might depend on the current firm value V_T^-, as we have seen for the block conversion. It is convenient to regard those firm values first, which result in a partial conversion at maturity. From the results in subsection 1a), we know that a partial conversion k_T^* occurs when the stock value $S_T\left(V_T^-, r_T, K_T, k_T^*\right)$ equals the value of a non-converted convertible $W_T^+\left(V_T^-, r_T, K_T, k_T^*\right)$ which is equal to F in this case. To analyze how a variation of r_T affects the equilibrium *conversion strategy* k_T^*, we have to evaluate how $S_T\left(V_T^-, r_T, K_T, k_T\right)$ is affected by a change of r_T. An increase in the stock value with the short rate r_T would correspond to an increase of the conversion volume because the conversion value would become more attractive with r_T. Due to the representation of the stock value by call values, we can see that in fact $S_T\left(V_T^-, r_T, K_T, k_T\right)$ increases with r_T for a fixed conversion volume k_T. Thus, after an increase of r_T every particular investor would have an incentive to convert the entire holdings if k_T was still the equilibrium strategy. If $k_T^* < m - K_T$, this effect results in a higher conversion volume k_T^* that decreases the stock value $S_T\left(V_T^-, r_T, K_T, k_T\right)$ due to the wealth transfer to the debt holders. In particular, k_T^* increases in such a way, that afterwards $S_T\left(V_T^-, r_T, K_T, k_T^*\right)$ equals F, i.e. the stock value $S_T\left(V_T^-, r_T, K_T, k_T\right)$ benefits from a higher short rate r_T as much as it suffers from the higher optimal conversion volume k_T^*.

If for a given firm value V_T^- and short rate r_T a partial conversion $0 < k_T^* < m - K_T$ is optimal, the short rate can be decreased such that no conversion occurs and also increased until a complete conversion takes place. The first part of this statement is easy to see, as $S_T\left(V_T^-, r_T, K_T, k_T\right)$ approaches zero when r_T tends to minus infinity. In the opposite case in which r_T tends to infinity, the debt value $D_T\left(V_T^-, r_T, K_T, k_T\right)$ becomes worthless and $S_T\left(V_T^-, r_T, K_T, k_T\right)$ approaches $\frac{V_T^- -(m-K_T-k_T)\cdot F}{n+K_T+k_T}$. Due to conversion condition (4.5), the firm value V_T^- has to be greater than $(n+m)\cdot F$ if a conversion occurs. Hence, the limit $\frac{V_T^- -(m-K_T-k_T)\cdot F}{n+K_T+k_T}$ of $S_T\left(V_T^-, r_T, K_T, k_T\right)$ is higher than F for all $k_T \in [0, m - K_T]$ such that $k_T^* = m - K_T$ is optimal for $r_T \to \infty$. These considerations enable us to define unique values for $\underline{r}_T$ and $\overline{r}_T$ as follows. The critical short rate $\underline{r}_T$ is defined such that $S_T\left(V_T^-, r_T, K_T, 0\right)$ given no conversion equals the value of a non-converted convertible bond $W_T^+\left(V_T^-, r_T, K_T, 0\right) = F$. Accordingly, $\overline{r}_T$ results from the stock value $S_T\left(V_T^-, r_T, K_T, m - K_T\right)$ after a complete conversion that equals F. As a consequence, a partial conversion is optimal for short rates between $\underline{r}_T$ and $\overline{r}_T$. For lower short rates, no conversion is optimal, but a complete conversion is optimal if the short rate is higher than $\overline{r}_T$. In particular, the optimal conversion volume k_T^* is a continuous strictly increasing function of r_T for short rates between $\underline{r}_T$ and $\overline{r}_T$. This finding can be verified by regarding the derivative $\frac{\partial k_T^*}{\partial r_T}$. This derivative exists for r_T between $\underline{r}_T$ and $\overline{r}_T$, as the stock value $S_T\left(V_T^-, r_T, K_T, k_T\right)$ is differentiable in r_T and k_T. In this case, we obtain $\frac{\partial k_T^*}{\partial r_T}$ analogously to the derivative in subsection 1a)

$$\frac{\partial k_T^*}{\partial r_T} = -\frac{\left.\frac{\partial S_T\left(V_T^-, r_T, K_T, k_T\right)}{\partial r_T}\right|_{k_T = k_T^*}}{\left.\frac{\partial S_T\left(V_T^-, r_T, K_T, k_T\right)}{\partial k_T}\right|_{k_T = k_T^*}}.$$

If the firm value V_T^- is $(n+m) \cdot F$ or lower, there is no short rate that leads to a conversion. This property is because the stock value $S_T\left(V_T^-, r_T, K_T, k_T\right)$ is lower than F for all r_T in this case. Otherwise, the two critical short rates $\underline{r}_T$ and $\overline{r}_T$ can be uniquely determined as shown above.

Values of the Convertible Bond and the Stock

The *value* of a *convertible bond* continuously increases with r_T. If the critical short rate $\overline{r}_T$ does not exist or the short rate is below this critical value $\overline{r}_T$, a complete conversion does not occur. Thus, $W_T\left(V_T^-, r_T, K_T, k_T^*\right)$ is equal to the value of a non-converted convertible bond $W_T^+\left(V_T^-, r_T, K_T, k_T^*\right)$ and does not depend on r_T. If r_T is above $\overline{r}_T$, a complete conversion occurs and $W_T\left(V_T^-, r_T, K_T, k_T^*\right)$ equals a call option value $\frac{1}{n+m} C_T\left(V_T^-\right)$ that increases with r_T.

The *stock value* $S_T\left(V_T^-, r_T, K_T, k_T^*\right)$ is zero independent of the short rate if the firm defaults at maturity, i.e. $V_T^- < (m - K_T) \cdot F$. For higher firm values, the stock value strictly and continuously increases with r_T as long as r_T is not in the interval between the two critical short rates $\underline{r}_T$ and $\overline{r}_T$. For short rates of this interval the stock value equals the redemption value F of a convertible bond. Figure 4.6 illustrates our findings for the optimal conversion strategy k_T^* and the values $W_T\left(V_T^-, r_T, K_T, k_T^*\right)$ and $S_T\left(V_T^-, r_T, K_T, k_T^*\right)$ when the short rate r_T is varied. These considerations provide us with the following result.

Result 7 *The optimal conversion volume k_T^* of the convertible bond at maturity T continuously increases with the short rate r_T. The optimal conversion strategy at maturity, given that the firm value V_T^- is above $(n+m) \cdot F$, shows the structure $k_T^* = 0$ for $r_T \leq \underline{r}_T$ and $k_T^* = m - K_T$ for $r_T \geq \overline{r}_T$. For $r_T \in (\underline{r}_T, \overline{r}_T)$, a partial conversion is the unique conversion strategy. For a given firm value V_T^- below $(n+m) \cdot F$, no critical short rate exists and no conversion is optimal for all r_T. The value of a convertible bond $W_T\left(V_T^-, r_T, K_T, k_T^*\right)$ before maturity T continuously increases with r_T. The stock value $S_T\left(V_T^-, r_T, K_T, k_T^*\right)$ at maturity T also continuously increases with the short rate. If default occurs or for $r_T \in (\underline{r}_T, \overline{r}_T)$, $S_T\left(V_T^-, r_T, K_T, k_T^*\right)$ is equal to a constant and otherwise it strictly increases with r_T.*

Figure 4.6: Optimal Conversion Strategy and Values of a Convertible Bond and a Stock at Maturity under Unrestricted Conversion

The left diagram shows the optimal conversion volume k_T^* in the unrestricted case at maturity as a function of the short rate r_T. The right diagram shows the related values of a convertible bond $W_T\left(V_T^-, r_T, 0, k_T^*\right)$ and a stock $S_T\left(V_T^-, r_T, 0, k_T^*\right)$. The parameter values are $n = 100$, $m = 100$, $F = 100$, $FD = 50,000$, $TD - T = 1$, $V_T^- = 60,000$, $\sigma = 0.5$, $\eta = 0.01097$, $\acute{\rho} = -0.1$, $\kappa = 0.16643$, $\theta = 0.0639$. The critical short rates $\underline{r}_T$ and $\overline{r}_T$ result in 0.002034 and 0.12898, respectively.

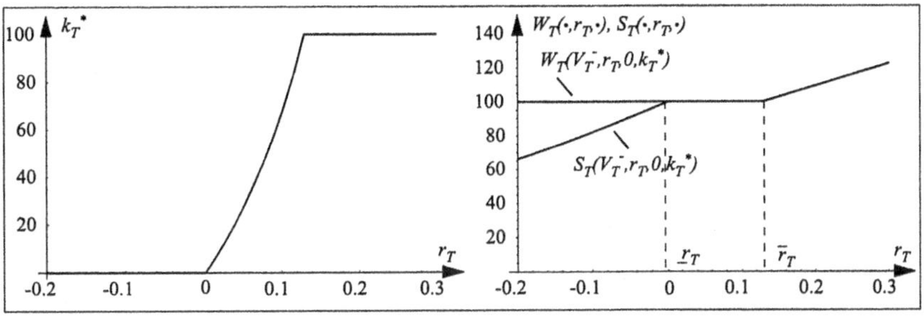

3) Conversion Strategy and the Values of a Convertible Bond and Stock as a Function of the Amount of Additional Debt

To determine the impact of the debt face value FD on the conversion strategy and the asset values, we can access our considerations in subsection 2). This possibility is because FD affects the conversion value $S_T\left(V_T^-, r_T, K_T, k_T\right)$ for a given conversion volume k_T in a way opposite to r_T. This effect means that $S_T\left(V_T^-, r_T, K_T, k_T\right)$ continuously decreases with FD from $\max\left(\frac{V_T^- - (m - K_T - k_T)\cdot F}{n + K_T + k_T}, 0\right)$ to zero. Therefore, the *conversion volume* k_T^* continuously decreases with FD. Accordingly, if and only if $V_T^- > (n+m)\cdot F$, there are two critical debt face values $\underline{FD}$ and $\overline{FD}$. Hence, k_T^* has the following structure. For $FD \leq \overline{FD}$, a complete conversion is optimal. A partial conversion takes place if $\underline{FD} > FD > \overline{FD}$, and no conversion occurs for $FD \geq \underline{FD}$. The derivative of k_T^* with respect to FD conditional to $\underline{FD} > FD > \overline{FD}$ is given by

$$\frac{\partial k_T^*}{\partial FD} = -\frac{\left.\frac{\partial S_T\left(V_T^-, r_T, K_T, k_T\right)}{\partial FD}\right|_{k_T = k_T^*}}{\left.\frac{\partial S_T\left(V_T^-, r_T, K_T, k_T\right)}{\partial k_T}\right|_{k_T = k_T^*}}.$$

If no finite critical debt face values exist, i.e. $V_T^- \geq (n+m)\cdot F$, no conversion is optimal. Moreover, the *convertible bond value* $W_T\left(V_T^-, r_T, K_T, k_T^*\right)$ is independent of FD if no complete conversion occurs and decreases with FD otherwise. Thus, $W_T\left(V_T^-, r_T, K_T, k_T^*\right)$ is a continuously decreasing function of FD.

Accordingly, the *stock value* $S_T\left(V_T^-, r_T, K_T, k_T^*\right)$ is a continuously decreasing function of FD. In particular, for $V_T^- \leq (m - K_T) \cdot F$, the firm defaults and $S_T\left(V_T^-, r_T, K_T, k_T^*\right)$ equals zero, for $\underline{FD} \geq FD \geq \overline{FD}$, a partial conversion together with $S_T\left(V_T^-, r_T, K_T, k_T^*\right)$ equal to F occurs, and otherwise $S_T\left(V_T^-, r_T, K_T, k_T^*\right)$ strictly decreases with FD. Therefore, we can summarize our findings in the next result.

Result 8 *The optimal conversion volume k_T^* of the convertible bond at maturity T continuously decreases with the debt face value FD. The optimal conversion strategy at maturity given that the firm value V_T^- is above $(n+m) \cdot F$ shows the structure $k_T^* = 0$ for $FD \geq \underline{FD}$ and $k_T^* = m - K_T$ for $FD \leq \overline{FD}$. For $FD \in \left(\overline{FD}, \underline{FD}\right)$, a partial conversion is the unique conversion strategy. For a given firm value V_T^- below $(n+m) \cdot F$, no critical debt face values exist and no conversion is optimal for all FD. The value of a convertible bond $W_T\left(V_T^-, r_T, K_T, k_T^*\right)$ before maturity T continuously decreases with FD. The stock value $S_T\left(V_T^-, r_T, K_T, k_T^*\right)$ at maturity T also continuously decreases with the debt face value. If default occurs or for $FD \in \left(\overline{FD}, \underline{FD}\right)$, $S_T\left(V_T^-, r_T, K_T, k_T^*\right)$ is equal to a constant and otherwise it strictly decreases with FD.*

The results obtained from the analysis of the conversion strategy k_T^* in the unrestricted case at maturity and the related values $W_T\left(V_T^-, r_T, K_T, k_T^*\right)$ and $S_T\left(V_T^-, r_T, K_T, k_T^*\right)$ correspond to our intuition. A higher firm or stock value encourages the convertible bond holders to convert more convertible bonds into stock and the values of a stock and a convertible bond are also higher. Accordingly, higher interest rates discriminate the debt value and a higher conversion volume occurs in conjunction with higher stock and convertible bond values. Conversely, if the debt face value increases, the conversion volume declines and the values of both a convertible bond and a stock also decrease.

We note that the conversion volume, the convertible bond value, and the stock value are always continuous functions of the firm value, the short rate, and the debt face value. Even the convertible bond value can be uniquely represented by the stock value if no default occurs. However, the conversion volume at maturity is not unique in the stock value if $S_T\left(V_T^-, r_T, 0, k_T^*\right)$ equals F.

An unexpected finding is that the stock value $S_T\left(V_T^-, r_T, 0, k_T^*\right)$ equals the redemption value of a convertible bond F for a whole range of the firm value, the short rate, and the debt face value. Thus, a stock value at maturity equal to F can occur with a positive probability, but all other stock values occur with a probability of zero. The reason for this finding is the equilibrium strategy followed by the convertible bond holders in the unrestricted case. At maturity, k_T^* is determined such that the stock value equals F whenever a partial conversion is optimal.

4.3 Monopolistic Conversion

1a) Conversion Strategy and the Values of a Convertible Bond and Stock as a Function of the Firm Value

Conversion Strategy

The monopolist is an investor who initially holds all m issued convertible bonds but no further securities. Since the monopolist still holds all stocks received by a prior conversion, her or his wealth consists of K_T stocks and $m - K_T$ convertible bonds at maturity. The optimal conversion strategy of the monopolist is to choose a conversion volume k_T that maximizes her or his wealth, which depends on K_T. Contrary to the block case, in the case of monopolistic conversion, any conversion volume $k_T \in [0, m - K_T]$ is a feasible strategy. Therefore, the optimization problem reads

$$\begin{aligned}
&\max_{k_T \in [0,m-K_T]} \left\{K_T \cdot S_T\left(V_T^-, r_T, K_T, k_T\right) + (m - K_T) \cdot W_T\left(V_T^-, r_T, K_T, k_T\right)\right\} \\
&= \max_{k_T \in [0,m-K_T]} \left\{(K_T + k_T) \cdot S_T\left(V_T^-, r_T, K_T, k_T\right)\right. \\
&\left. + (m - K_T - k_T) \cdot W_T^+\left(V_T^-, r_T, K_T, k_T\right)\right\}.
\end{aligned}$$

According to this representation, we can either regard the value of a convertible bond before conversion $W_T\left(V_T^-, r_T, K_T, k_T\right)$ or the identical representation by values of a non-converted convertible bond $W_T^+\left(V_T^-, r_T, K_T, k_T\right)$ and a stock $S_T\left(V_T^-, r_T, K_T, k_T\right)$. The identity between these two representations and the values a stock and a non-converted convertible bond were given in section 3.3. Since the objective function is continuous in k_T and the set of feasible k_T is compact, a solution k_T^* for this optimization problem always exists. We can find a solution for this optimal *conversion volume* k_T^* by taking the first order condition and accounting for certain boundary conditions for k_T. Before doing so, we will provide an intuition for the basic mechanism that drives the following results.

For a low firm value, $V_T^- < (m - K_T - k_T) \cdot F$, there is a possibility for a default resulting in a total value of the convertible bonds equal to the firm value V_T^-. Thus in this case, no conversion, $k_T^* = 0$, would lead to a default, and this is an optimal strategy as the monopolist cannot otherwise attain a higher value than the firm value.[6]

Due to the result that $k_T^* = 0$ is the optimal strategy in the case of bankruptcy $V_T^- < (m - K_T) \cdot F$, we focus on the non-default case $V_T^- \geq (m - K_T) \cdot F$ in the following analysis under 1a), i.e. $W_T^+ (V_T^-, r_T, K_T, k_T) \equiv F$. According to our experiences of the behavior of $S_T (V_T^-, r_T, K_T, k_T)$ when discussing the unrestricted conversion, we are aware of the fact that $S_T (V_T^-, r_T, K_T, k_T)$ decreases with k_T for those firm values associated with a positive conversion volume, but the value of a non-converted convertible bond $W_T^+ (V_T^-, r_T, K_T, k_T)$ is identical to the redemption value F. Therefore, the determination of the optimal conversion volume k_T^* is a balance between two effects. The first effect is that a higher conversion volume k_T allows the monopolist to participate more in the stock value $S_T (V_T^-, r_T, K_T, k_T)$. However, the countereffect is that both the value of a converted convertible bond $S_T (V_T^-, r_T, K_T, k_T)$ at maturity and the value of the holdings of the prematurely converted bonds decrease with k_T. This is the reason why in fact a partial conversion can be optimal at maturity.

We will show that analogously to the unrestricted conversion, there exist two critical values $\underline{V}_T (K_T)$ and $\overline{V}_T (K_T)$ such that $k_T^* = 0$ for $V_T^- \leq \underline{V}_T (K_T)$, $k_T^* = m - K_T$ for $V_T^- \geq \overline{V}_T (K_T)$, and $0 < k_T^* < m - K_T$ for $V_T^- \in (\underline{V}_T (K_T), \overline{V}_T (K_T))$. Contrary to the unrestricted case, $\overline{V}_T (K_T)$ will depend on the prior conversion volume. Obviously, after a conversion the stock value has to be at least equal to F. Otherwise, the total convertible bond value would lie below $(m - K_T) \cdot F$ and the K_T stocks would suffer from the wealth transfer to the debt holders. In this case, the strategy $k_T^* = 0$ had the two advantages that no wealth transfer to debt holders occurred and that a higher value of the convertible bonds $(m - K_T) \cdot F$ was achieved. The critical firm value $\underline{V}_T (K_T)$ for $K_T = 0$ is determined according to (4.4) by the condition

$$S_T (\underline{V}_T (0), r_T, 0, 0) = F.$$

The reason why $\underline{V}_T (0)$ is as in the unrestricted case can be shown as follows. As the stock value strictly decreases with the conversion volume k_T for these firm values, $k_T > 0$ would lead to a stock value below F for $V_T^- < \underline{V}_T (0)$. Conversely, a positive conversion volume $k_T^* > 0$, is optimal if the firm value V_T^- exceeds the critical value $\underline{V}_T (0)$. This effect follows from the strict monotonicity of $S_T (V_T^-, r_T, 0, k_T)$ in V_T^- for fixed k_T. Therefore, if no conversion occurred, the stock value $S_T (V_T^-, r_T, 0, 0)$ would lie above F. Hence, there exists a positive conversion volume k_T such that $k_T \cdot S_T (V_T^-, r_T, 0, k_T) > k_T \cdot F$ holds.

---

6 In the case of bankruptcy, all conversion volumes k_T with $V_T^- < (m - K_T - k_T) \cdot F$ are optimal because they all result in a total value of convertible bonds equal to V_T^-. As all these strategies basically represent the same economic situation namely that the firm value is transferred to the monopolist, we assume $k_T^* = 0$ in this case to avoid an extensive discussion of a trivial case.

From the continuity of $S_T\left(V_T^-, r_T, 0, k_T\right)$ in k_T follows that an optimal conversion volume $k_T^* > 0$ exists and that $\underline{V}_T(0)$ separates the conversion region from the non-conversion region.

When a premature conversion has already occurred, i.e. $K_T > 0$, the critical firm value $\underline{V}_T(K_T)$ that triggers a positive conversion is such that the stock value $S_T(\underline{V}_T(K_T), r_T, K_T, 0)$, given no conversion, is strictly above F. This effect is a result of the stock holdings of the monopolist. As the value of the stock holdings suffer from a conversion, the conversion incentive of a monopolist is inhibited. We can verify this intuition by taking the first derivative of the monopolist's objective function

$$\begin{aligned}&\frac{\partial\left(K_T+k_T\right)\cdot S_T\left(V_T^-, r_T, K_T, k_T\right)+\left(m-K_T-k_T\right)\cdot W_T^+\left(V_T^-, r_T, K_T, k_T\right)}{\partial k_T} \\ &= S_T\left(V_T^-, r_T, K_T, k_T\right)-F-\left(K_T+k_T\right)\cdot\frac{\partial S_T\left(V_T^-, r_T, K_T, k_T\right)}{\partial k_T}\end{aligned} \tag{4.6}$$

which is negative for all k_T when $S_T\left(V_T^-, r_T, K_T, 0\right) - F = 0$ is valid. The existence of $\underline{V}_T(K_T)$ follows from the intermediate value theorem, because the derivative is negative for low firm values and positive for high firm values. Moreover, $\underline{V}_T(K_T)$ is unique as we will see below.

Next, we prove the existence of $\overline{V}_T(K_T)$ which separates the firm values for which a complete or an incomplete conversion is optimal. The existence means that a complete conversion occurs for sufficiently high firm values. The intuitive rationale for this finding is that the debt value $D_T\left(V_T^-, r_T, K_T, k_T\right)$ for very large firm values is approximately equal to $FD \cdot B_T(TD)$ and

$$S_T\left(V_T^-, r_T, K_T, k_T\right) \approx \frac{V_T^- - \left(m-K_T-k_T\right)\cdot F - FD\cdot B_T(TD)}{n+K_T+k_T}$$

holds. Using this representation for the stock value, we can see that a higher conversion volume increases the monopolist's wealth and therefore a complete conversion $k_T^* = m - K_T$ is optimal. The critical value $\overline{V}_T(K_T)$ can be obtained — in a similar way to $\underline{V}_T(K_T)$ — as a solution of the first order condition.

To show the uniqueness of both critical firm values, $\underline{V}_T(K_T)$ and $\overline{V}_T(K_T)$, we prove that the conversion volume k_T^* is increasing with the firm value V_T^-. This property is an immediate result of the fact that $\frac{\partial^2 (m-K_T)\cdot W_T\left(V_T^-, r_T, K_T, k_T\right)+K_T\cdot S_T\left(V_T^-, r_T, K_T, k_T\right)}{\partial V_T^- \partial k_T}$ is strictly positive.[7] Intuitively, this property of the second partial derivative means that

[7] Representing the monopolist's objective function by the value of a call option as $(m-K_T-k_T)\cdot F + (K_T+k_T)\cdot\frac{C_T\left(V_T^- -(m-K_T-k_T)\cdot F\right)}{n+K_T+k_T}$, we can verify that the derivative $\frac{\partial^2 (m-K_T)\cdot W_T\left(V_T^-, r_T, K_T, k_T\right)+K_T\cdot S_T\left(V_T^-, r_T, K_T, k_T\right)}{\partial V_T^- \partial k_T}$ results in $\frac{n}{(n+K_T+k_T)^2}$Call-Delta$_T$ + $F\frac{K_T+k_T}{n+K_T+k_T}$Call-Gamma$_T$. Since the Call-Delta and Call-Gamma are always positive, this second derivative must have a positive sign.

the higher the conversion volume k_T, the higher the increase of the objective function $(m - K_T) \cdot W_T(V_T^-, r_T, K_T, k_T) + K_T \cdot S_T(V_T^-, r_T, K_T, k_T)$ with V_T^-. Hence, if the conversion volume was decreasing as a reaction to a higher firm value, it always leads to a value of the monopolist's wealth which is lower than that achieved by still selecting the former conversion volume k_T^*.

The optimal conversion strategy is obviously no conversion or a complete conversion for firm values below $\underline{V}_T(K_T)$ or above $\overline{V}_T(K_T)$. Thus, we focus on the other firm values $V_T^- \in [\underline{V}_T(K_T), \overline{V}_T(K_T)]$, because it is not clear whether the optimal conversion volume k_T^* is unique and continuous in the firm value V_T^-. For this purpose, we consider two cases illustrated in figures 4.7 and 4.8.

Figure 4.7: Optimal Conversion Strategy and Values of a Convertible Bond and a Stock at Maturity under Monopolistic Conversion

The left diagram shows the optimal conversion volume k_T^* in the monopolistic case at maturity as a function of the firm value V_T^-. The right diagram shows the related values of a convertible bond $W_T(V_T^-, r_T, 0, k_T^*)$ and a stock $S_T(V_T^-, r_T, 0, k_T^*)$. The parameter values are $n = 100$, $m = 100$, $F = 100$, $FD = 50,000$, $TD - T = 1$, $r_T = 0.05$, $\sigma = 0.5$, $\eta = 0.01097$, $\rho = -0.1$, $\kappa = 0.16643$, $\theta = 0.0639$. The critical firm values $\underline{V}(0)$ and $\overline{V}_T$ result in 58,547.8 and 66,955.4, respectively.

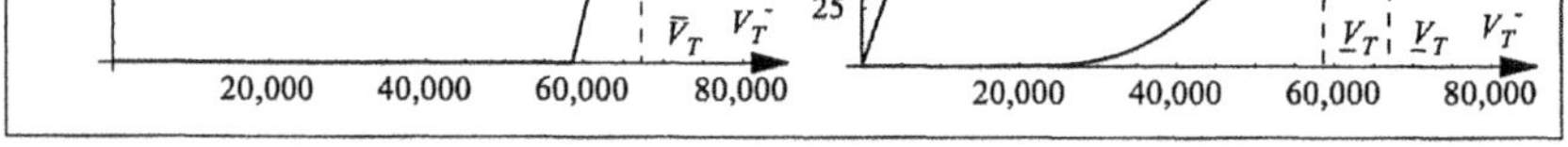

In the first case presented in figure 4.7, the optimal conversion volume is unique and continuously increasing with V_T^-. This case is associated with an objective function $(m - K_T) \cdot W_T(V_T^-, r_T, K_T, k_T) + K_T \cdot S_T(V_T^-, r_T, K_T, k_T)$ that has exactly one local maximum at $0 < k_T^* < m - K_T$ which is also the global one. Then, the derivative $\frac{\partial k_T^*}{\partial V_T^-}$ exists for $V_T^- \in (\underline{V}_T(K_T), \overline{V}_T(K_T))$ by the implicit function theorem, because the derivative (4.6) is continuous in both V_T^- and k_T.

However, the optimal conversion volume k_T^* need not be continuous in the firm value. This case occurs in the example presented in figure 4.8. In this figure, k_T^* first continuously

Figure 4.8: Optimal Conversion Strategy and Values of a Convertible Bond and a Stock at Maturity under Monopolistic Conversion

The left diagram shows the optimal conversion volume k_T^* in the monopolistic case at maturity as a function of the firm value V_T^-. The right diagram shows the related values of a convertible bond $W_T(V_T^-, r_T, 0, k_T^*)$ and a stock $S_T(V_T^-, r_T, 0, k_T^*)$. The parameter values differ from those used in the figures above. In particular, we have $n = 100$, $m = 100$, $F = 100$, $FD = 10{,}000$, $TD - T = 1$, $r_T = 0.05$, $\sigma = 0.25$, $\eta = 0.01097$, $\rho = -0.1$, $\kappa = 0.16643$, $\theta = 0.0639$. The critical firm values $\underline{V}_T(0)$ and $\overline{V}_T$ result in 29,500.1 and 29,502.3, respectively.

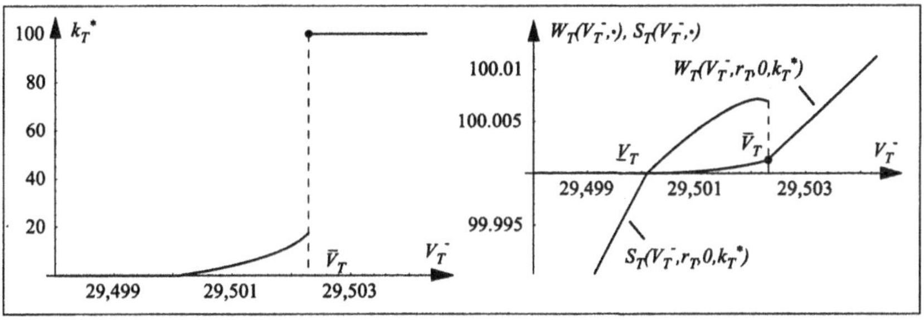

increases with V_T^- to a volume of 17.6 and then jumps from 17.6 to $m = 100$ at the critical firm value $\overline{V}_T(0) = 29{,}502.3$.[8] As a consequence, conversion volumes in the interval $(17.6, m)$ are not optimal for any firm value. To avoid uninteresting subcases, we assume $k_T^* = m$ for $V_T^- = \overline{V}_T(0)$.

The reason for the jump of k_T^* is that the objective function $(m - K_T) \cdot W_T(V_T^-, r_T, K_T, k_T) + K_T \cdot S_T(V_T^-, r_T, K_T, k_T)$ at $V_T^- = 29{,}502{,}3$ has two maxima, one at $k_T^* = 17.6$ and one at $k_T^* = m$. Figure 4.9 illustrates this situation. For three firm values the wealth of the monopolist is shown as a function of the conversion volume k_T. In each case, this wealth function has a local maximum. For the lowest firm value, this is also the global maximum. In the medium case, the wealth in the local maximum and for a complete conversion are equal, but for the largest firm value a complete conversion results in a higher wealth.

---

8 In case that the objective function $(m - K_T) \cdot W_T(V_T^-, r_T, K_T, k_T) + K_T \cdot S_T(V_T^-, r_T, K_T, k_T)$ has two maxima, the critical firm value might depend on the prior conversion volume. This effect is illustrated by the example of figure 4.8 for $V_T^- = 29{,}502.25$. If the prior conversion volume K_T sufficiently higher than 17.6 but not complete, then a complete conversion is the unique optimal strategy at time T. In the case of a prior conversion volume lower than 17.6, no complete conversion, $k_T^* = 17.6 - K_T < m - K_T$ is optimal.

Figure 4.9: Value of the outstanding Convertible Bonds at Maturity

The figure shows $m \cdot W_T\left(V_T^-, r_T, 0, k_T\right)$, the value of the outstanding convertible bonds, as a function of the conversion volume k_T for three different firm values $V_T^- = 29,502.25$, $V_T^- = 29,502.3$, and $V_T^- = 29,502.4$, respectively. The parameter values are $n = 100$, $m = 100$, $F = 100$, $FD = 10,000$, $TD - T = 1$, $r_T = 0.05$, $\sigma = 0.25$, $\eta = 0.01097$, $\rho = -0.1$, $\kappa = 0.16643$, $\theta = 0.0639$.

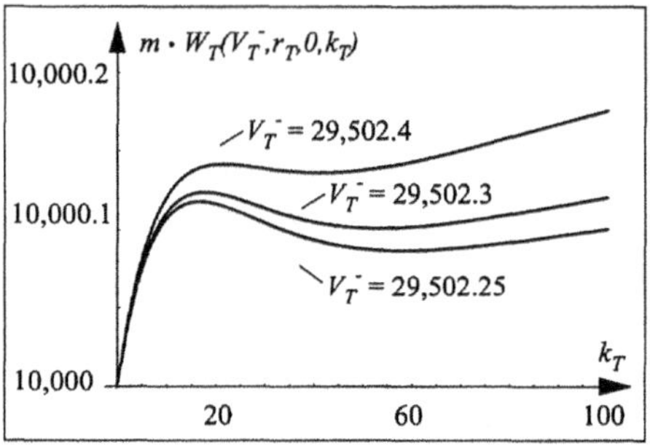

Values of the Convertible Bond and the Stock

The *value* of a *convertible bond* $W_T\left(V_T^-, r_T, K_T, k_T^*\right)$ immediately before maturity is a continuously increasing function of the firm value V_T^- as long as $K_T = 0$. This property is a consequence of the objective function $m \cdot W_T\left(V_T^-, r_T, K_T, k_T\right)$, which is continuous in all arguments and increasing with V_T^-.

In the case of a prior conversion $K_T > 0$, the value of a convertible bond $W_T\left(V_T^-, r_T, K_T, k_T^*\right)$ can have a jump in the firm value V_T^-. This jump occurs if and only if k_T^* has a jump. In this case the stock value has a drop because it suffers from the wealth transfer to the debt holders. As the objective function $(m - K_T) \cdot W_T\left(V_T^-, r_T, K_T, k_T\right) + K_T \cdot S_T\left(V_T^-, r_T, K_T, k_T\right)$ is continuous in all arguments, $W_T\left(V_T^-, r_T, K_T, k_T^*\right)$ must jump. According to the optimal conversion strategy, $W_T\left(V_T^-, r_T, K_T, k_T^*\right)$ reads:

$$W_T\left(V_T^-, r_T, K_T, k_T^*\right) = \begin{cases} \frac{V_T^-}{m-K_T}, \text{ for } V_T^- < (m - K_T) \cdot F \\ F, \text{ for } (m - K_T) \cdot F \leq V_T^- < \underline{V}_T(K_T) \\ \frac{k_T^* \cdot S_T\left(V_T^-, r_T, K_T, k_T^*\right) + \left(m - K_T - k_T^*\right) \cdot F}{m - K_T}, \text{ for } \underline{V}_T(K_T) \\ \leq V_T^- < \overline{V}_T(K_T) \\ S_T\left(V_T^-, r_T, K_T, k_T^*\right), \text{ for } V_T^- \geq \overline{V}_T(K_T) \end{cases}$$

For firm values greater than $\underline{V}_T(K_T)$, a conversion occurs and the convertible bond value $W_T\left(V_T^-, r_T, K_T, k_T^*\right)$ is higher than its redemption value F and lower than the value of a stock $S_T\left(V_T^-, r_T, K_T, k_T^*\right)$. We can see this effect for $K_T = 0$ in figures 4.7 and 4.8.

The reason for this property is that $W_T\left(V_T^-, r_T, K_T, k_T^*\right)$ is a convex combination of both values F and $S_T\left(V_T^-, r_T, K_T, k_T^*\right) > F$. Though an incomplete conversion is optimal for these firm values, $W_T\left(V_T^-, r_T, K_T, k_T^*\right)$ is different from the value obtained with a non-converted convertible bond $W_T^+\left(V_T^-, r_T, K_T, k_T^*\right) = F$ for firm values between $\underline{V}_T(K_T)$ and $\overline{V}_T(K_T)$.

The *value* of a *stock* is given by:

$$S_T\left(V_T^-, r_T, K_T, k_T^*\right) = \begin{cases} 0, \text{ for } V_T^- < (m - K_T) \cdot F \\ S_T\left(V_T^-, r_T, K_T, 0\right), \text{ for } (m - K_T) \cdot F \leq V_T^- < \underline{V}_T(K_T) \\ S_T\left(V_T^-, r_T, K_T, k_T^*\right), \text{ for } \underline{V}_T(K_T) \leq V_T^- < \overline{V}_T(K_T) \\ S_T\left(V_T^-, r_T, K_T, m - K_T\right), \text{ for } V_T^- \geq \overline{V}_T(K_T) \end{cases}$$

If the optimal conversion volume k_T^* is continuous in the firm value V_T^-, $S_T\left(V_T^-, r_T, K_T, k_T^*\right)$ is also a continuous function of V_T^-. However, $S_T\left(V_T^-, r_T, K_T, k_T^*\right)$ can increase or decrease with the firm value. A decrease occurs if k_T^* increases with V_T^- strongly enough that the wealth transfer from the stockholders to the debt holders dominates the positive effect of a higher firm value. Figure 4.8 shows this effect for firm values slightly below 29, 502.3. In this figure, $S_T\left(V_T^-, r_T, K_T, k_T^*\right)$ first increases with V_T^- up to a local maximum, then it continuously declines and exhibits a drop. Afterwards it is equal to $W_T\left(V_T^-, r_T, K_T, k_T^*\right)$ and increases again. In other words, the increase of the conversion volume with a higher firm value can be so strong that a lower stock value is accepted by the monopolist. When k_T^* exhibits an upward jump with V_T^-, the stock value — analogous to the block case — shows a downward jump.

We summarize these findings in the following result.

Result 9 *The optimal conversion volume k_T^* at maturity T increases with the firm value V_T^- but not necessarily continuously. The optimal monopolistic conversion strategy at maturity has the structure $k_T^* = 0$ for $V_T^- \leq \underline{V}_T(K_T)$ and $k_T^* = m$ for $V_T^- \geq \overline{V}(K_T)$. For firm values $V_T^- \in \left(\underline{V}_T(K_T), \overline{V}(K_T)\right)$, a partial conversion is the optimal strategy. It is possible that a conversion volume of a certain interval cannot be optimal for any firm value. The value of a convertible bond $W_T\left(V_T^-, r_T, K_T, k_T^*\right)$ before conversion at maturity T continuously increases with V_T^- if $K_T = 0$. For $K_T > 0$, the convertible bond value has a jump if k_T^* jumps. Moreover, the convertible bond value lies strictly between its redemption value F and the stock value $S_T\left(V_T^-, r_T, 0, k_T^*\right)$ when a partial conversion is optimal, i.e. if $V_T^- \in \left(\underline{V}_T(K_T), \overline{V}(K_T)\right)$. The stock value $S_T\left(V_T^-, r_T, K_T, k_T^*\right)$ can continuously increase or decrease or discontinuously decrease with the firm value.*

1b) Conversion Strategy and the Value of a Convertible Bond as a Function of the Stock Value

To analyze how the stock value $S_T\left(V_T^-, r_T, K_T, k_T^*\right)$ affects the optimal conversion volume k_T^* and the convertible bond value $W_T\left(V_T^-, r_T, 0, k_T^*\right)$ immediately before conversion, we map $S_T\left(V_T^-, r_T, K_T, k_T^*\right)$ with the corresponding values of k_T^* and $W_T\left(V_T^-, r_T, K_T, k_T^*\right)$. Figure 4.10 gives the result of these mappings. The optimal *conversion volume* k_T^* equals

Figure 4.10: Optimal Conversion Strategy and Value of a Convertible Bond at Maturity under Monopolistic Conversion

The left diagram shows the optimal conversion volume k_T^* in the monopolistic case at maturity as a function of the stock value $S_T\left(V_T^-, r_T, 0, k_T^*\right)$. The right diagram shows the related value of a convertible bond $W_T\left(V_T^-, r_T, 0, k_T^*\right)$. The parameter values are $n = 100$, $m = 100$, $F = 100$, $FD = 50{,}000$, $TD - T = 1$, $r_T = 0.05$, $\sigma = 0.5$, $\eta = 0.01097$, $\rho = -0.1$, $\kappa = 0.16643$, $\theta = 0.0639$.

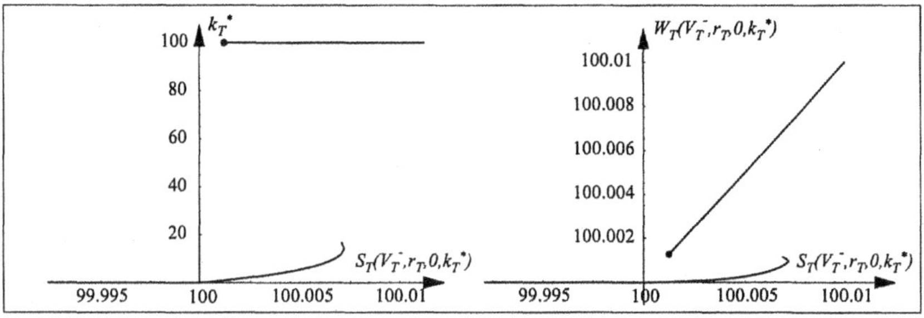

zero for stock values below the redemption value F. When $S_T\left(V_T^-, r_T, K_T, k_T^*\right)$ is above F and a partial conversion is optimal, there is not necessarily a unique relation between the stock value and the optimal conversion volume. In particular, there can be two or three different optimal conversion volumes for one given stock value. This unusual shape is a result of the fact that k_T^* increases with the firm value, but the stock value can continuously and discontinuously decrease with V_T^-. For high stock values a complete conversion is optimal.

Analogously, the *convertible bond value* $W_T\left(V_T^-, r_T, K_T, k_T^*\right)$ is partly not unique in the stock value. This is because for those stock values, which are associated with more than one optimal conversion volume, there are also two or three different convertible bond values related to this particular stock value. In addition, for a stock value equal to zero, $W_T\left(V_T^-, r_T, K_T, k_T^*\right)$ is not unique and can attain every value between zero and its redemption value F. For the other stock values, $W_T\left(V_T^-, r_T, K_T, k_T^*\right)$ is a unique, continuous, and strictly increasing function of the stock value $S_T\left(V_T^-, r_T, K_T, k_T^*\right)$.

The consequence of the shapes of these curves is that the optimal conversion volume k_T^* and the convertible bond value $W_T\left(V_T^-, r_T, K_T, k_T^*\right)$ cannot be uniquely determined given that only the stock value rather than the firm value is known. In particular, a lower stock value can be associated with a higher conversion volume and a higher convertible bond value. Only in the special case in that $S_T\left(V_T^-, r_T, K_T, k_T^*\right)$ is strictly increasing with the firm value V_T^-, the conversion volume k_T^* and the convertible bond value $W_T\left(V_T^-, r_T, K_T, k_T^*\right)$ are uniquely determined by the stock value.

These considerations lead us to the next result.

Result 10 *The conversion strategy k_T^* and the convertible bond value $W_T\left(V_T^-, r_T, K_T, k_T^*\right)$ are not always uniquely defined by the stock value. For a given stock value, two or three different conversion strategies k_T^* can be optimal depending on the firm value. Analogously, two or three different convertible bond values can be related to those stock values. In addition, the value of a convertible bond is not unique if bankruptcy occurs, $S_T\left(V_T^-, r_T, 0, k_T^*\right) = 0$. Otherwise, both k_T^* and $W_T\left(V_T^-, r_T, K_T, k_T^*\right)$ are continuously increasing with $S_T\left(V_T^-, r_T, K_T, k_T^*\right)$.*

2) Conversion Strategy and the Values of a Convertible Bond and Stock as a Function of the Short Rate

Conversion Strategy

The optimal *conversion volume* k_T^* under monopolistic conversion results from maximizing the total value of the prematurely-converted and the non-prematurely converted bonds $(m - K_T - k_T) \cdot W_T^+\left(V_T^-, r_T, K_T, k_T\right) + (K_T + k_T) \cdot S_T\left(V_T^-, r_T, K_T, k_T\right)$. No conversion takes place independent of the short rate, if the firm value V_T^- satisfies $V_T^- \leq (n+m) \cdot F$. As we have seen in the unrestricted case, the stock value for those firm values is below F and therefore a necessary condition for a conversion in the monopolistic case is violated.

For a higher firm value, $V_T^- > (n+m) \cdot F$ a change of the short rate only affects the stock value $S_T\left(V_T^-, r_T, K_T, k_T\right)$ but not the value of a non-converted convertible bond $W_T^+\left(V_T^-, r_T, K_T, k_T\right)$, which equals the redemption value F. In this case, the short rate can change such that no conversion or a complete conversion become optimal. This effect is shown as follows. When r_T becomes sufficiently large, the debt value $D_T\left(V_T^-, r_T, K_T, k_T\right)$ approaches zero and therefore the stock value $S_T\left(V_T^-, r_T, K_T, k_T\right)$ is approximately $\frac{V_T^- - (m - K_T - k_T) \cdot F}{n + K_T + k_T} > F$. This equation reveals that it is optimal for the monopolist to convert the entire holdings to get a stake of the firm as high as possible. Conversely, when r_T becomes sufficiently low the stock value $S_T\left(V_T^-, r_T, K_T, 0\right)$, given no conversion, lies below F. According to the considerations in subsection 1a), no conversion is optimal in this case. As a result, two finite critical short rates, $\underline{r}_T$ and $\overline{r}_T$, always exist for $V_T^- > (n+m) \cdot F$, but there are no critical short rates for a lower firm value. We define $\underline{r}_T$ and $\overline{r}_T$ in an analogous way as under unrestricted conversion as the critical short rates that trigger a positive conversion volume and a complete conversion, respectively.

Moreover, $\underline{r}_T$ and $\overline{r}_T$ are unique, which follows from the fact that the conversion volume k_T^* increases with r_T. The rationale for this monotonicity is — similar to the consideration of the effect of V_T^- in subsection 1a) — that the higher k_T, the higher the increase of the objective function $(m - K_T - k_T) \cdot W_T^+ (V_T^-, r_T, K_T, k_T) + (K_T + k_T) \cdot S_T (V_T^-, r_T, K_T, k_T)$ with r_T. This effect is a consequence of a positive derivative $\frac{\partial^2 (m-K_T-k_T) \cdot W_T^+ (V_T^-, r_T, K_T, k_T) + (K_T+k_T) \cdot S_T (V_T^-, r_T, K_T, k_T)}{\partial k_T \partial r_T}$.[9] Figure 4.11 shows an example for the optimal conversion volume as a function of the short rate r_T. In this particular

Figure 4.11: Optimal Conversion Strategy and Values of a Convertible Bond and a Stock at Maturity under Monopolistic Conversion

The left diagram shows the optimal conversion volume k_T^* in the unrestricted case at maturity as a function of the short rate r_T. The right diagram shows the related values of a convertible bond $W_T(V_T^-, r_T, 0, k_T^*)$ and a stock $S_T(V_T^-, r_T, 0, k_T^*)$. The parameter values are $n = 100$, $m = 100$, $F = 100$, $FD = 50{,}000$, $TD - T = 1$, $V_T^- = 60{,}000$, $\sigma = 0.5$, $\eta = 0.01097$, $\rho = -0.1$, $\kappa = 0.16643$, $\theta = 0.0639$. The critical short rates $\underline{r}_T$ and $\overline{r}_T$ result in 0.002034 and 0.2384, respectively.

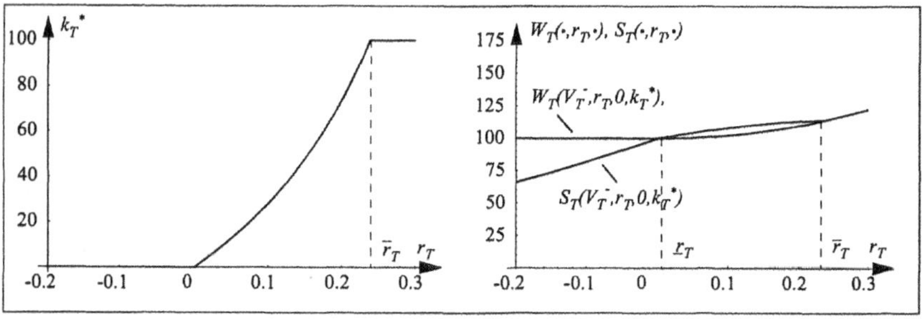

example, k_T^* continuously increases from zero to $m - K_T$ with the short rate r_T. However, the continuity does not necessarily hold. In other examples, k_T^* exhibits jumps from a fixed conversion volume below $m - K_T$ to a complete conversion $m - K_T$. The reason is analogous to that under 1a) for the firm value. The objective function

[9] $\frac{\partial^2 (m-K_T) \cdot W_T (V_T^-, r_T, K_T, k_T) + K_T \cdot S_T (V_T^-, r_T, K_T, k_T)}{\partial k_T \partial r_T}$ is equal to $\frac{1}{(n+K_T+k_T)^2} \left(n \cdot \text{Call-Rho}_T + (K_T + k_T \cdot F) \cdot (n + K_T + k_T) \frac{\partial \text{Call-Delta}_T}{\partial r_T} \right).$

$(m - K_T - k_T) \cdot W_T^+ (V_T^-, r_T, K_T, k_T) + (K_T + k_T) \cdot S_T (V_T^-, r_T, K_T, k_T)$ can have a local maximum and a local minimum in k_T such that the interior maximum is the global maximum for certain short rates, but the boundary solution $k_T^* = m - K_T$ yields a value of $(m - K_T) \cdot W_T (V_T^-, r_T, K_T, m - K_T) + K_T \cdot S_T (V_T^-, r_T, K_T, m - K_T)$ above the local maximum for higher short rates.

As long as the objective function has always exactly one local maximum which is also the global one, the optimal conversion volume k_T^* is differentiable in r_T for short rates between $\underline{r}_T$ and $\overline{r}_T$ by analogous arguments as for the differentiability in V_T^- presented in subsection 1a).

Values of the Convertible Bond and the Stock

The *value* of a *convertible bond* $W_T (V_T^-, r_T, K_T, k_T^*)$ is a continuously increasing function of the short rate r_T if $K_T = 0$. This finding is because the objective function $m \cdot W_T (V_T^-, r_T, 0, k_T)$ is continuous in r_T and k_T. If $K_T > 0$, the convertible bond value can have a jump in r_T. The reason for the jump is the same as for the jump in the firm value presented in subsection 1a).

In general, for short rates below $\underline{r}_T$, no conversion is optimal and $W_T (V_T^-, r_T, K_T, k_T^*)$ is equal to the value of a non-converted convertible bond $W_T^+ (V_T^-, r_T, K_T, k_T^*)$ which is independent of r_T. When r_T is between $\underline{r}_T$ and $\overline{r}_T$, a partial conversion is optimal. The convertible bond value $W_T (V_T^-, r_T, K_T, k_T^*)$ lies between the stock value $S_T (V_T^-, r_T, K_T, k_T^*)$ and the value of a non-converted convertible bond F. For a high short rate above $\overline{r}_T$, a complete conversion is optimal and $W_T (V_T^-, r_T, K_T, k_T^*)$ equals $S_T (V_T^-, r_T, K_T, k_T^*)$. Hence, $W_T (V_T^-, r_T, K_T, k_T^*)$ increases with r_T because an increase of r_T causes a wealth transfer from debt holders to stockholders. Only if V_T^- is not above $(n + m) \cdot F$, finite critical short rates do not exist, no conversion occurs, and $W_T (V_T^-, r_T, K_T, k_T^*)$ is equal to the value of a non-converted convertible bond $W_T^+ (V_T^-, r_T, K_T, k_T^*)$ for all r_T.

The *value* of a *stock* $S_T (V_T^-, r_T, K_T, k_T^*)$ can continuously increase, continuously decrease, and discontinuously decrease with r_T. If no conversion is optimal, $r_T < \underline{r}_T$, $S_T (V_T^-, r_T, K_T, k_T^*)$ continuously increases with r_T. Then, for a partial conversion, $S_T (V_T^-, r_T, K_T, k_T^*)$ can continuously increase, continuously decrease, or drop. The reason is that the benefit of $S_T (V_T^-, r_T, K_T, k_T^*)$ from a higher short rate can be lower than the disadvantage from a higher conversion volume which is indicated by a continuous and a discontinuous decrease of $S_T (V_T^-, r_T, K_T, k_T^*)$ in the example of figure 4.8. The drop results from the jump of the optimal conversion volume k_T^* in r_T. For short rates higher than $\overline{r}_T$, $S_T (V_T^-, r_T, K_T, k_T^*)$ is again continuously and strictly increasing. In the example of figure 4.11, $S_T (V_T^-, r_T, K_T, k_T^*)$ continuously and strictly increases for all r_T.

As a result, we obtain the following.

Result 11 *The optimal conversion volume k_T^* of the convertible bond at maturity T increases with the short rate r_T. However, k_T^* can continuously or discontinuously increase. If V_T^- is not larger than $(n+m) \cdot F$, no finite critical short rates exist as no conversion is optimal for all r_T. Otherwise, the optimal conversion volume has the structure $k_T^* = 0$ for $r_T \leq \underline{r}_T$, $k_T^* = m - K_T$ for $r_T \geq \overline{r}_T$, and a partial conversion occurs for the other short rates. The value of a convertible bond $W_T\left(V_T^-, r_T, K_T, k_T^*\right)$ before conversion at maturity T continuously increases with r_T for $K_T = 0$. Otherwise, the convertible bond value has a jump when the conversion volume jumps. The stock value $S_T\left(V_T^-, r_T, K_T, k_T^*\right)$ at maturity T can continuously increase, decrease, or drop when the short rate rises.*

3) Conversion Strategy and the Values of a Convertible Bond and Stock as a Function of the Amount of Additional Debt

The determination of the properties of the optimal conversion volume k_T^* and the values $W_T\left(V_T^-, r_T, K_T, k_T^*\right)$ and $S_T\left(V_T^-, r_T, K_T, k_T^*\right)$ for a variation of the debt face value FD is similar to the corresponding analysis for the short rate r_T under 2). However, the debt face value affects the stock value $S_T\left(V_T^-, r_T, K_T, k_T\right)$ and therefore the objective function $(m - K_T - k_T) \cdot W_T^+\left(V_T^-, r_T, K_T, k_T\right) + (K_T + k_T) \cdot S_T\left(V_T^-, r_T, K_T, k_T\right)$ in the opposite way as r_T does.

For $V_T^- \leq (n+m) \cdot F$, no conversion is optimal as under 2). In the opposite case, the stock value $S_T\left(V_T^-, r_T, K_T, k_T\right)$ for a given conversion volume decreases from $\max\left(\frac{V_T^- - (m-K_T-k_T) \cdot F}{n+K_T+k_T}, 0\right)$ to zero. Therefore, the corresponding critical debt face values $\underline{FD}$ and $\overline{FD}$ in the monopolistic case exist for $V_T^- > (n+m) \cdot F$ but not for lower firm values. To illustrate this effect, we can argue that a complete conversion is optimal for those firm values if the debt face value is close to zero. The reason why for a high FD no conversion is optimal is because the stock value $S_T\left(V_T^-, r_T, K_T, 0\right)$ becomes lower than F which is a necessary condition for a conversion.

The uniqueness of $\underline{FD}$ and $\overline{FD}$ that trigger a partial and a complete conversion, respectively, results from the fact that the optimal *conversion volume* k_T^* decreases with FD. This property follows from $\frac{\partial^2 (m-K_T-k_T) \cdot W_T^+\left(V_T^-, r_T, K_T, k_T\right) + (K_T+k_T) \cdot S_T\left(V_T^-, r_T, K_T, k_T\right)}{\partial FD \partial k_T} < 0$, as the objective function decreases more severely when k_T is high.

The *convertible bond value* $W_T\left(V_T^-, r_T, K_T, k_T^*\right)$ is a continuous decreasing function of FD for $K_T = 0$, because the objective function $m \cdot W_T\left(V_T^-, r_T, 0, k_T\right)$ is continuously decreasing with FD for all k_T and is continuous in k_T. Otherwise, $W_T\left(V_T^-, r_T, K_T, k_T\right)$ can have a drop in FD. This drop occurs if the optimal conversion volume has a drop in the debt face value in favor of the stock value. Nevertheless, the monopolist's wealth is continuous in FD under the optimal strategy. This is the opposite effect to that we have seen for V_T^- and r_T in subsections 1a) and 2).

The *stock value* $S_T\left(V_T^-, r_T, K_T, k_T^*\right)$ continuously decreases with FD if the conversion volume k_T^* is not impacted. Otherwise, $S_T\left(V_T^-, r_T, K_T, k_T^*\right)$ can increase or decrease depending on which of the two effects, the decrease of $S_T\left(V_T^-, r_T, K_T, k_T\right)$ with FD or the increase of $S_T\left(V_T^-, r_T, K_T, k_T\right)$ due to a lower optimal conversion volume, dominates. In general, $S_T\left(V_T^-, r_T, K_T, k_T^*\right)$ can continuously increase or continuously decrease with FD. If the optimal conversion volume shows a drop in FD, the stock value $S_T\left(V_T^-, r_T, K_T, k_T^*\right)$ has an upward jump.

These considerations provide us with the following result.

Result 12 *The optimal conversion volume k_T^* of the convertible bond at maturity T decreases with the debt face value FD. However, k_T^* can continuously or discontinuously decrease. If V_T^- is not larger than $(n+m) \cdot F$, no finite critical debt face values exist as no conversion is optimal for all FD. Otherwise, the optimal conversion volume has the structure $k_T^* = 0$ for $FD \geq \underline{FD}$, $k_T^* = m - K_T$ for $FD \leq \overline{FD}$ and a partial conversion occurs for the other debt face values. The value of a convertible bond $W_T\left(V_T^-, r_T, K_T, k_T^*\right)$ before conversion at maturity T continuously decreases with FD for $K_T = 0$. Otherwise, the convertible bond value has a drop when the conversion volume jumps. The stock value $S_T\left(V_T^-, r_T, K_T, k_T^*\right)$ at maturity T can continuously increase, decrease, or jump when the debt face value rises.*

The general tendency of the optimal conversion volume k_T^* and the values $W_T\left(V_T^-, r_T, K_T, k_T^*\right)$ and $S_T\left(V_T^-, r_T, K_T, k_T^*\right)$ in the monopolistic case parallels our intuition. The conversion volume and the asset values at maturity T increase with the firm value and the short rate and decrease with the debt face value.

However, there are some surprising findings regarding the optimal conversion strategy and the values of a convertible bond and a stock. The optimal conversion volume k_T^* might show jumps in V_T^-, r_T, and FD. In these cases, some but not all partial conversion volumes can occur. Whenever the optimal conversion volume is discontinuous and $K_T > 0$, the convertible bond value is also discontinuous in V_T^-, r_T, and FD. This finding is a result of the continuity of the monopolist's objective function in conjunction with the stock value drop (jump) in V_T^- and r_T (FD).

Because of these properties of the stock value, neither the optimal conversion volume nor the convertible bond value are unique in the stock value. In particular, three different conversion volumes and three different convertible bond values can be associated with some fixed stock values.

4.4 Analysis without additional Debt

The different properties of the conversion strategy at maturity and the related asset values for the three conversion variants are primarily driven by the existence of additional debt. This is because for every conversion variant, a different way of coping with the additional debt and the potential wealth transfer to the debt holders is selected. Now, we want to examine whether without additional debt the strategies for the three conversion variants still differ.

Without additional debt, $FD = 0$, the optimal *conversion strategy* at maturity immediately results from the value of a non-converted convertible bond $W_T^+(V_T^-, r_T, K_T, k_T) = \min\left(\frac{V_T^-}{m-K_T-k_T}, F\right)$ and a stock $S_T(V_T^-, r_T, K_T, k_T) = \max\left(0, \frac{V_T^- -(m-K_T-k_T)\cdot F}{n+K_T+k_T}\right)$.

If the firm value V_T^- is higher than $(n+m)\cdot F$, the stock value is $\frac{V_T^- -(m-K_T-k_T)\cdot F}{n+K_T+k_T} > F$ for all k_T, where $W_T^+(V_T^-, r_T, K_T, k_T)$ equals F. As a consequence, a complete conversion is optimal in the block case $\left(S_T(V_T^-, r_T, 0, m) > W_T^+(V_T^-, r_T, 0, 0)\right)$ and in the unrestricted case $\left(S_T(V_T^-, r_T, K_T, m) > W_T^+(V_T^-, r_T, K_T, m)\right)$. A complete conversion is also optimal under monopolistic conversion. This effect can be shown with the derivative of the monopolist's objective function $\frac{\partial (m-K_T)\cdot W_T\left(V_T^-, r_T, K_T, k_T\right) + K_T \cdot S_T\left(V_T^-, r_T, K_T, k_T\right)}{\partial k_T}$ which results in $n\frac{V_T^- -(n+m)\cdot F}{n+K_T+k_T}$ and is therefore always positive for those firm values.

In the opposite case, $V_T^- < (n+m)\cdot F$, the relations between $W_T^+(V_T^-, r_T, K_T, k_T)$ and $S_T(V_T^-, r_T, K_T, k_T)$ are all reversed such that no conversion is optimal for the three conversion variants.

In the special case $V_T^- = (n+m)\cdot F$, every conversion volume k_T leads to a stock and a convertible bond value equal to F. Consequently, the block strategy, like every other strategy, results in the same asset values. Thus, every conversion volume $k_T \in [0, m-K_T]$ is an equilibrium strategy in the unrestricted and monopolistic case, but $k_T^* = m$ is the only feasible strategy by definition in the block case. These considerations demonstrate that the initial conversion condition (2.2) employed by the traditional approaches in the absence of debt are equilibrium strategies, even if more advanced conversion strategies, like unrestricted or monopolistic conversion, are considered.

As a consequence, the asset *values* of a *convertible bond*

$$W_T(V_T^-, r_T, K_T, k_T^*) = \max\left(\frac{V_T^-}{n+m}, \min\left(\frac{V_T^-}{m-K_T}, F\right)\right)$$

and a *stock*

$$S_T(V_T^-, r_T, K_T, k_T^*) = \min\left(\frac{V_T^-}{n+m}, \max\left(\frac{V_T^- -(m-K_T)\cdot F}{n+K_T}, 0\right)\right)$$

are the same for every conversion variant. Thus, both the value of a convertible bond and a stock are continuous and increasing functions of the firm value. Moreover, neither the conversion volume nor the asset values depend on the short rate r_T anymore. Furthermore, the convertible bond value is a unique function of the stock value given no default at maturity.

We obtain the following result.

Result 13 *If the firm has no additional debt outstanding, the block strategy is an optimal strategy at maturity for all three conversion variants. The optimal block strategy is* $k_T^* = 0$ *for* $V_T^- < \overline{V}_T = (n+m) \cdot F$ *and* $k_T^* = m$ *for* $V_T^- \geq (n+m) \cdot F$. *The values of a convertible bond* $W_T\left(V_T^-, r_T, 0, k_T^*\right)$ *before conversion at maturity* T *and a stock* $S_T\left(V_T^-, r_T, 0, k_T^*\right)$ *continuously increase with* V_T^-. *If no default occurs at maturity, the convertible bond value is uniquely determined by the stock value for all variants. Moreover, the stock value can never lie above the convertible bond value.*

Chapter 5

Optimal Conversion Strategies and Valuation of Convertible Bonds before Maturity

In this chapter, we conduct the corresponding analysis to the previous chapter, but for a conversion date before maturity. As the effects at every premature conversion date are basically the same, it is reasonable to employ a two conversion date model to emphasize the basic properties of the conversion strategy and the related asset values. In chapter 7, we will explicitly discuss the differences between the properties at the last and an arbitrary premature conversion date. For the ease of notation, we set the last premature conversion date t_N equal to zero throughout this chapter. Since the total conversion volume before time $t = 0$, which is denoted by K_0, is zero if only two conversion dates are considered, we can write for the values $W_0\left(V_0^-, r_0, k_0\right)$, $W_0^+\left(V_0^-, r_0, k_0\right)$, $S_0\left(V_0^-, r_0, k_0\right)$, and $D_0\left(V_0^-, r_0, k_0\right)$ instead of the more sophisticated notation.[1]

The results for the optimal conversion volume and the asset values at maturity allow us to determine the values of a convertible bond $W_0\left(V_0^-, r_0, k_0\right)$ before conversion, $W_0^+\left(V_0^-, r_0, k_0\right)$ after conversion, and a stock $S_0\left(V_0^-, r_0, k_0\right)$ for an exogenous conversion volume k_0. For this purpose, we can apply equations (3.15), (3.16), and (3.14) if we employ the conversion strategy found for the corresponding conversion variant. The equilibrium concept to determine the optimal conversion volume k_0^* at the first conversion date is analogous to that used for the analysis at maturity. However, the conversion decision is driven by other factors especially the dividend, which does not play any role at maturity.

---

[1] If we assume that the firm already exists before time $t = 0$, we can think of V_0^-, which has been introduced as the left limit of the firm value process at time $t = 0$, as the firm value before the coupon payment.

There are two cases which have identical consequences for the strategies of the three conversion variants. The first case is that the firm value at time $t = 0$ is not above the promised coupon payment, $m \cdot c$, and the second one concerns a dividend rate δ equal to zero. Therefore, we begin with these simple cases to prevent a repetition of similar arguments for all conversion variants.

For $V_0^- \leq m \cdot c$, default occurs, if the convertible bond holders do not convert. Since the consequences of a default before maturity are analogous to those at maturity, as the claim of the convertible bond holders is senior to the other claims, the situation $V_0^- \leq m \cdot c$ at time $t = 0$ is analogous to $V_T^- \leq (m - K_T) \cdot F$ at maturity. As a consequence of the considerations at maturity, the optimal strategy is not to convert whenever a default can be triggered.

In the absence of dividends, $\delta = 0$, a conversion cannot occur. The intuitive rationale for this property in the block and monopolistic case is as follows. A conversion is associated with a loss of the coupon payment and the flexibility to convert at a later date, but a prior conversion has no advantage in the absence of a dividend payment.[2] Similarly, in the unrestricted case the value of a non-converted convertible bond for a given strategy must be higher than the stock value for the same strategy. Therefore, every investor prefers not to convert and $k_0^* = 0$ is also the optimal aggregate conversion strategy without dividends.

Due to the fact that no conversion occurs for $V_0^- \leq m \cdot c$ or $\delta = 0$ under all three conversion variants, the following analysis focuses on firm values for which the firm survives at time $t = 0$ and on dividend rates, $\delta > 0$ for which a conversion probably occurs.

In addition, it is appropriate to stress four general properties, which will be helpful for the following examination. These properties result from the analysis at maturity.

(1) The values $W_0\left(V_0^-, r_0, k_0\right)$, $W_0^+\left(V_0^-, r_0, k_0\right)$, $S_0\left(V_0^-, r_0, k_0\right)$, and $D_0\left(V_0^-, r_0, k_0\right)$ given by (3.15), (3.16), (3.13), and (3.14), respectively, are obviously continuous and arbitrarily often differentiable functions of all arguments.

(2) The conversion volume k_T^* at maturity is a random variable depending on the realizations of the firm value V_T^- and the short rate r_T. However, we can show that the total

---

[2] Under Monopolistic conversion, this argument is straightforward in the absence of coupon payments. If the firm makes coupon payments, the incentive not to convert is even higher, because the coupons represent a portion of the firm value which is exclusively reserved for the monopolist. In the case of a conversion, all three groups of shareholders benefit from the saved coupon payments and not only the monopolist. If, in contrast to our framework, the saved coupon payment had side-effects e.g. on the firm value risk, a conversion without dividend payments could be advantageous.

conversion volume $k_T^* + k_0$ increases with the conversion volume k_0 prior to maturity.[3] For the block case, this statement is obvious, as a complete conversion at time $t = 0$ cannot be exceeded anymore. In the unrestricted and monopolistic case, we first consider a fixed firm value V_T^- and a fixed short rate r_T at maturity. In this case, a premature conversion has the same effect as a conversion at maturity. Thus, a lower k_0 cannot result in a higher total conversion volume $k_T^* + k_0$. We then take into account that the firm value V_T^- at maturity increases with k_0 because of the lower coupon payment due at time $t = 0$. As the optimal conversion volume k_T^* increases with the firm value independent of the conversion variant and as the short rate r_T is not affected by k_0, we can finally conclude that the total conversion volume $k_T^* + k_0$ increases with the prior conversion volume k_0.

(3) The debt value $D_0\left(V_0^-, r_0, k_0\right)$ increases with k_0 for all conversion variants. This property is a consequence of two facts. First, the debt value at maturity $D_T\left(V_T^-, r_T, k_0, k_T\right)$ increases with both the firm value V_T^- and the total conversion volume $k_T^* + k_0$. Second, according to remark (2), V_T^- and $k_T^* + k_0$ increase with k_0. Thus, the higher k_0, the higher the debt value at maturity. Therefore, a conversion in $t = 0$ also results in a wealth transfer to the debt holders. If the dividend rate δ is strictly below one and no default occurs, the debt value strictly increases with k_0. Only in the special case of $\delta = 1$ or a default, the debt value $D_0\left(V_0^-, r_0, k_0\right) = 0$ is independent of k_0.

(4) If the short rate becomes very low, the expectation of the firm value under the relevant measure $\mathbb{P}_T$ tends to zero. Thus, if the firm does not default at time $t = 0$, it will (almost surely) go bankrupt at maturity. Therefore, the limit of the total value of all non-converted convertible bonds is equal to the firm value V_0^- minus the dividend payment $\max\left(V_0^- - (m - k_0) \cdot c, 0\right) \cdot \delta$. Defining $W_0^+\left(V_0^-, -\infty, k_0\right)$ as $\lim_{r_0 \to -\infty} W_0^+\left(V_0^-, r_0, k_0\right)$, we obtain $W_0^+\left(V_0^-, -\infty, k_0\right) = \frac{V_0^- - \max\left(V_0^- - (m-k_0)\cdot c, 0\right)\cdot\delta}{m-k_0}$. As a consequence, the stock value equals the value of the dividend payment which is $\lim_{r_0 \to -\infty} S_0\left(V_0^-, r_0, k_0\right) := S_0\left(V_0^-, -\infty, k_0\right) = \frac{\max\left(V_0^- - (m-k_0)\cdot c, 0\right)\cdot\delta}{n+k_0}$.

5.1 Block Conversion

1a) Conversion Strategy and the Values of a Convertible Bond and Stock as a Function of the Firm Value

[3] This statement is not trivial. When dealing with corporate warrants, which are generally regarded as a similar instrument as convertible bonds, Koziol (2002) shows that a higher premature exercise volume k_0 can be associated with a lower total exercise volume $k_T^* + k_0$.

Conversion Strategy

Block conversion requires a unique conversion decision for all convertible bonds. Therefore, the optimal *conversion volume* $k_0^* \in \{0, m\}$ is chosen such that the value obtained with the convertible bonds is maximized. This value either equals m times the stock value after a complete conversion or m times the value of a non-converted convertible bond:

$$\begin{aligned} & \max_{k_0 \in \{0,m\}} k_0 \cdot S_0 \left(V_0^-, r_0, k_0\right) + (m - k_0) \cdot W_0^+ \left(V_0^-, r_0, k_0\right) \\ = \; & m \cdot \max \left\{ S_0 \left(V_0^-, r_0, m\right), W_0^+ \left(V_0^-, r_0, 0\right) \right\} \end{aligned}$$

For the determination of k_0^*, we simply have to compare the conversion value $S_0 \left(V_0^-, r_0, m\right)$ with the value of a non-converted convertible bond $W_0^+ \left(V_0^-, r_0, 0\right)$.

Comparing the advantages of the values $S_0 \left(V_0^-, r_0, m\right)$ and $W_0^+ \left(V_0^-, r_0, 0\right)$, we see that a full conversion in $t = 0$ is associated with a dividend payment having a present value equal to $\delta \frac{V_0^-}{n+m}$ and that the firm value does not suffer from the coupon payment at time $t = 0$. On the other hand, the convertible bond provides its holders with a coupon right and a better downside protection as the stock at maturity.

In the following, we consider the difference between the value of the convertible bond and the stock at maturity T as a function of the firm value $\mathbb{V}$. The value $\mathbb{V}$ is defined as the firm value at time T before maturity that results from a given firm value V_0^- when no coupon payment but a total dividend payment at time τ $(0 < \tau < T)$ equal to $V_\tau^- \cdot \delta$ is made. Then, the value of one share at time T is given by its call value representation as follows

$$S_T \left(\mathbb{V}, r_T, m, 0\right) = \frac{C_T \left(\mathbb{V}\right)}{n + m}.$$

We must distinguish the firm value $\mathbb{V}$ from a further relevant but similar firm value. Since after a coupon payment at time $t = 0$, the firm value at maturity is smaller, namely $\left(V_0^- - m \cdot c\right) \frac{\mathbb{V}}{V_0^-}$, we must use $\left(V_0^- - m \cdot c\right) \frac{\mathbb{V}}{V_0^-}$ for the firm value at maturity that determines the value of the convertible bonds. Thus, the value of a non-converted convertible bond at maturity in terms of $\mathbb{V}$ is:

$$W_T \left(\left(V_0^- - m \cdot c\right) \frac{\mathbb{V}}{V_0^-}, r_T, 0, k_T^* \right) =$$

$$\begin{cases} \frac{\left(V_0^- - m \cdot c\right) \frac{\mathbb{V}}{V_0^-}}{m}, & \text{if } \left(V_0^- - m \cdot c\right) \frac{\mathbb{V}}{V_0^-} < m \cdot F \\ F, & \text{if } m \cdot F \leq \left(V_0^- - m \cdot c\right) \frac{\mathbb{V}}{V_0^-} \text{ and } F > \frac{C_T\left(\left(V_0^- - m \cdot c\right) \frac{\mathbb{V}}{V_0^-}\right)}{n+m} \\ \frac{C_T\left(\left(V_0^- - m \cdot c\right) \frac{\mathbb{V}}{V_0^-}\right)}{n+m}, & \text{if } F \leq \frac{C_T\left(\left(V_0^- - m \cdot c\right) \frac{\mathbb{V}}{V_0^-}\right)}{n+m} \end{cases}$$

Under our general assumption, $V_0^- > m \cdot c$, imposed at the beginning of this chapter, the

Figure 5.1: Differences between the Values of a Convertible Bond and a Stock at Maturity under Block Conversion

The diagram shows the value of a stock $S_T(\mathbb{V}, 0, m)$ as a function of the firm value $\mathbb{V}$ at maturity that arises after a complete premature conversion. In addition, the diagram shows the value obtained with a convertible bond at maturity (after the coupon payment at time 0), $W_T\left(\left(V_0^- - m \cdot c\right) \frac{\mathbb{V}}{V_0^-}, 0, k_T^*\right)$, and the difference of both assets, $dif_T\left(\mathbb{V}, V_0^-, r_T\right)$ as a function of $\mathbb{V}$. The dashed line indicates the asymptote $-\frac{m \cdot c}{n+m} \frac{\mathbb{V}}{V_0^-}$. The parameter values are $n = 100$, $m = 100$, $F = 100$, $FD = 50{,}000$, $c = 5$, $TD - T = 1$, $V_0^- = 100{,}000$, $r_T = 0.05$, $\sigma = 0.5$, $\eta = 0.01097$, $\rho = -0.1$, $\kappa = 0.16643$, $\theta = 0.0639$.

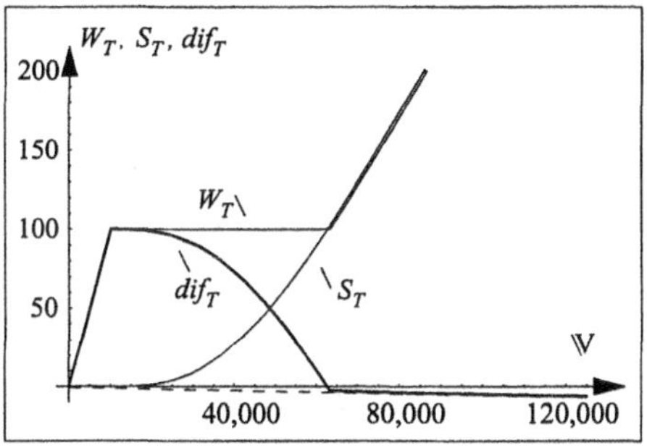

difference

$$dif_T\left(\mathbb{V}, V_0^-, r_T\right) := W_T\left(\left(V_0^- - m \cdot c\right) \frac{\mathbb{V}}{V_0^-}, r_T, 0, k_T^*\right) - S_T\left(\mathbb{V}, r_T, 0, m\right)$$

has a general pattern that is shown in figure 5.1. This difference increases first with $\mathbb{V}$ and then decreases to the value of the function $-\frac{m \cdot c}{n+m} \frac{\mathbb{V}}{V_0^-}$. For low firm values $\mathbb{V}$, $dif_T\left(\mathbb{V}, V_0^-, r_T\right)$ is positive and increases because the convertible bond at maturity, given no conversion, equals the total firm value divided by the number of outstanding convertible bonds, but the stock value after conversion is close to zero as the firm will probably default at the debt's maturity TD. Since due to the coupon payment at time $t = 0$, the difference between the relevant firm value of a convertible bond and the stock after a prior conversion is $-m \cdot c \frac{\mathbb{V}}{V_0^-}$, the difference between the value of a convertible bond at maturity and a prematurely converted bond for high firm values is approximately this firm value difference divided by $n + m$, i.e. $-\frac{m \cdot c}{n+m} \frac{\mathbb{V}}{V_0^-}$.

The value of this difference $dif_0\left(V_0^-, r_0\right)$ at time $t = 0$ results in $B_0(T) \cdot \mathbb{E}_0^{\mathbb{P}_T}\left(dif_T\left(\mathbb{V}, V_0^-, r_T\right)\right)$. Hence, we can consider $dif_0\left(V_0^-, r_0\right)$ as the value of a financial claim that provides the difference at time T between the convertible bond value when no conversion would have taken place at time $t = 0$ and the stock value after a complete conversion prior to maturity. According to our intuition $dif_0(V_0^-, r_0)$ has a similar qualitative pattern in V_0^- as $dif_T(\mathbb{V}, V_0^-, r_T)$ in $\mathbb{V}$. Therefore, $dif_0(V_0^-, r_0)$ is close to zero for low firm values V_0^- and then it might attain a maximum. For large V_0^-, the difference approaches $-\frac{m \cdot c}{n+m} \cdot (1-\delta)$ which is the current value of a payment equal to the lower bound, $-\frac{m \cdot c}{n+m} \frac{\mathbb{V}}{V_0^-}$, of $dif_T(\mathbb{V}, V_0^-, r_T)$ in figure 5.1.

The definition of $dif_0(V_0^-, r_0)$ allows us to represent the important difference $W_0^+(V_0^-, r_0, 0) - S_0(V_0^-, r_0, m)$ by $dif_0(V_0^-, r_0)$ plus the value of the exclusive payment from a convertible bond minus the value of the exclusive payment of a stock. As this payment is the coupon c for a convertible bond and the dividend with a value of $\delta \frac{V_0^-}{n+m}$ per stock, the difference $W_0^+(V_0^-, r_0, 0) - S_0(V_0^-, r_0, m)$ reads:

$$W_0^+(V_0^-, r_0, 0) - S_0(V_0^-, r_0, m) = dif_0(V_0^-, r_0) + c - \delta \frac{V_0^-}{n+m} \tag{5.1}$$

Again, the sign of (5.1) determines whether a conversion occurs or not, i.e. no conversion is optimal for a positive sign, but a complete conversion takes place for a negative one. In the case of indifference, i.e. $W_0^+(V_0^-, r_0, 0) - S_0(V_0^-, r_0, m) = 0$, we assume $k_0^* = m$ as we did at maturity. These considerations lead us to the following representation of k_0^*:

$$k_0^* = \begin{cases} 0, & \text{if } dif_0(V_0^-, r_0) + c - \delta \frac{V_0^-}{n+m} > 0 \\ m, & \text{if } dif_0(V_0^-, r_0) + c - \delta \frac{V_0^-}{n+m} \leq 0 \end{cases} \tag{5.2}$$

As we can see in representation (5.2), the optimal conversion strategy, depends on both the coupon c and the dividend rate δ. Moreover, we use the property introduced above that $dif_0(V_0^-, r_0)$ is always above $-\frac{m \cdot c}{n+m} \cdot (1-\delta)$ for the analysis of (5.2). Therefore, we obtain the following properties:

- No conversion is optimal for all firm values V_0^- if the dividend rate δ is zero, as illustrated at the beginning of this chapter.

- The opposite case, in which a conversion is optimal for all firm values V_0^-, can also occur. This scenario occurs if the dividend rate δ is sufficiently close to one and no coupon payment is made. According to equation (5.2), the relevant difference between the value of a non-converted convertible bond and a stock equals $dif_0(V_0^-, r_0) - \delta \frac{V_0^-}{n+m}$ in this case. Since $dif_0(V_0^-, r_0)$ approaches zero when δ tends to one, we obtain a negative difference implying a complete conversion independent of the firm value V_0^-.

- In all other cases a positive critical firm value $\overline{V}_0$ must exist that triggers a conversion. This is because a complete conversion is optimal if the firm value V_0^- is sufficiently high, given a positive dividend rate $\delta > 0$. In this case, the value of the flexibility to convert at a later date is almost worthless, and the value of the dividend payment $\delta \cdot V_0$ is higher than the coupon payment. We can analogously derive this property from equation (5.2). Since $dif_0\left(V_0^-, r_0\right)$ is bounded, the sign of representation (5.2) becomes negative for high firm values indicating that a complete conversion is then optimal. Thus, a critical firm value $\overline{V}_0$ exists that $k_0^* = m$ for $V_0^- \geq \overline{V}_0$. If $dif_0\left(V_0^-, r_0\right)$ is a concave function in V_0^- first and subsequently convex, the critical firm value $\overline{V}_0$ is unique.[4] However, we were unable to rule out the possibility that k_0^* jumps from m to zero and back to m, if V_0^- increases to infinity.

- If the coupon c is positive, no conversion is optimal for low firm values because it is optimal to force the firm into default if the firm value is not sufficient to make the coupon payment. As a consequence, a *positive* critical firm value $\overline{V}_0$ that triggers a conversion exists in the case with a positive coupon and dividend rate.

Values of the Convertible Bond and the Stock

The optimal conversion strategy k_0^* results in the following representation for the *value* of a *convertible bond* $W_0\left(V_0^-, r_0, k_0^*\right)$:

$$W_0\left(V_0^-, r_0, k_0^*\right) = \begin{cases} W_0^+\left(V_0^-, r_0, 0\right), & \text{if } k_0^* = 0 \\ S_0\left(V_0^-, r_0, m\right), & \text{if } k_0^* = m \end{cases}$$

According to this representation, $W_0\left(V_0, r_0, k_0^*\right)$ is a continuous strictly increasing function of the firm value V_0^-. The continuity and the strict monotonicity are a result of the fact that $W_0\left(V_0^-, r_0, k_0^*\right)$ is equal to the maximum of the two functions $W_0^+\left(V_0^-, r_0, 0\right)$ and $S_0\left(V_0^-, r_0, m\right)$ each of which is continuous and strictly increasing in V_0^-. These properties of $W_0^+\left(V_0^-, r_0, 0\right)$ and $S_0\left(V_0^-, r_0, m\right)$ are an immediate result of representations (3.16) and (3.14) together with the optimal conversion volume k_T^* at maturity as derived in the previous chapter.

Likewise, the *value* of a *stock* is given by:

$$S_0\left(V_0^-, r_0, k_0^*\right) = \begin{cases} S_0\left(V_0^-, r_0, 0\right), & \text{if } k_0^* = 0 \\ S_0\left(V_0^-, r_0, m\right), & \text{if } k_0^* = m \end{cases}$$

$S_0\left(V_0^-, r_0, k_0^*\right)$ can continuously increase with the firm value V_0^- as long as a change of V_0^- does not affect the optimal conversion volume k_0^*. According to remark (3) at the beginning of this chapter, the debt value $D_0\left(V_0^-, r_0, m\right)$ after a conversion is higher

---

4 In this case, the function $dif_0\left(V_0^-, r_0\right) + c$ and the linear term $\left(V_0^- - m \cdot c\right)\delta$ can only coincide in one positive V_0^- at most. This intersection is the critical firm value. If no intersection exists, $\overline{V}_0$ equals zero and a conversion is optimal for all firm values.

than the debt value $D_0(V_0^-, r_0, 0)$ without a conversion. This property is the reason why the stock value $S_0(V_0^-, r_0, k_0^*)$ can lie above the value of a non-converted convertible $W_0^+(V_0^-, r_0, 0)$ and no conversion is optimal. This effect, as we have seen at maturity, is based on the fact that a conversion is associated with a drop of the stock value due to a wealth transfer to the debt holders. Hence, a conversion only occurs if the stock value after conversion is not below $W_0^+(V_0^-, r_0, 0)$. For this reason, a second critical firm value $\underline{V}_0$ with $S_0(\underline{V}_0, r_0, 0) = W_0^+(\underline{V}_0, r_0, 0)$ exists (as long as a positive $\overline{V}_0$ exists and a conversion is not optimal for all V_0^-). For firm values V_0^- in the interval $(\underline{V}_0, \overline{V}_0)$, $S_0(V_0^-, r_0, 0)$ is higher than $W_0(V_0^-, r_0, 0)$. Then, at $\overline{V}_0$ the stock value drops and is equal to $W_0^+(\overline{V}_0, r_0, 0)$ thereafter. The optimal conversion volume and the values of a convertible bond and a stock are illustrated in figure 5.2 for a typical example.

Figure 5.2: Optimal Conversion Strategy and Values of a Convertible Bond and a Stock before Maturity under Block Conversion

The left diagram shows the optimal conversion volume k_0^* in the block case before maturity as a function of the firm value V_0^-. The right diagram shows the related values of a convertible bond $W_0(V_0^-, r_0, k_0^*)$ and a stock $S_0(V_0^-, r_0, k_0^*)$. The parameter values are $n = 100$, $m = 100$, $F = 100$, $FD = 50,000$, $c = 5$, $\delta = 0.03$, $T = 1$, $TD = 2$, $r_0 = 0.05$, $\sigma = 0.5$, $\eta = 0.01097$, $\rho = -0.1$, $\kappa = 0.16643$, $\theta = 0.0639$. The critical firm value $\overline{V}_0$ is 96,825.2.

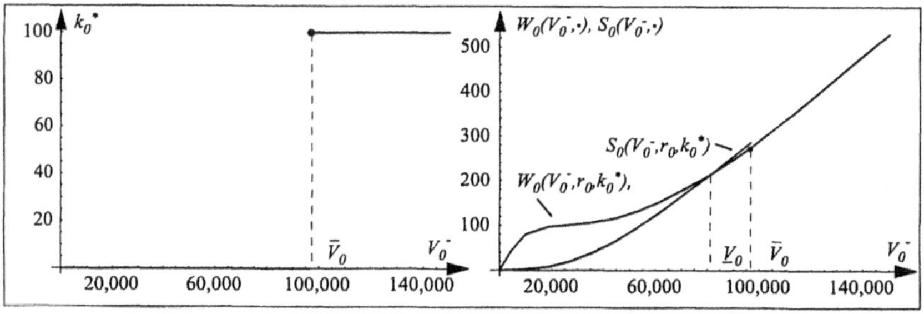

Moreover, the stock value $S_0(V_0^-, r_0, k_0^*)$ might continuously decrease with V_0^-. This effect can happen for firm values V_0 in a neighborhood of $\overline{V}_T$ because $S_0(V_0^-, r_0, k_0^*)$ can reflect the drop of the stock value at maturity in a continuous form.

As a result, we summarize the properties of the optimal block conversion strategy and those of the related values of a convertible bond and a stock.

Result 14 *The optimal conversion volume k_0^* is zero for all firm values if and only if the dividend rate δ equals zero. A complete conversion for all firm values can be optimal, if the*

coupon is zero and the dividend rate is positive. Otherwise, a positive critical firm value exists that triggers conversion. The value of a convertible bond $W_0\left(V_0^-, r_0, k_0^*\right)$ *strictly and continuously increases with* V_0^-. *The stock value* $S_0\left(V_0^-, r_0, k_0^*\right)$ *can continuously increase or decrease with the firm value* V_0^-. *At the critical firm value* $\overline{V}_0$, *the stock value has a drop. Therefore, the stock value can lie above the convertible bond value, even though no conversion is advantageous.*

1b) Conversion Strategy and the Value of a Convertible Bond as a Function of the Stock Value

At this point, we consider the optimal conversion strategy and the convertible bond value as a function of the stock value. Analogous to the considerations at maturity, we can represent both k_0^* and $W_0\left(V_0^-, r_0, k_0^*\right)$ as a function of $S_0\left(V_0^-, r_0, k_0^*\right)$ by determining the combinations $\left(S_0\left(V_0^-, r_0, k_0^*\right), k_0^*\right)$ and $\left(S_0\left(V_0^-, r_0, k_0^*\right), W_0\left(V_0^-, r_0, k_0^*\right)\right)$ for every firm value V_0^-.

A typical example that demonstrates the general structure of k_0^* and $W_0\left(V_0^-, r_0, k_0^*\right)$ for the case with a positive coupon and dividend is given in figure 5.3. This figure shows that

Figure 5.3: Optimal Conversion Strategy and Value of a Convertible Bond before Maturity under Block Conversion

The left diagram shows the optimal conversion volume k_0^* *in the block case before maturity as a function of the stock value* $S_0\left(V_0^-, r_0, k_0^*\right)$. *The right diagram shows the related value of a convertible bond* $W_0\left(V_0^-, r_0, k_0^*\right)$. *The parameter values are* $n = 100$, $m = 100$, $F = 100$, $FD = 50,000$, $c = 5$, $\delta = 0.03$, $T = 1$, $TD = 2$, $r_0 = 0.05$, $\sigma = 0.5$, $\eta = 0.01097$, $\rho = -0.1$, $\kappa = 0.16643$, $\theta = 0.0639$.

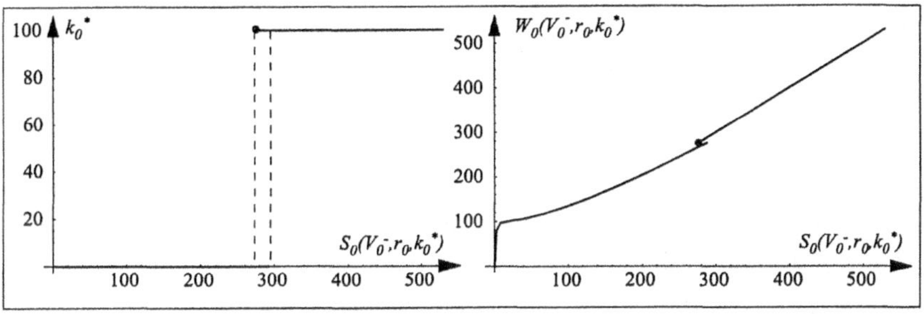

the optimal *conversion volume* k_0^* is zero for low stock values and equals m for high stock values. However, k_0^* is not unique in the stock value for a certain interval. This interval is spanned by the stock value $S_0\left(\overline{V}_0, r_0, m\right)$ after the drop in V_0^- and $S_0\left(\overline{V}_0, r_0, 0\right)$ before the drop. For stock values in this interval both feasible conversion volumes zero and m can be optimal. Therefore, the exact fixing of k_0^* requires the knowledge of the firm value. Knowledge only of the stock value $S_0(V_0^-, r_0, k_0^*)$ is not sufficient in this case.

In subsection 1a), we derived the properties of k_0^* if the dividend rate δ and the coupon c vary. These properties also hold if k_0^* is considered as a function of the stock value and are repeated here for completeness. The primary reason for the adaption of these findings is that the stock value $S_0(V_0^-, r_0, k_0^*)$ approaches zero (infinity) when V_0^- tends to zero (infinity).

- No conversion is optimal for any stock value $S_0(V_0^-, r_0, k_0^*)$ when the dividend rate δ is zero.
- If no coupon payment is made and the dividend rate is sufficiently high, a conversion can be optimal for all stock values $S_0(V_0^-, r_0, k_0^*)$.
- A complete conversion is optimal if the stock value $S_0(V_0^-, r_0, k_0^*)$ is sufficiently high, given a positive dividend rate $\delta > 0$.
- If the coupon c is positive, it is optimal not to convert for low stock values.

The *convertible bond* value $W_0(V_0^-, r_0, k_0^*)$ generally increases with the stock value. A typical example is given in figure 5.3.

However, there are three possibilities for which the convertible bond value is not unique in the stock value. The first possibility for a non-uniqueness of $W_0(V_0^-, r_0, k_0^*)$ in $S_0(V_0^-, r_0, k_0^*)$ is in the case of bankruptcy when $S_0(V_0^-, r_0, k_0^*) = 0$. In this case, the convertible bond value $W_0(V_0^-, r_0, k_0^*)$ can attain values between zero and c depending on the magnitude of the firm value. The second possibility includes the stock values for which the conversion volume is not unique. In this case two different firm values lead to the same stock value but to different convertible bond values. The convertible bond value associated with the higher firm value is always the higher one. The third possibility arises if $S_0(V_0^-, r_0, k_0^*)$ continuously decreases with V_0^-. Then, the convertible bond value $W_0(V_0^-, r_0, k_0^*)$ does not necessarily have to be unique in $S_0(V_0^-, r_0, k_0^*)$, even though k_0^* does not change. As a consequence, three different convertible bond values $W_0(V_0^-, r_0, k_0^*)$ can be associated with one particular stock value, in this case.

The shape of $W_0(V_0^-, r_0, k_0^*)$ depends on the optimal conversion strategy. If $k_0^* \equiv 0$ for all stock values because of no dividend payments, the convertible bond value $W_0(V_0^-, r_0, k_0^*)$ is not unique in the case of bankruptcy but in general it is a unique, continuous, and strictly increasing function of $S_0(V_0^-, r_0, k_0^*)$ for positive stock values $S_0(V_0^-, r_0, k_0^*) > 0$. The only exception is that $S_0(V_0^-, r_0, k_0^*)$ discontinuously or continuously decreases with

V_0^-. Then, the convertible bond value $W_0\left(V_0^-, r_0, k_0^*\right)$ is not unique in $S_0\left(V_0^-, r_0, k_0^*\right)$, but two or three different convertible bond values can be related to one stock value.

If a complete conversion is optimal for all stock values, the convertible bond value $W_0\left(V_0^-, r_0, k_0^*\right)$ is a unique, continuous, and strictly increasing function of $S_0\left(V_0^-, r_0, k_0^*\right)$ even for $S_0\left(V_0^-, r_0, k_0^*\right) = 0$. The reason is that $W_0\left(V_0^-, r_0, k_0^*\right)$ is identical to $S_0\left(V_0^-, r_0, k_0^*\right)$ for all $S_0\left(V_0^-, r_0, k_0^*\right)$ as a complete conversion is always optimal. These findings are summarized in the following result.

Result 15 *The optimal conversion volume k_0^* can be either equal to zero or equal to m for all stock values. Otherwise, k_0^* is non-unique in the stock value, because for every stock value of the interval $\left(S_0\left(\overline{V}_0, r_0, m\right), S_0\left(\overline{V}_0, r_0, 0\right)\right)$ both conversion strategies $k_0^* = 0$ and $k_0^* = m$ are optimal. The convertible bond value $W_0\left(V_0^-, r_0, k_0^*\right)$ is also non-unique in the stock value interval $\left(S_0\left(\overline{V}_0, r_0, m\right), S_0\left(\overline{V}_0, r_0, 0\right)\right)$ for which no unique conversion volume is optimal and for a stock value equal to zero as long as the coupon c is positive. Moreover, it is possible that three different convertible bond values are related to one stock value.*

2) Conversion Strategy and the Values of a Convertible Bond and Stock as a Function of the Short Rate

Conversion Strategy

To analyze the effect of the short rate r_0 on the *conversion strategy* k_0^*, we first provide an intuitive discussion of how the optimal conversion volume behaves if the short rate r_0 rises. For this purpose, we consider the difference $W_0^+\left(V_0^-, r_0, 0\right) - S_0\left(V_0^-, r_0, m\right)$ which is also given by $dif_0\left(V_0^-, r_0\right) + c - \delta \frac{V_0^-}{n+m}$. As after a conversion at time $t = 0$, the firm only consists of stocks and debt, the stock value $S_0\left(V_0^-, r_0, m\right)$ can be represented by $\frac{1}{n+m}$ European call options written on the firm value with strike price FD and maturity TD. As seen at maturity, the call value and therefore the stock value increase with the short rate.

The convertible bond value $W_0^+\left(V_0^-, r_0, 0\right)$ partly behaves like a bond and partly like a stock such that the effect of a higher short rate is not obvious. For low firm values, $W_0^+\left(V_0^-, r_0, 0\right)$ behaves like a bond which suffers from a higher short rate r_0. For high firm values, both the convertible bond value and the stock value have a similar character and benefit from the wealth transfer at the cost of the debt holders caused by a higher r_0.

It seems plausible that the the stock value $S_0\left(V_0^-, r_0, m\right)$ increases more strongly with r_0 than the convertible bond value $W_0^+\left(V_0^-, r_0, 0\right)$, as the convertible bond is a hybrid security. Then, the difference $W_0^+\left(V_0^-, r_0, 0\right) - S_0\left(V_0^-, r_0, m\right)$ decreases with r_0 which implies a higher conversion incentive with r_0. In other words, if the firm value V_0^- is such that the short rate is equal to a critical level $\overline{r}_0$ given by $W_0^+\left(V_0^-,\overline{r}_0,0\right)-S_0\left(V_0^-,\overline{r}_0,m\right)=0$, k_0^* is expected to increase from zero to m if r_0 increases. However, we were unable to prove or to nullify the property that $W_0^+\left(V_0^-,r_0,0\right)-S_0\left(V_0^-,r_0,m\right)$ cannot have a second root.

To see how the conversion volume can behave as a function of r_0, we discuss the properties of k_0^* in detail. The properties of the optimal conversion volume k_0^*, given a fixed firm value V_0^-, are as follows:

- No conversion is optimal for all short rates r_0 if the dividend rate δ is not higher than $\frac{c\cdot n}{V_0^- - c\cdot m}$. This relation results from weighing up the coupon c, the constant dividend payment $\delta\frac{V_0^-}{n+m}$, and the current value $dif_0\left(V_0^-,r_0\right)$ of the difference at maturity T which are contained in equation (5.1). Since $dif_0\left(V_0^-,r_0\right)$ is higher than $-\frac{m\cdot c}{n+m}\left(1-\delta\right)$, the statement above follows.

- A complete conversion can be optimal for all short rates. If the limit $W_0^+\left(V_0^-,-\infty,0\right)=\frac{V_0^- - \left(V_0^- - m\cdot c\right)\cdot\delta}{m}$ presented in remark (4) is lower than the limit $S_0\left(V_0^-,-\infty,m\right)=\frac{V_0^-\cdot\delta}{n+m}$ a conversion occurs even if r_0 approaches minus infinity. As according to our intuition the incentive to convert rises with r_0, we can see why a conversion for all r_0 can occur.

- In all other cases a positive critical value $\overline{r}_0$ must exist that triggers a conversion. In particular, if δ is above $\frac{c\cdot n}{V_0^- - c\cdot m}$, a conversion occurs for a high short rate r_0. When the short rate r_0 tends to infinity, the value of debt $D_0\left(V_0^-,r_0,k_0\right)$ and also the value at time $t=0$ embedded in a convertible bond to receive a bond with redemption value F at time T instead of a stock become worthless. Then, it is more favorable to participate in the dividend payment and to abandon the coupon payment. Therefore, if r_0 is sufficiently high, a conversion is optimal. This effect can also be shown using equation (5.1) in conjunction with the fact that for large r_0 $dif_0\left(V_0^-,r_0\right)$ approaches $-\frac{m\cdot c}{n+m}\left(1-\delta\right)$. We note that the fact that the firm value V_T after no conversion at time $t=0$ is lower than after a conversion can lead to a complete conversion even though the coupon c is higher than the value of the dividend per stock $\delta\frac{V_0^-}{n+m}$.

- If the short rate is sufficiently low, it is not optimal to convert when $\delta<\frac{V_0^-}{\frac{2m+n}{n+m}V_0^- - c\cdot m}$ holds. This effect follows from the limits $W_0^+\left(V_0^-,-\infty,0\right)=\frac{V_0^- - \left(V_0^- - m\cdot c\right)\cdot\delta}{m}$ and $S_0\left(V_0^-,-\infty,m\right)=\frac{V_0^-\cdot\delta}{n+m}$. As a consequence, a *finite* critical short rate $\overline{r}_0$ that triggers a conversion exists if $\frac{c\cdot n}{V_0^- - c\cdot m}<\delta<\frac{V_0^-}{\frac{2m+n}{n+m}V_0^- - c\cdot m}$.

An example for the optimal conversion volume k_0^* and the values $W_0\left(V_0^-, r_0, k_0^*\right)$ and $S_0\left(V_0^-, r_0, k_0^*\right)$ is given in figure 5.4.

Figure 5.4: Optimal Conversion Strategy and Values of a Convertible Bond and a Stock before Maturity under Block Conversion

The left diagram shows the optimal conversion volume k_0^* in the block case before maturity as a function of the short rate r_0. The right diagram shows the related values of a convertible bond $W_0\left(V_0^-, r_0, k_0^*\right)$ and a stock $S_0\left(V_0^-, r_0, k_0^*\right)$. The parameter values are $n = 100$, $m = 100$, $F = 100$, $FD = 50{,}000$, $c = 5$, $\delta = 0.03$, $T = 1$, $TD = 2$, $V_0^- = 100{,}000$, $\sigma = 0.5$, $\eta = 0.01097$, $\rho = -0.1$, $\kappa = 0.16643$, $\theta = 0.0639$. *The critical short rate $\overline{r}_0$ is* 0.02512.

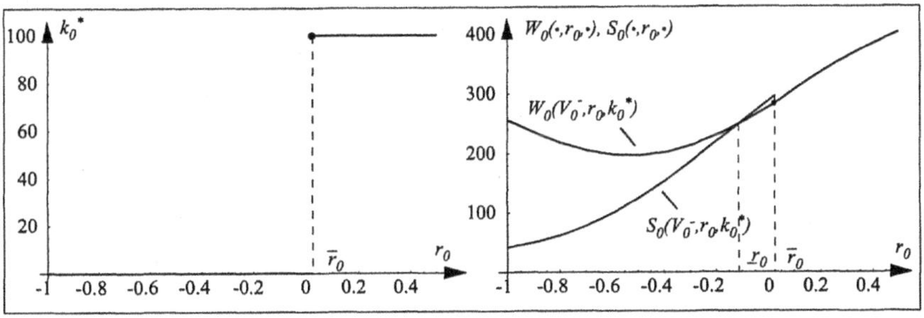

Values of the Convertible Bond and the Stock

The *value* of a *convertible bond* $W_0\left(V_0^-, r_0, k_0^*\right)$, which is the maximum of two continuous functions $W_0^+\left(V_0^-, r_0, 0\right)$ and $S_0\left(V_0^-, r_0, m\right)$ in r_0, is again continuous in r_0. If k_0^* is equal to m, $W_0\left(V_0^-, r_0, k_0^*\right)$ increases with r_0 as $W_0\left(V_0^-, r_0, k_0^*\right)$ is equal to the stock value $S_0\left(V_0^-, r_0, m\right)$ due to the call value property. When k_0^* is zero, $W_0\left(V_0^-, r_0, k_0^*\right)$ can decrease or increase with r_0 as we have shown above.

The *stock value* $S_0\left(V_0^-, r_0, k_0^*\right)$ in figure 5.4 increases with r_0 until the critical value $\overline{r}_0$ that causes a conversion. At this level a downward jump occurs as the stock value suffers from the wealth transfer to the debt holders associated with the conversion. Then, the stock value increases continuously with r_0 due to the call value property. In particular, a second critical short rate $\underline{r}_0 < \overline{r}_0$ defined by $W_0^+\left(V_0^-, \underline{r}_0, 0\right) = S_0\left(V_0^- \underline{r}_0, 0\right)$, for which the stock value is equal to the convertible bond value $W_0\left(V_0^-, r_0, k_0^*\right)$, can exist. In this case for all short rates between $\underline{r}_0$ and $\overline{r}_0$, the stock value is higher than the convertible bond value, but a conversion is not optimal as a conversion would result in a stock value below $W_0\left(V_0^-, r_0, k_0^*\right)$.

We note that even if a positive and finite $\overline{r}_0$ exists, a finite $\underline{r}_0$ need not exist, i.e.

for all short rates below $\overline{r}_0$ the stock value is higher than the convertible bond value. To illustrate this assertion, we compare the limits $W_0^+(V_0^-, -\infty, 0) = \frac{V_0^- - (V_0^- - m \cdot c) \cdot \delta}{m}$, $S_0(V_0^-, -\infty, 0) = \frac{(V_0^- - m \cdot c) \cdot \delta}{n}$, and $S_0(V_0^-, -\infty, m) = \frac{V_0^- \cdot \delta}{n+m}$. In certain examples, we can see that $S_0(V_0^-, -\infty, 0) > W_0^+(V_0^-, -\infty, 0) > S_0(V_0^-, -\infty, m)$ holds and that $S_0(V_0^-, r_0, 0)$ rises more sharply with r_0 than $W_0^+(V_0^-, r_0, 0)$.

In general, $S_0(V_0^-, r_0, k_0^*)$ increases with r_0 but it can also continuously decrease with the short rate. This effect is similar to that for V_0^-. The downward jump at maturity of the stock value triggered by a higher short rate can be adapted by $S_0(V_0^-, r_0, k_0^*)$ in a continuous form for short rates in a neighborhood of $\overline{r}_T$. As a result, we obtain:

Result 16 *The optimal conversion volume k_0^* for a fixed firm value V_0^- is zero for all short rates if and only if the dividend rate δ is not higher than $\frac{c \cdot n}{V_0^- - m \cdot c}$ and the firm value is not higher than $m \cdot c$. A complete conversion can be optimal for all short rates, if the dividend rate is sufficiently high. Otherwise, a finite critical short rate exists that triggers a conversion. The value of a convertible bond $W_0(V_0^-, r_0, k_0^*)$ is continuous but not necessarily monotonous in r_0. The stock value $S_0(V_0^-, r_0, k_0^*)$ continuously and strictly increases with the short rate r_0 for $r_0 > \overline{r}_0$. If $r_0 < \overline{r}_0$, the stock value is not necessarily monotonous in r_0. At the critical short rate $\overline{r}_0$, the stock value has a drop. Therefore, the stock value can lie above the convertible bond value, even though no conversion is advantageous.*

3) Conversion Strategy and the Values of a Convertible Bond and Stock as a Function of the Dividend Rate and the Debt Face Value

At this point we analyze the effect caused by a variation of the dividend rate δ and the debt face value FD. First, we vary the dividend rate.

The optimal *conversion volume* k_0^* is zero for $\delta = 0$, as we have shown above. The incentive to convert increases when the dividend rate increases from zero to one. This is because $S_0(V_0^-, r_0, m)$ increases with δ but $W_0^+(V_0^-, r_0, 0)$ decreases. The property of $S_0(V_0^-, r_0, m)$ is obvious. The decrease of $W_0^+(V_0^-, r_0, 0)$ from a higher dividend rate δ is a result of a lower firm value V_T^- at maturity T. Therefore, the implication is that the conversion volume k_0^* cannot decrease with δ.

It is optimal not to convert for any dividend rate δ if $V_0^- < (n+m) \cdot c$ holds, because even for $\delta = 1$ the conversion value $S_0(V_0^-, r_0, m)$ is lower than the value of a non-converted convertible bond $W_0^+(V_0^-, r_0, 0)$. In the case of default, this relation is obvious. For higher firm values below $(n+m) \cdot c$, the convertible bond value is equal to c, but the stock value equal to $\frac{V_0^- - m \cdot c}{n}$ must be lower.

In the opposite case, $V_0^- \geq (n+m) \cdot c$, a conversion is optimal for high dividend rates, because the dividend of a stock after conversion $\frac{V_0^- \cdot \delta}{n+m}$ exceeds the convertible bond value equal to c. Moreover, a unique critical dividend rate $\overline{\delta}$ must exist in this case for which

$$W_0^+ \left(V_0^-, r_0, 0\right) = S_0 \left(V_0^-, r_0, m\right)$$

holds, because both values are continuous in δ as demonstrated in remark (1) at the beginning of this chapter.

Figure 5.5: Optimal Conversion Strategy and Values of a Convertible Bond and a Stock before Maturity under Block Conversion

The left diagram shows the optimal conversion volume k_0^* in the block case before maturity as a function of the dividend rate δ. The right diagram shows the related values of a convertible bond $W_0\left(V_0^-, r_0, k_0^*\right)$ and a stock $S_0\left(V_0^-, r_0, k_0^*\right)$. The parameter values are $n = 100$, $m = 100$, $F = 100$, $FD = 50{,}000$, $c = 5$, $T = 1$, $TD = 2$, $V_0^- = 100{,}000$, $r_0 = 0.05$, $\sigma = 0.5$, $\eta = 0.01097$, $\rho = -0.1$, $\kappa = 0.16643$, $\theta = 0.0639$. *The critical dividend rate $\overline{\delta}$ is* 0.02651.

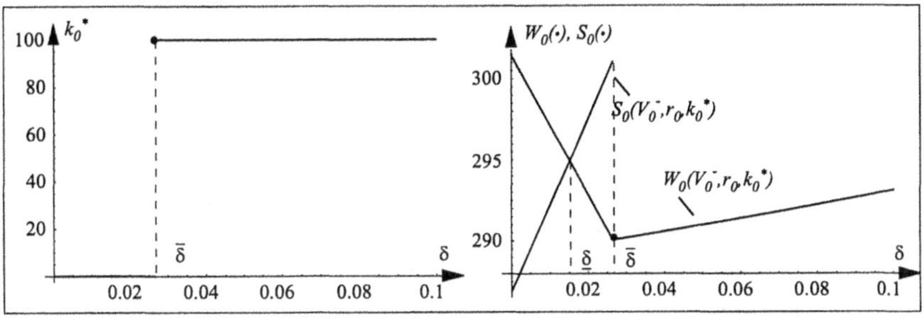

The *value* of a *convertible bond* is continuous in δ. As seen above, it decreases with δ if $k_0^* = 0$ is optimal and it increases with δ, like a stock, at the costs of the debt holders if a complete conversion is optimal.

The *stock value* is a continuous increasing function of δ if k_0^* does not change with δ. It equals zero if $V_0^- \leq m \cdot c$, because the firm is liquidated after the coupon payment. For higher firm values, it strictly increases in δ for $\delta < \overline{\delta}$. At $\overline{\delta}$ if it exists, the stock value has a drop because of the wealth transfer to the debt holders. Thus, whenever a critical dividend rate $\overline{\delta} \leq 1$ exists, there is also a positive $\underline{\delta}$, such that the stock value is higher than the convertible bond value for $\underline{\delta} < \delta < \overline{\delta}$ and no conversion is optimal.

We note that if a critical dividend rate $\overline{\delta} \leq 1$ does not exist, i.e. $V_0^- < (n+m) \cdot c$, there is no critical value of $\underline{\delta}$. If such a $\underline{\delta}$ existed, $W_0^+ \left(V_0^-, r_0, 0\right) < S_0 \left(V_0^-, r_0, 0\right)$ would hold for $\delta = 1$. However, for these firm values V_0^- and $\delta = 1$, the value of $W_0^+(V_0^-, r_0, 0) = \max\left(\frac{V_0^-}{m}, c\right)$ is higher than $S_0(V_0^-, r_0, 0) = \max\left(\frac{V_0^- - m \cdot c}{n}, 0\right)$.

These considerations provide us with the next result.

Result 17 *The optimal conversion volume k_0^* for a fixed firm value V_0^- is zero for all dividend rates if and only if $V_0^- < (n+m) \cdot c$. Otherwise, a finite critical dividend rate exists that triggers a conversion. The convertible bond value $W_0(V_0^-, r_0, k_0^*)$ is continuous but not necessarily monotonous in δ. The stock value strictly and continuously increases with δ as long as $V_0^- > m \cdot c$ holds and the conversion volume is not affected by δ. For the critical dividend rate $\overline{\delta}$ for which a conversion occurs, the stock value drops with δ.*

In the next step, we consider the effects associated with the debt face value FD given a positive fixed firm value V_0^-. The optimal *conversion volume* k_0^* decreases with the debt face value, as the conversion value $S_0(V_0^-, r_0, m)$ decreases with FD more strongly than the value of a non-converted convertible bond $W_0^+(V_0^-, r_0, 0)$. This is because $dif_T(V_T^-, V_0^-, r_T)$ at maturity T increases with FD, because the stock value at maturity is always affected by an increase of FD where the convertible bond value only suffers after a conversion and if both instruments are affected the size of the variation of the convertible bond value is lower. As a consequence, $dif_0(V_0^-, r_0)$ and therefore the difference $W_0^+(V_0^-, r_0, 0) - S_0(V_0^-, r_0, m)$ increase in FD.

It can be optimal not to convert independent of the debt face value, because for some firm values no conversion is optimal even in the case of no debt. Conversely, a complete conversion can be optimal even for large debt face values. This effect occurs, if the present value of the dividend payment $\delta \frac{V_0^-}{n+m}$ exceeds the value of a non-converted convertible bond $W_0^+(V_0^-, r_0, 0)$, which is then nearly as high as a corresponding straight bond of the firm without any conversion rights.

In the other cases, there is a unique critical debt face value $\overline{FD}'$ that triggers a conversion. The uniqueness results from the monotonicity of k_0^*.

The *convertible bond value* $W_0(V_0^-, r_0, k_0^*)$ continuously decreases with the debt face value FD, as both the conversion value and the value of a non-converted convertible bond decrease with FD which follows from the analysis at maturity T.

The *stock value* $S_0(V_0^-, r_0, k_0^*)$ generally decreases with FD. However, $S_0(V_0^-, r_0, k_0^*)$ can also increase with FD by a jump. This effect happens, if a higher debt face value prevents a conversion of the convertible bonds and the associated wealth transfer from stockholders to the debt holders. Moreover, $S_0(V_0^-, r_0, k_0^*)$ can continuously increase with FD due to the fact that the shape of $S_T(V_T^-, r_T, k_0, k_T^*)$ at maturity is adapted by $S_0(V_0^-, r_0, k_0^*)$ in a continuous form. If $\overline{FD}'$ exists, a second critical debt face value $\underline{FD}' > \overline{FD}'$ defined by

$W_0^+ \left(V_0^-, r_0, 0\right) = S_0 \left(V_0^-, r_0, 0\right)$ can also exist but does not in every case. If it exists, the stock value $S_0 \left(V_0^-, r_0, k_0^*\right)$ is higher than the convertible bond value for debt face values between $\overline{FD}'$ and $\underline{FD}'$.

This leads to the following result.

Result 18 *The optimal conversion volume k_0^* for a fixed firm value V_0^- can be zero for all debt face values or it can be m for all FD. Otherwise, a unique critical debt face value exists that triggers a conversion. The convertible bond value $W_0 \left(V_0^-, r_0, k_0^*\right)$ is continuously decreasing in FD. The stock value can continuously increase or decrease with FD given that k_0^* does not change. For the critical debt face value $\overline{FD}'$ for which a conversion occurs, the stock value increases with FD by a jump. If the critical value $\overline{\delta}$ exists, the related value of $\underline{\delta}$ must also exist such that the stock value is higher than the convertible bond value for certain intervals of the dividend rate.*

The properties of the conversion strategy k_0^* in the block case before maturity and the related values $W_0 \left(V_0^-, r_0, k_0^*\right)$ and $S_0 \left(V_0^-, r_0, k_0^*\right)$ are in several cases similar to that at maturity.

The higher the firm value, the higher the conversion volume and the values of a convertible bond and a stock in general. If the short rate r_0 increases, the conversion volume and the values of a stock and a convertible bond can increase. A higher debt face value results in a lower conversion volume and reduces the value of a convertible bond, where the stock value might also decline. In line with the behavior at maturity, there are also some perhaps surprising properties before maturity. The stock value can drop with the firm value, the short rate, and a lower debt face value. Therefore, the conversion volume and the value of a convertible bond cannot be uniquely represented by the stock value.

Contrary to these results before maturity which coincide with those at maturity, we find some differences between these two conversion dates. First, the optimal conversion volume shows different patterns in the considered variables. In addition to the standard case with one critical parameter that triggers a conversion, it can be optimal to convert for all firm values, short rates, or debt face values, or a conversion is never optimal.

The stock value can continuously decrease with the firm value or the short rate and continuously increase with FD and not only by a jump as at maturity. This effect is because $S_0 \left(V_0^-, r_0, k_0^*\right)$ can have the character of a continuous version of the functional shape of a stock value at maturity. Due to the fact that the stock value can continuously decrease and drop in the firm value, while the convertible bond value increases, three different convertible bond values can be associated with one stock value.

In contrast to the behavior at maturity, $W_0 \left(V_0^-, r_0, k_0^*\right)$ can also decrease with the short rate, because the convertible bond value before maturity can have the character of a straight bond.

Unlike at maturity, we can also vary the dividend rate before maturity. The higher the dividend rate, the higher the conversion incentive. In general, the stockholders benefit from a higher dividend as it is a higher extra payment especially reserved for them, but the debt holders suffer. Only if a higher dividend rate increases the conversion volume, does the stock value drop due to the wealth transfer from the debt holders. The convertible bond holders also benefit from a higher dividend, if a conversion is optimal, but they suffer otherwise.

5.2 Unrestricted Conversion

In addition to the remarks at the beginning of this chapter, we note a further property exclusively concerning the value of a non-converted convertible $W_0^+\left(V_0^-, r_0, k_0\right)$ under unrestricted conversion: The value of a non-converted convertible bond $W_0^+\left(V_0^-, r_0, k_0\right)$ under unrestricted conversion increases with the conversion volume k_0. The reason is that its value at maturity $W_T\left(V_T^-, r_T, k_0, k_T^*\right)$ for a given firm value V_T^- increases with k_0 when default occurs $\left(V_T^- < (m - k_0) \cdot F\right)$ as the number of outstanding convertible bonds decreases with k_0. Its value is independent of k_0, otherwise. Furthermore, $W_T\left(V_T^-, r_T, k_0, k_T^*\right)$ increases with the firm value V_T^- and V_T^- increases with k_0 due to the coupon effect. Thus, we find that the value of $W_0^+\left(V_0^-, r_0, k_0\right)$ benefits from a higher conversion volume k_0. For $\delta < 1$, the strict monotonicity holds, but in the special case $\delta = 1$, $W_0^+\left(V_0^-, r_0, k_0\right) = \min\left(\frac{V_0^-}{m-k_0}, c\right)$ can be independent of k_0.

Under monopolistic conversion, $W_0^+\left(V_0^-, r_0, k_0\right)$ increases with k_0 in several cases. However, as figure 4.9 suggests, $W_0^+\left(V_0^-, r_0, k_0\right)$ can also decrease with k_0, because the convertible bond value at maturity $W_T\left(V_T^-, r_T, k_0, k_T^*\right)$ can decrease with k_0.

1a) Conversion Strategy and the Values of a Convertible Bond and Stock as a Function of the Firm Value

Conversion Strategy

Under the conversion variant unrestricted conversion, every investor decides on a value basis between the two possibilities "holding the convertible bonds" or "conversion". In the case of a conversion, the investor obtains the conversion value $S_0\left(V_0^-, r_0, k_0\right)$ per converted bond if the aggregate conversion volume is k_0. Accordingly, if she or he decides not to convert, the value obtained with one convertible bond is equal to the value of a non-converted convertible bond $W_0^+(V_0^-, r_0, k_0)$. Thus, analogous to section 4.2, we get the following characterization for the aggregate *conversion volume* k_0^* in any Nash equilibrium:

$$k_0^* = \begin{cases} 0, & \text{if } S_0(V_0^-, r_0, 0) < W_0^+(V_0^-, r_0, 0) \\ x, & \text{if } S_0(V_0^-, r_0, x) = W_0^+(V_0^-, r_0, x) \\ m, & \text{if } S_0(V_0^-, r_0, m) > W_0^+(V_0^-, r_0, m) \end{cases} \tag{5.3}$$

The Nash equilibrium (5.3) on the aggregate level is unique for $\delta < 1$, as the three different possibilities in (5.3) are mutually exclusive. We will deal with the special case of $\delta = 1$ in more detail in subsection 3). The uniqueness can be shown as follows. According to remark (3) and the note at the beginning of this section, $W_0^+(V_0^-, r_0, k_0)$ is strictly and $D_0(V_0^-, r_0, k_0)$ monotonously increasing in the conversion volume k_0. As the firm value

$$V_0^- = (n + k_0) \cdot S_0(V_0^-, r_0, k_0) + (m - k_0) \cdot W_0^+(V_0^-, r_0, k_0) + D_0(V_0^-, r_0, k_0)$$

is independent of the conversion volume k_0, the equilibrium condition $W_0^+(V_0^-, r_0, x) = S_0(V_0^-, r_0, x)$ can hold for one particular conversion volume k_0 at most.[5] If $W_0^+(V_0^-, x, r_0,) = S_0(V_0^-, r_0, x)$ does not have a solution, either $S_0(V_0^-, r_0, k_0) < W_0^+(V_0^-, r_0, k_0)$ or $S_0(V_0^-, r_0, k_0) > W_0^+(V_0^-, r_0, k_0)$ must hold for all k_0. In the first case, $k_0^* = 0$ is optimal, and in the second, k_0^* equals m.

Moreover, the optimal conversion volume k_0^* is always continuous in the firm value V_0^- and it is differentiable for firm values for which $0 < k_0^* < m$ holds. In addition, the differentiability is obviously satisfied for those firm values for which k_0^* is constant, namely equal to zero or m. The differentiability for $k_0^* \in (0, m)$ is a result of the implicit function theorem that can be applied to the conversion condition $W_0^+(V_0^-, r_0, x) = S_0(V_0^-, r_0, x)$ in a similar way as at maturity because both functions $W_0^+(V_0^-, r_0, k_0)$ and $S_0(V_0^-, r_0, k_0)$ are differentiable in all arguments.

From the considerations at the beginning of this chapter, we know that no conversion occurs if $V_0^- \leq m \cdot c$ holds. Thus, we analyze the other cases, $V_0^- > m \cdot c$ by regarding — similar as in the block case — the difference $dif_T(V_T^-, V_0^-, r_T, k_0)$ of the value obtained with a non-converted convertible bond and a stock at maturity given a firm value V_0^- and a premature conversion volume k_0. Contrary to the block case, in which we had to consider two different firm values at maturity T, namely $\mathbb{V}$ after a full premature conversion and

---

[5] If for $\overline{k}_0$ and $\widehat{k}_0$ $\left(\overline{k}_0 < \widehat{k}_0\right)$ the stock value and the value of a convertible bond were to coincide, the firm value for $\overline{k}_0$, i.e. $V_0^- = (n+m) \cdot W_0(V_0^-, r_0, \overline{k}_0) + D_0(V_0^-, r_0, \overline{k}_0)$, would be lower than that for $\widehat{k}_0$, $V_0^- = (n+m) \cdot W_0\left(V_0^-, r_0, \widehat{k}_0\right) + D_0\left(V_0^-, r_0, \widehat{k}_0\right)$. This effect contradicts the property that the firm value is independent of the conversion volume.

$\left(V_0^- - m \cdot c\right) \cdot \frac{\mathbf{V}}{V_0^-}$ after the coupon payment, we can deal with one firm value V_T^-. The difference $dif_T\left(V_T^-, V_0^-, r_T, k_0\right) := W_T\left(V_T^-, r_T, k_0, k_T^*\right) - S_T\left(V_T^-, r_T, k_0, k_T^*\right)$ reads:

$$dif_T\left(V_T^-, V_0^-, r_T, k_0\right) = \begin{cases} \frac{V_T^-}{m-k_0}, & \text{if } V_T^- < (m-k_0)\cdot F \\ F - \frac{C_T\left(V_T^- - (m-k_0)\cdot F\right)}{n+k_0}, & \text{if } (m-k_0)\cdot F \leq V_T^- < \underline{V}_T(k_0) \\ 0, & \text{if } \underline{V}_T(k_0) \leq V_T^- \end{cases}$$

The difference $dif_T\left(V_T^-, V_0^-, r_T, k_0\right)$ strictly increases with V_T^- in the case of default at maturity, and strictly decreases with V_T^- if no default occurs and no conversion is optimal at maturity. For higher firm values, $dif_T\left(V_T^-, V_0^-, r_T, k_0\right)$ is zero. Its current value $dif_0\left(V_0^-, r_0, k_0\right)$ is a continuous positive function of V_0^- that increases for low firm values V_0^- and approaches zero if V_0^- is high. The difference $W_0^+\left(V_0^-, r_0, k_0\right) - S_0\left(V_0^-, r_0, k_0\right)$ amounts to

$$W_0^+\left(V_0^-, r_0, k_0\right) - S_0\left(V_0^-, r_0, k_0\right) = dif_0\left(V_0^-, r_0, k_0\right) + c - \delta\frac{V_0^- - (m-k_0)\cdot c}{n+k_0}, \qquad (5.4)$$

if $V_0^- > (m-k_0)\cdot c$. This representation reveals the behavior of the optimal conversion volume as a function of the firm value V_0^-.

- No conversion is optimal for all firm values V_0^- if the dividend rate δ is zero, as illustrated at the beginning of this chapter.

- The opposite case that a conversion is optimal for all firm values V_0^- can also occur. This effect occurs under similar conditions as in the block case, namely if δ is sufficiently high and c equals zero. Then, the difference $W_0^+\left(V_0^-, r_0, k_0\right) - S_0\left(V_0^-, r_0, k_0\right)$, given in equation (5.4), is non-positive for all k_0. This is because $dif_0\left(V_0^-, r_0, k_0\right)$ tends to zero if δ approaches one, but $\delta\frac{V_0^-}{n+k_0}$ is positive. Consequently, $k_0^* = m$ for all V_0^- can be optimal in this special case.

- If these two presented possibilities do not occur, then a critical firm value $\overline{V}_0$ must exist that triggers a complete conversion. The reason is that for $\delta > 0$, a complete conversion is optimal if the firm value V_0^- is sufficiently high. This is because the convertible bond will probably be converted at maturity. Since for high firm values the current value of the dividend payment is above the coupon payment, a prompt conversion with the reception of the dividend is more attractive than receiving the lower coupon payment and converting at maturity. This intuition is again in line with equation (5.4). If the firm value is very high, $dif_0\left(V_0^-, r_0, k_0\right)$ tends to zero, and the difference $W_0^+\left(V_0^-, r_0, k_0\right) - S_0\left(V_0^-, r_0, k_0\right)$ converges to $c - \delta\frac{V_0^- - (m-k_0)\cdot c}{n+k_0}$ which is negative for all k_0 for sufficiently high V_0^-. Consequently, $k_0^* = m$ is the equilibrium strategy.

In general, we expect that the stock value $S_0(V_0^-, r_0, k_0)$ benefits more from a higher firm value V_0^- than the value of a non-converted convertible bond $W_0^+(V_0^-, r_0, k_0)$ if the conversion volume k_0 equals k_0^* with $0 < k_0^* < m$. Then, k_0^* increases with V_0^- as the conversion incentive rises with V_0^-. However, we were unable to prove this assertion.

- If the coupon c is positive, no conversion is optimal for low firm values. In this case with $c > 0$ and $\delta > 0$, we obtain two finite critical firm values $\underline{V}_0$ and $\overline{V}_0$ analogously defined as at maturity. $\underline{V}_0$ is the highest firm value such that no conversion takes place for lower firm values. Accordingly, $\overline{V}_0$ denotes the lowest firm value such that a complete conversion occurs for all firm values above $\overline{V}_0$. The fact that both $\underline{V}_0$ and $\overline{V}_0$ are finite in the case of $c > 0$ and $\delta > 0$ is a consequence of the finding that $k_0^* = 0$ occurs for sufficiently low firm values and that $k_0^* = m$ takes place if V_0^- is sufficiently high. We note that for $c = 0$ a critical value $\underline{V}_0$ need not exist even though a positive $\overline{V}_0$ exists. This is the case in which a partial but no complete conversion is optimal for low firm values and it increases towards m with a higher firm value.

Values of the Convertible Bond and the Stock

The optimal conversion strategy results in a *value* of a *convertible bond* $W_0(V_0^-, r_0, k_0^*)$ as follows. If no conversion or a complete conversion is optimal $W_0(V_0^-, r_0, k_0^*)$ is equal to $W_0^+(V_0^-, r_0, 0)$ or $S_0(V_0^-, r_0, m)$, respectively. If a sequential conversion occurs, we have

$$\begin{aligned} W_0^+(V_0^-, r_0, k_0^*) &= \frac{V_0^- - (m - k_0^*) \cdot S_0(V_0^-, r_0, k_0^*) - D_0(V_0^-, r_0, k_0^*)}{m - k_0^*} \\ &= \frac{V_0^- - D_0(V_0^-, r_0, k_0^*)}{n + m}, \end{aligned} \tag{5.5}$$

where the second equation follows from $W_0^+(V_0^-, r_0, k_0^*) = S_0(V_0^-, r_0, k_0^*)$.

This representation allows us to interpret the value of a convertible bond and accordingly the value of a stock given a partial conversion as the value after a complete conversion, where the debt value $D_0(V_0^-, r_0, k_0^*)$ results from the equilibrium conversion volume k_0^*. Therefore, the value of a convertible bond $W_0(V_0^-, r_0, k_0^*)$ is:

$$W_0(V_0^-, r_0, k_0^*) = \begin{cases} W_0^+(V_0^-, r_0, 0), & \text{if } k_0^* = 0 \\ \frac{V_0^- - D_0(V_0^-, r_0, k_0^*)}{n+m}, & \text{if } k_0^* > 0 \end{cases} \tag{5.6}$$

As k_0^* and the values $W_0^+(V_0^-, r_0, k_0)$ and $D_0(V_0^-, r_0, k_0)$ are continuous in all arguments due to (3.16) and (3.13), the convertible bond value $W_0(V_0^-, r_0, k_0^*)$ is continuous in V_0^-. In addition, $W_0(V_0^-, r_0, k_0^*)$ is strictly increasing in the firm value V_0^-. For $k_0^* = 0$ or $k_0^* = m$, this assertion clearly follows from equation (3.16) and (3.14). If a partial conversion is optimal, we have to distinguish between the case $\frac{\partial k_0^*}{\partial V_0^-} \geq 0$ and $\frac{\partial k_0^*}{\partial V_0^-} < 0$. In the first case, $\frac{\partial k_0^*}{\partial V_0^-} \geq 0$, $W_0\left(V_0^-, r_0, k_0^*\right)$ benefits from two effects. First, $W_0\left(V_0^-, r_0, k_0\right)$ increases with V_0^- for a fixed conversion volume. Second, according to the note at the beginning of this section, $W_0\left(V_0^-, r_0, k_0^*\right)$ benefits from the higher equilibrium conversion volume k_0^* caused by a higher firm value. In the opposite case $\frac{\partial k_0^*}{\partial V_0^-} < 0$, we consider the relation $W_0\left(V_0^-, r_0, k_0^*\right) = \frac{V_0^- - D_0\left(V_0^-, r_0, k_0^*\right)}{n+m}$. Regarding the debt value, we can argue that for a fixed conversion volume, $D_0\left(V_0^-, r_0, k_0\right)$ increases by less than one marginal unit if V_0^- increases by one marginal unit due to representation (3.13). In addition, $D_0\left(V_0^-, r_0, k_0^*\right)$ suffers from a lower conversion volume k_0^* mentioned in remark (3). Hence, the derivative $\frac{\partial D_0\left(V_0^-, r_0, k_0^*\right)}{\partial V_0^-}$ is strictly below one. Therefore, $W_0\left(V_0^-, r_0, k_0^*\right) = \frac{V_0^- - D_0\left(V_0^-, r_0, k_0^*\right)}{n+m}$ must increase with V_0^-.

Moreover, we can see that the convertible bond value $W_0\left(V_0^-, r_0, k_0^*\right)$ is equal to the value of a non-converted convertible bond $W_0^+\left(V_0^-, r_0, k_0^*\right)$ as long as $W_0^+\left(V_0^-, r_0, k_0^*\right)$ is reasonably defined, i.e. no complete conversion is optimal. Thus, the value of a convertible bond has no jumps in t at time $t = 0$ that do not stem from the coupon payment. As a result of this equivalence, we do not explicitly discuss the properties of $W_0^+\left(V_0^-, r_0, k_0^*\right)$ immediately after conversion, as they are analogous to those of $W_0\left(V_0^-, r_0, k_0^*\right)$ for $k_0^* < m$ before conversion.

Accordingly, the *value* of a *stock* is given by:

$$S_0\left(V_0^-, r_0, k_0^*\right) = \begin{cases} S_0\left(V_0^-, r_0, 0\right), & \text{if } k_0^* = 0 \\ W_0\left(V_0^-, r_0, k_0^*\right) = \frac{V_0^- - D_0\left(V_0^-, r_0, k_0^*\right)}{n+m}, & \text{if } k_0^* > 0 \end{cases}$$

The same argumentation as for the convertible bond value explains that $S_0\left(V_0^-, r_0, k_0^*\right)$ is a continuous and increasing function of the firm value. If no default occurs at time $t = 0$, $S_0\left(V_0^-, r_0, k_0^*\right)$ is in fact strictly increasing. For $k_0^* = 0$, this is a consequence of representation (3.14). Otherwise, the stock value is equal to the convertible bond value. We note that the stock value can never be above the convertible bond value $W_0\left(V_0^-, r_0, k_0^*\right)$.

An example for the optimal conversion volume k_0^* and the values of a convertible bond and a stock is shown in figure 5.6.

Our findings are summarized in the next result.

Result 19 *The optimal conversion volume k_0^* is continuous in the firm value. It is zero for all firm values if and only if the dividend rate δ equals zero. A complete conversion for all firm values can be optimal, if the coupon is zero and the dividend rate is positive. Otherwise, a positive critical firm value exists that triggers a complete conversion.*

Figure 5.6: Optimal Conversion Strategy and Values of a Convertible Bond and a Stock before Maturity under Unrestricted Conversion

The left diagram shows the optimal conversion volume k_0^* in the unrestricted case before maturity as a function of the firm value V_0^-. The right diagram shows the related values of a convertible bond $W_0(V_0^-, r_0, k_0^*)$ and a stock $S_0(V_0^-, r_0, k_0^*)$. The parameter values are $n = 100$, $m = 100$, $F = 100$, $FD = 50{,}000$, $c = 5$, $\delta = 0.03$, $T = 1$, $TD = 2$, $r_0 = 0.05$, $\sigma = 0.5$, $\eta = 0.01097$, $\rho = -0.1$, $\kappa = 0.16643$, $\theta = 0.0639$. The critical firm values $\underline{V}_0$ and $\overline{V}_0$ result in 81,598.0 and 100,964.3, respectively.

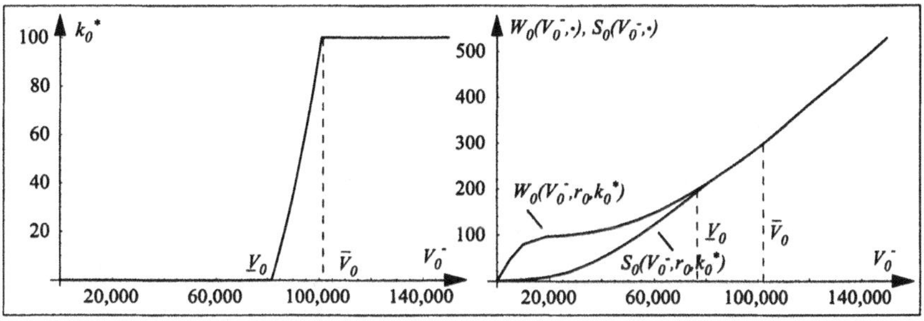

If the coupon is positive, no conversion is optimal for low firm values and a second critical firm value exists that triggers a partial conversion. The value of a convertible bond $W_0(V_0^-, r_0, k_0^*)$ before conversion strictly and continuously increases with V_0^-. It equals the convertible bond value $W_0^+(V_0^-, r_0, k_0^*)$ after conversion as long as $W_0^+(V_0^-, r_0, k_0^*)$ is reasonably defined. The stock value $S_0(V_0^-, r_0, k_0^*)$ is also continuous in the firm value V_0^-. It is equal to zero in the case of default and strictly increases with V_0^-, otherwise. Moreover, the stock value cannot lie above the convertible bond value.

1b) Conversion Strategy and the Value of a Convertible Bond as a Function of the Stock Value

As an alternative to the firm value, we represent the optimal conversion volume k_0^* and the value of a convertible bond $W_0(V_0^-, r_0, k_0^*)$ as a function of the stock value $S_0(V_0^-, r_0, k_0^*)$. As a positive stock value $S_0(V_0^-, r_0, k_0^*)$ strictly and continuously increases with the firm value, the conversion volume k_0^* is also unique and continuous in $S_0(V_0^-, r_0, k_0^*)$. We note that even in the case of bankruptcy, $0 \leq V_0^- < m \cdot c$, the optimal conversion volume is unique, namely zero, as the stock value is also equal to zero. A typical example is given in figure 5.7.

According to this figure, k_0^* strictly and continuously increases with the stock value from

Figure 5.7: Optimal Conversion Strategy and Value of a Convertible Bond before Maturity under Unrestricted Conversion

The left diagram shows the optimal conversion volume k_0^* in the unrestricted case before maturity as a function of the stock value $S_0(V_0^-, r_0, k_0^*)$. The right diagram shows the related value of a convertible bond $W_0(V_0^-, r_0, k_0^*)$. The parameter values are $n = 100$, $m = 100$, $F = 100$, $FD = 50{,}000$, $c = 5$, $\delta = 0.03$, $T = 1$, $TD = 2$, $r_0 = 0.05$, $\sigma = 0.5$, $\eta = 0.01097$, $\rho = -0.1$, $\kappa = 0.16643$, $\theta = 0.0639$.

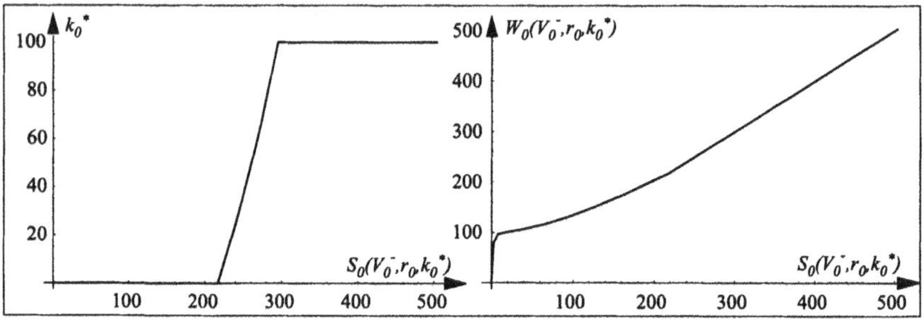

zero to m. In general, the optimal conversion volume shows properties that correspond to those obtained in subsection 1a) for the consideration as a function of the firm value.

- No conversion is optimal for all stock values $S_0(V_0^-, r_0, k_0^*)$ if the dividend rate δ is equal to zero.
- If no coupon payment is made and the dividend rate is sufficiently high, a complete conversion might be optimal for all stock values $S_0(V_0^-, r_0, k_0^*)$.
- A complete conversion is optimal if the stock value $S_0(V_0^-, r_0, k_0^*)$ is sufficiently high, given a positive dividend rate $\delta > 0$.
- If the coupon c is positive, no conversion is optimal for low stock values. Conversely, in the case of no coupon payments, a sequential conversion can be optimal for low stock values.

The *convertible bond* value $W_0(V_0^-, r_0, k_0^*)$ shown in figure 5.7 exhibits the typical shape. It continuously and strictly increases with the stock value as long as $S_0(V_0^-, r_0, k_0^*)$ is positive. This property is again a direct consequence of the fact that a positive $S_0(V_0^-, r_0, k_0^*)$ strictly and continuously increases with the firm value V_0^-. For $S_0(V_0^-, r_0, k_0^*) = 0$, the firm is bankrupt and the total value of all convertible bonds equals the firm value. Thus, in the case of bankruptcy the determination of the convertible bond value cannot be uniquely achieved from the stock value but requires the knowledge of the firm value. This effect is analogous as at maturity of the convertible bond. The only difference is that before maturity the critical firm value below which default occurs is $m \cdot c$, rather than $(m - k_0) \cdot F$. If no coupon is paid, $c = 0$, this non-uniqueness does not occur and $W_0\left(V_0^-, r_0, k_0^*\right)$ is always uniquely determined by $S_0\left(V_0^-, r_0, k_0^*\right)$.

Result 20 *The optimal conversion volume k_0^* is a unique and continuous function of the stock value. It can equal either zero or m for all stock values. Otherwise, k_0^* is equal to zero or at least below m for low stock values and equals m for high stock values. The convertible bond value $W_0\left(V_0^-, r_0, k_0^*\right)$ is non-unique for a stock value equal to zero as long as the coupon c is positive. For positive stock values, $W_0\left(V_0^-, r_0, k_0^*\right)$ strictly and continuously increases with $S_0\left(V_0^-, r_0, k_0^*\right)$. Only if $c = 0$, the convertible bond value $W_0\left(V_0^-, r_0, k_0^*\right)$ is always unique in the stock value.*

2) Conversion Strategy and the Values of a Convertible Bond and Stock as a Function of the Short Rate

Conversion Strategy

We know from the considerations at the beginning of this chapter that in the simple case in which the firm is liquidated at time $t = 0$, $V_0^- \leq m \cdot c$, the optimal conversion volume is zero independent of the short rate. In the other cases, we know that that the difference

$$W_0^+\left(V_0^-, r_0, k_0\right) - S_0\left(V_0^-, r_0, k_0\right) = dif_0\left(V_0^-, r_0, k_0\right) + c - \delta \frac{V_0^- - (m - k_0) \cdot c}{n + k_0}$$

reveals the effect of the short rate r_0 on the *conversion volume* k_0^* as the higher this difference the lower the incentive to convert. According to this equation, only $dif_0\left(V_0^-, r_0, k_0\right)$ depends on the short rate r_0, but the coupon and the dividend term are independent of r_0. Intuition tells us that $dif_0\left(V_0^-, r_0, k_0\right)$ decreases with r_0, because the difference $dif_T\left(V_T^-, V_0^-, r_T, k_0\right)$ between the stock value and a convertible bond value at maturity for every fixed V_T^- declines with the short rate r_T. As a higher short rate r_0 is associated with a higher r_T and a lower discount factor $B_0(T)$ used to discount the expectation of $dif_T\left(V_T^-, V_0^-, r_T, k_0\right)$ in order to determine $dif_0\left(V_0^-, r_0, k_0\right)$, we can see why $dif_0\left(V_0^-, r_0, k_0\right)$ might decrease with r_0. However, this argumentation is solely an intuition which we cannot prove. Alternatively, we can argue in a similar way to the block case that $S_0\left(V_0^-, r_0, k_0\right)$ increases with r_0 more sharply than $W_0^+\left(V_0^-, r_0, k_0\right)$. This suggestion is because the convertible bond is a hybrid instrument consisting of a bond and a stock component. In general the value of the bond component decreases with r_0, but the stock component increases.

Moreover, the optimal conversion volume is continuous in r_0 and differentiable in r_0 if $k_0^* \in (0, m)$ or k_0^* does not change. These properties result from the implicit function theorem in an analogous way as for V_0^- discussed in subsection 1a). An example for the optimal conversion volume k_0^* is given in figure 5.8. In this figure the optimal conversion volume is zero for short rates below a critical value of $\underline{r}_0$, then it increases with r_0, and it attains m for short rates higher than a second critical short rate $\overline{r}_0$.[6]

Figure 5.8: Optimal Conversion Strategy and Values of a Convertible Bond and a Stock before Maturity under Unrestricted Conversion

The left diagram shows the optimal conversion volume k_0^* in the unrestricted case before maturity as a function of the short rate r_0. The right diagram shows the related values of a convertible bond $W_0(V_0^-, r_0, k_0^*)$ and a stock $S_0(V_0^-, r_0, k_0^*)$. The parameter values are $n = 100$, $m = 100$, $F = 100$, $FD = 50{,}000$, $c = 5$, $\delta = 0.03$, $T = 1$, $TD = 2$, $V_0^- = 100{,}000$, $\sigma = 0.5$, $\eta = 0.01097$, $\rho = -0.1$, $\kappa = 0.16643$, $\theta = 0.0639$. *The critical firm values $\underline{r}_0$ and $\overline{r}_0$ result in* -0.1170 *and* 0.0578*, respectively.*

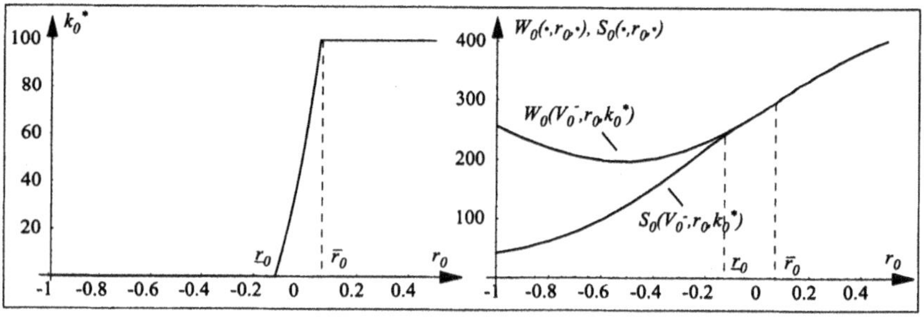

In general, the optimal conversion volume k_0^* for a fixed firm value V_0^- can have the following properties:

- No conversion is optimal for all short rates r_0 if the dividend rate δ is not higher than $\frac{c \cdot n}{V_0^- - c \cdot m}$. If this condition $\delta \leq \frac{c \cdot n}{V_0^- - c \cdot m}$ holds, the value of the dividend payment per stock is at most $\delta \frac{V_0^- - c \cdot m}{n} = c$ for $k_0 = 0$. Thus, the dividend cannot lie above the coupon c. Moreover, the value obtained with a convertible bond at maturity is as high or even higher than the value obtained with a stock. Consequently, the value of a non-converted convertible bond $W_0^+(V_0^-, r_0, 0)$ including the coupon payment

6 $\underline{r}_0$ and $\overline{r}_0$ are defined by $W_0^+(V_0^-, \underline{r}_0, 0) = S_0(V_0^-, \underline{r}_0, 0)$ and $W_0^+(V_0^-, \overline{r}_0, m) = S_0(V_0^-, \overline{r}_0, m)$ respectively. In this case these values are unique. However, we were not able to show that they are always uniquely defined by these definitions.

at time zero is higher than the corresponding stock value $S_0\left(V_0^-, r_0, 0\right)$ with the dividend payment. Therefore, no conversion is optimal.

- A complete conversion can be the optimal strategy for all short rates. This special case occurs for a dividend rate $\delta = 1$ and a coupon c lower than the value of the dividend per stock.

- In what follows, we consider the case that a conversion can be possible, i.e. $\delta > \frac{c \cdot n}{V_0^- - c \cdot m}$. If the short rate r_0 is sufficiently high, a conversion but not necessarily a complete conversion is optimal. This property results from the conversion conditions for a partial, $W_0^+\left(V_0^-, r_0, 0\right) - S_0\left(V_0^-, r_0, 0\right) \leq 0$, and a complete conversion, $W_0^+\left(V_0^-, r_0, m\right) - S_0\left(V_0^-, r_0, m\right) \leq 0$. Since the value $dif_0\left(V_0^-, r_0, k_0\right)$ at time $t = 0$ tends to zero for increasing r_0, we can represent the difference $W_0^+\left(V_0^-, r_0, k_0\right) - S_0\left(V_0^-, r_0, k_0\right)$ in the limit by $c - \delta \frac{V_0^- - k_0 \cdot c}{n + k_0}$. Thus, we can see that for every fixed $\delta > \frac{c \cdot n}{V_0^- - c \cdot m}$ the condition for a partial conversion is satisfied for high r_0. Analogously, we can find that a complete conversion for high short rates requires a higher dividend rate $\delta > \frac{n+m}{V_0^-} c$.

- If the short rate r_0 becomes arbitrarily small, the limits of a non-converted convertible bond and a stock are $W_0^+\left(V_0^-, -\infty, k_0\right) = \frac{V_0^- - \delta\left(V_0^- - (m - k_0) \cdot c\right)}{m - k_0}$ and $S_0\left(V_0^-, -\infty, k_0\right) = \delta \frac{V_0^- - (m - k_0) \cdot c}{n + k_0}$ according to remark (4). Thus, the conversion condition $W_0^+\left(V_0^-, r_0, 0\right) - S_0\left(V_0^-, r_0, 0\right) \leq 0$ reveals that if and only if $\delta > \frac{n V_0^-}{(n+m)\left(V_0^- - m \cdot c\right)}$, a conversion occurs for sufficiently low short rates. Moreover, we can see that a complete conversion requires a dividend rate δ equal to one.

  As a result of these considerations, it is possible that no critical short rate or only one finite critical short rate, $\overline{r}_0$ or $\underline{r}_0$, exists. The case with no critical short rate can occur if a partial conversion is optimal for all r_0. The other effect with only one critical short rate occurs in those cases in which the conversion volume k_0^* is monotonous and $k_0^* = 0$ $(0 < k_0^* < m)$ is optimal for $r_0 \to -\infty$ and $0 < k_0^* < m$ $(k_0^* = m)$ for $r_0 \to \infty$.

Values of the Convertible Bond and the Stock

The *value* of a *convertible bond* $W_0\left(V_0^-, r_0, k_0^*\right)$ is a continuous function of r_0. The continuity follows from the fact that $W_0\left(V_0^-, r_0, k_0\right)$ is continuous in r_0 and k_0 and that k_0^* is continuous in r_0. In particular, $W_0\left(V_0^-, r_0, k_0^*\right)$ can increase or decrease with r_0. The short rate has three effects on the convertible bond value which can be positive or negative. First, the value of the bond component of a non-converted convertible bond $W_0^+\left(V_0^-, r_0, k_0\right)$ decreases with r_0 for a fixed conversion volume. Second, the wealth transfer from the debt holders caused by a higher short rate has a positive effect. Third,

$W_0^+(V_0^-, r_0, k_0^*)$ benefits from a possible increase of k_0^* triggered by a higher short rate. This property is shown in figure 5.8.

Following the considerations for the convertible bond value, we find that the *stock value* is also a continuous function of the short rate that can increase or decrease. A typical example for $S_0(V_0^-, r_0, k_0^*)$ in that $S_0(V_0^-, r_0, k_0^*)$ always increases with r_0 is given in figure 5.8. These effects give the following result.

Result 21 *The optimal conversion volume k_0^* for a fixed firm value V_0^- is zero for all short rates if and only if the dividend rate δ is not higher than $\frac{c \cdot n}{V_0^- - c \cdot m} > 0$. A complete conversion can be optimal if the dividend rate equals one. Otherwise, a critical short rate that triggers a partial or a complete conversion can exist but does not have to. The values of a convertible bond $W_0(V_0^-, r_0, k_0^*)$ and a stock $S_0(V_0^-, r_0, k_0^*)$ are continuous in r_0 and can increase or decrease.*

3) Conversion Strategy and the Values of a Convertible Bond and Stock as a Function of the Dividend Rate and the Debt Face Value

In what follows, we consider the effects of the dividend rate δ and the debt face value FD.

The optimal *conversion volume* k_0^* increases with the dividend rate δ. The reason is that the conversion value $S_0(V_0^-, r_0, k_0)$ increases with δ but the value of a non-converted convertible bond $W_0^+(V_0^-, r_0, k_0)$ declines for every k_0. Given an optimal sequential conversion k_0^*, we know from subsection 1a) that the difference, $W_0^+(V_0^-, r_0, k_0) - S_0(V_0^-, r_0, k_0)$, is negative for all $k_0 < k_0^*$ and positive for $k_0 > k_0^*$. Therefore, a higher dividend rate results in a higher conversion volume $k_0 > k_0^*$ with $W_0^+(V_0^-, r_0, k_0) - S_0(V_0^-, r_0, k_0) \leq 0$.

Analogous to subsections 1a) and 2), the optimal conversion volume is a continuous function in the dividend rate δ that is also differentiable if $k_0^* \in (0, m)$ or k_0^* does not change.

If the firm value is below $(n+m) \cdot c$, no conversion occurs for any δ. Otherwise, for $V_0^- \geq (n+m) \cdot c$, the dividend can be increased until a complete conversion is optimal. To show these assertions, we regard the values of $W_0^+(V_0^-, r_0, k_0)$ and $S_0(V_0^-, r_0, k_0)$ for the highest feasible dividend rate $\delta = 1$. $W_0^+(V_0^-, r_0, k_0) = c$ holds as the convertible bond value at maturity is zero due to the total liquidation of the firm at the dividend date. For the stock value $S_0(V_0^-, r_0, k_0) = \frac{V_0^- - (m-k_0) \cdot c}{n+k_0}$ holds. If $V_0^- < (n+m) \cdot c$ for $\delta = 1$, the stock value for every conversion volume is below $S_0((n+m) \cdot c, r_0, k_0) = \frac{(n+m) \cdot c - (m-k_0) \cdot c}{n+k_0} = c$ and no conversion can optimally occur. Conversely, for $V_0^- \geq (n+m) \cdot c$, the stock value $S_0(V_0^-, r_0, m)$ is at least c, indicating that a complete conversion is optimal. As in the optimal conversion strategy of an unlevered firm at maturity, for $V_0^- = (n+m) \cdot c$ the optimal conversion volume can be arbitrarily chosen. For lower firm values, no conversion is optimal, but for higher firm values a complete conversion occurs. This analysis shows that k_0^* is not necessarily continuous in V_0^- for $\delta = 1$, even though it is continuous for $\delta < 1$.

Since a dividend rate of zero results in no conversion, there are always two finite and unique critical dividend rates $\underline{\delta}$ and $\overline{\delta}$ that trigger a positive conversion volume and a complete conversion for $V_0^- > (n+m) \cdot c$. $\underline{\delta}$ and $\overline{\delta}$ are defined by $W_0^+ \left(V_0^-, r_0, 0\right) = S_0 \left(V_0^-, r_0, 0\right)$ and $W_0^+ \left(V_0^-, r_0, m\right) = S_0 \left(V_0^-, r_0, m\right)$. In the opposite case $V_0^- < (n+m) \cdot c$, no critical dividend rates exist. An example for the optimal conversion volume is shown in figure 5.9.

Figure 5.9: Optimal Conversion Strategy and Values of a Convertible Bond and a Stock before Maturity under Unrestricted Conversion

The left diagram shows the optimal conversion volume k_0^* in the unrestricted case before maturity as a function of the dividend rate δ. The right diagram shows the related values of a convertible bond $W_0 \left(V_0^-, r_0, k_0^*\right)$ and a stock $S_0 \left(V_0^-, r_0, k_0^*\right)$. The parameter values are $n = 100$, $m = 100$, $F = 100$, $FD = 50{,}000$, $c = 5$, $T = 1$, $TD = 2$, $V_0^- = 100{,}000$, $r_0 = 0.05$, $\sigma = 0.5$, $\eta = 0.01097$, $\rho = -0.1$, $\kappa = 0.16643$, $\theta = 0.0639$. The critical dividend rates $\underline{\delta}$ and $\overline{\delta}$ result in 0.0151 and 0.0310, respectively.

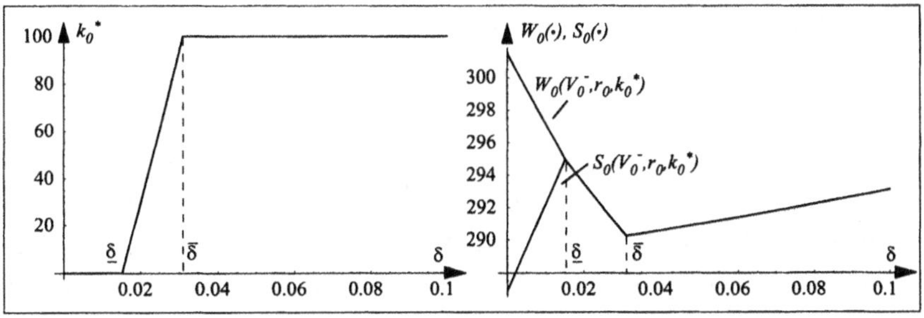

The value of a *convertible bond* $W_0 \left(V_0^-, r_0, k_0^*\right)$ is continuous in δ, because the optimal conversion volume k_0^* is also continuous in δ. $W_0 \left(V_0^-, r_0, k_0^*\right)$ can increase or decrease with δ. It decreases with δ if $k_0^* = 0$ is optimal and it increases with δ at the cost of the debt holders if a complete conversion is optimal. If a partial conversion occurs, the effect of a variation of δ on $W_0 \left(V_0^-, r_0, k_0^*\right)$ is not unique. $W_0 \left(V_0^-, r_0, k_0\right)$ for a fixed conversion volume suffers from a higher dividend rate, but $W_0 \left(V_0^-, r_0, k_0^*\right)$ benefits from the higher conversion volume caused by the higher dividend rate. In the example of figure

5.9, $W_0\left(V_0^-, r_0, k_0^*\right)$ first decreases with δ and then increases.

The value of a *stock* $S_0\left(V_0^-, r_0, k_0^*\right)$ is also a continuous function of the dividend rate δ. If k_0^* equals zero or m, the stock value benefits from the higher dividend. If a change of δ also affects the optimal conversion volume, the stock value equals the convertible bond value due to the conversion condition $S_0\left(V_0^-, r_0, k_0^*\right) = W_0\left(V_0^-, r_0, k_0^*\right)$ required for a positive conversion volume. Thus, the stock value can decrease with δ, if a sequential conversion occurs.

Result 22 *The optimal conversion volume k_0^* for a fixed firm value V_0^- continuously increases with δ. It is zero for all dividend rates if $V_0^- < (n+m)\cdot c$. For $V_0^- > (n+m)\cdot c$ two finite critical dividend rate exists that trigger a partial and a complete conversion. If $V_0^- = (n+m)\cdot c$ a conversion can only occur for $\delta = 1$. The values of a convertible bond value $W_0\left(V_0^-, r_0, k_0^*\right)$ and a stock $S_0\left(V_0^-, r_0, k_0^*\right)$ are continuous but not necessarily monotonous in δ.*

If the debt face value FD rises, the optimal *conversion volume* k_0^* continuously decreases. The rationale for this property — analogous to that presented for a variation of the dividend — is that the difference $W_0^+\left(V_0^-, r_0, k_0\right) - S_0\left(V_0^-, r_0, k_0\right)$ increases with the debt face value FD for every k_0. This property follows from the fact that at maturity T the convertible bond value does not depend on FD or is equal to the stock value which suffers from a higher FD. Therefore, $dif_T\left(V_T^-, V_0^-, r_T, k_0\right)$ and as a consequence $dif_0\left(V_0^-, r_0, k_0\right)$ and $W_0^+\left(V_0^-, r_0, k_0\right) - S_0\left(V_0^-, r_0, k_0\right)$ increase with FD.

It can be optimal not to convert independent of the debt face value. This effect occurs, because even without additional debt $FD = 0$, no conversion can be optimal.

Conversely, a complete conversion can be optimal for all debt face values FD, if the value of the dividend payment $\delta\frac{V_0^-}{n+m}$ after a complete conversion is higher than the value of the bond component of a non-converted convertible bond. In this case even for very high debt face values FD, a complete conversion associated with the participation in the dividend is more favorable than holding some bonds.

In addition to these two scenarios, critical values of $\underline{FD}'$ and $\overline{FD}'$ can exist which trigger a partial and a complete conversion, respectively. In the standard case, k_0^* equals zero for high FD, then at $\underline{FD}'$ a sequential conversion is triggered and k_0^* increases as FD declines. At $\overline{FD}'$ a complete conversion occurs. If these critical values $\underline{FD}'$ and $\overline{FD}'$ exist, they are uniquely defined by $W_0^+\left(V_0^-, r_0, 0\right) = S_0\left(V_0^-, r_0, 0\right)$ and $W_0^+\left(V_0^-, r_0, m\right) = S_0\left(V_0^-, r_0, m\right)$, respectively. The uniqueness results from the monotonicity of k_0^* in FD.

Analogous to the critical short rates presented in subsection 2), a finite $\underline{FD}'$ or $\overline{FD}'$ can but need not exist. The reason for this finding can be shown as follows. In the case without debt, $FD = 0$, every conversion volume can be optimal. Moreover, if the debt face value is very high, the stock value approaches the value of the dividend payment, where the value of the non-converted bond converges to the value of the bond component. Since for high FD either the bond value or the conversion value can be higher depending on the other parameters, the optimal conversion volume can range from zero to m. As k_0^* monotonously decreases with FD, k_0^* can be above zero for all FD and no $\underline{FD}'$ exists, k_0^* can be below m for all FD and no $\overline{FD}'$ exists, and a sequential conversion can be optimal for all FD such that no critical debt face values exist at all.

The *convertible bond value* $W_0\left(V_0^-, r_0, k_0^*\right)$ continuously decreases with the debt face value FD. The continuity is due to the fact that the optimal conversion volume k_0^* is continuous in FD, as shown for the other parameters. The fact that $W_0\left(V_0^-, r_0, k_0^*\right)$ decreases with FD is because a higher debt face value FD has two effects on the convertible bond value. First, the value of $W_0\left(V_0^-, r_0, k_0\right)$ for a fixed conversion volume declines. Second, $W_0\left(V_0^-, r_0, k_0^*\right)$ also suffers from a possibly lower conversion volume. Only in the case of default does $W_0\left(V_0^-, r_0, k_0^*\right)$ not depend on FD.

Analogously, the *stock value* $S_0\left(V_0^-, r_0, k_0^*\right)$ is also a continuously decreasing function of FD. If default occurs, the stock value is zero. Otherwise, it strictly decreases like the convertible bond. This effect is obvious if the block strategy $k_0^* \in \{0, m\}$ is optimal. Otherwise, the stock value is identical to the convertible bond value. Therefore, we obtain the following result.

Result 23 *The optimal conversion volume k_0^* for a fixed firm value V_0^- continuously decreases with FD. It can be zero for all debt face values or a complete conversion can be optimal for all FD. Otherwise, a critical debt face value that triggers a partial or a complete conversion can exist but does not have to. The values of a convertible bond $W_0\left(V_0^-, r_0, k_0^*\right)$ and a stock $S_0\left(V_0^-, r_0, k_0^*\right)$ are continuously decreasing in FD.*

The properties of the optimal conversion volume k_0^* before maturity and the values of both a convertible bond $W_0\left(V_0^-, r_0, k_0^*\right)$ and a stock $S_0\left(V_0^-, r_0, k_0^*\right)$ are intuitive and coincide with those at maturity in several cases. The higher the firm value, the higher the values of $W_0\left(V_0^-, r_0, k_0^*\right)$ and $S_0\left(V_0^-, r_0, k_0^*\right)$. Accordingly, $W_0\left(V_0^-, r_0, k_0^*\right)$ is a unique and strictly increasing function of $S_0\left(V_0^-, r_0, k_0^*\right)$ as long as the stock value is positive. Moreover, when FD increases, the conversion incentive decreases, resulting in a lower k_0^*. As a consequence, the values of $W_0\left(V_0^-, r_0, k_0^*\right)$ and $S_0\left(V_0^-, r_0, k_0^*\right)$ decrease with the debt face value.

Since the convertible bond value under the unrestricted conversion variant is continuous in t at time $t = 0$, the convertible bond value $W_0\left(V_0^-, r_0, k_0^*\right)$ before conversion is equal to the convertible bond value $W_0^+\left(V_0^-, r_0, k_0^*\right)$ after conversion if $W_0^+\left(V_0^-, r_0, k_0^*\right)$ still exists. Hence, the properties of $W_0\left(V_0^-, r_0, k_0^*\right)$ for $k_0^* < m$ are also valid for $W_0^+\left(V_0^-, r_0, k_0^*\right)$.

There are some different properties at a point in time before maturity than at maturity. The optimal conversion volume k_0^* at time $t = 0$ can have more feasible patterns, i.e. k_0^* can be either identical to zero, positive, or identical to m for all firm values, short rates, or debt face values. In particular, a partial conversion can be optimal for all short rates or debt face values.

Conversely, at time T, the optimal conversion volume is always a function increasing from zero to $m - k_0$ with the firm value V_T^-. In addition, the optimal conversion volume k_T^* at maturity cannot be positive for very low short rates or very high debt face values.

Furthermore, the optimal conversion volume k_0^* can be unique in the stock value $S_0\left(V_0^-, r_0, k_0^*\right)$, but at time T all feasible conversion volumes can occur for a stock value equal to the redemption value F .

Another difference between these two conversion dates is that the value of a convertible bond and a stock at time $t = 0$ can increase or decrease with the short rate r_0 due to the hybrid structure of a convertible bond. At maturity, a higher short rate is always associated with higher convertible bond and stock values.

In addition to the analysis at maturity, the dividend rate at time $t = 0$ can also be considered. The optimal conversion volume benefits from a higher dividend rate. However, the corresponding values $W_0\left(V_0^-, r_0, k_0^*\right)$ and $S_0\left(V_0^-, r_0, k_0^*\right)$ can increase or decrease, as the effect of δ for the convertible bond (the stock) is negative (positive) but the change of k_0^* has a positive (negative) effect.

5.3 Monopolistic Conversion

1a) Conversion Strategy and the Values of a Convertible Bond and Stock as a Function of the Firm Value

Conversion Strategy

In the case of monopolistic conversion, the optimal conversion strategy k_0^* is driven by the goal to maximize the total value of the convertible bonds, i.e.

$$\begin{aligned} k_0^* &= \arg\max_{0 \le k_0 \le m} m \cdot W_0\left(V_0^-, r_0, k_0\right) \\ &= \arg\max_{0 \le k_0 \le m} \left(m - k_0\right) \cdot W_0^+\left(V_0^-, r_0, k_0\right) + k_0 \cdot S_0\left(V_0^-, r_0, k_0\right). \end{aligned}$$

A solution k_0^* always exists for this optimization problem, as the objective function is continuous in k_0 and the set of feasible values for k_0 is compact.

Intuitively, a conversion means that the coupon payment and the downward protection of a convertible bond over a stock at maturity T are given up for the converted bonds in favor of a participation in the dividend payment. Thus, an interior solution $0 < k_0^* < m$ might be optimal as we have seen at maturity T. Figure 5.10 provides us with an example in which a sequential conversion takes place. In this example, the value of a non-converted convertible $W_0^+\left(V_0^-, r_0, k_0\right)$ increases with k_0, but the value obtained with a converted convertible bond $S_0\left(V_0^-, r_0, k_0\right)$ decreases with k_0. These properties demonstrate why a sequential conversion can be optimal. When the conversion volume k_0 rises, the number of non-converted convertible bonds held decreases, but the remaining $W_0^+\left(V_0^-, r_0, k_0\right)$ increases in value. Conversely, the number of stocks held increases in k_0 but their value subsequently decreases. These two opposite effects can result in a sequential conversion strategy.

The fact that the holdings of the instrument $W_0^+\left(V_0^-, r_0, k_0\right)$ that increases with k_0 decrease with k_0 and conversely that the holdings of the instrument $S_0\left(V_0^-, r_0, k_0\right)$ that suffers from a higher k_0 increase with k_0 lead to a sequential conversion in this case.

Figure 5.10: Values of a Convertible Bond before and after Conversion and a Stock

The diagram shows the values of a stock $S_0\left(V_0^-, r_0, k_0\right)$ and a convertible bond before conversion, $W_0\left(V_0^-, r_0, k_0\right)$, and after conversion, $W_0^+\left(V_0^-, r_0, k_0\right)$ in the monopolistic case as a function of the conversion volume k_0. The parameter values are $n = 100$, $m = 100$, $F = 100$, $FD = 50{,}000$, $c = 5$, $\delta = 0.03$, $T = 1$, $TD = 2$, $V_0^- = 100{,}000$, $r_0 = 0.05$, $\sigma = 0.5$, $\eta = 0.01097$, $\rho = -0.1$, $\kappa = 0.16643$, $\theta = 0.0639$.

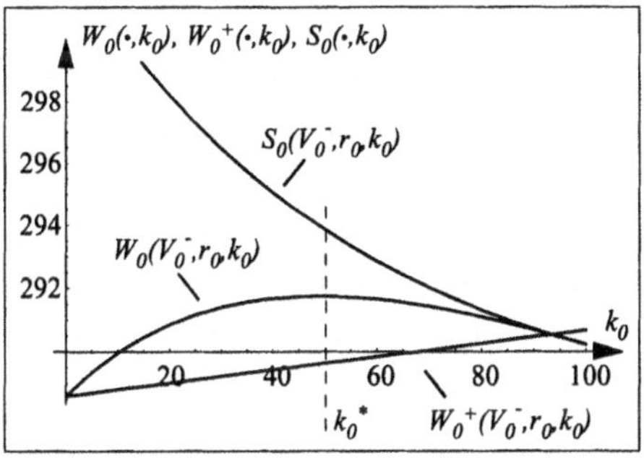

If the objective function $m \cdot W_0\left(V_0^-, r_0, k_0\right)$ has one local maximum and no local minimum in k_0, the optimal conversion volume k_0^* immediately results from the first order condition and is unique. If in addition the objective function has at most one local maximum in k_0 for all firm values, we can apply the implicit function theorem to characterize the derivative of k_0^* for V_0^-. We note that all the required assumptions for the implicit function theorem are satisfied, as $W_0^+(V_0^-, r_0, k_0)$ and $S_0(V_0^-, r_0, k_0)$ are both continuous and arbitrarily often differentiable by remark (1). As a result, the optimal conversion volume is continuous and differentiable for $0 < k_0^* < m$ under these assumptions. Figure 5.11 shows an example for this case.

Figure 5.11: Optimal Conversion Strategy before Maturity and Values of a Convertible Bond before and after Conversion and a Stock under Monopolistic Conversion

The left diagram shows the optimal conversion volume k_0^* in the monopolistic case before maturity as a function of the firm value V_0^-. The right diagram shows the related values of a stock $S_0(V_0^-, r_0, k_0^*)$ and a convertible bond before conversion $W_0(V_0^-, r_0, k_0^*)$ and after conversion $W_0^+(V_0^-, r_0, k_0^*)$. The parameter values are $n = 100$, $m = 100$, $F = 100$, $FD = 50,000$, $c = 5$, $\delta = 0.03$, $T = 1$, $TD = 2$, $r_0 = 0.05$, $\sigma = 0.5$, $\eta = 0.01097$, $\rho = -0.1$, $\kappa = 0.16643$, $\theta = 0.0639$. The critical firm values $\underline{V}_0$ and $\overline{V}_0$ result in 79,968.2 and 115,633.0, respectively.

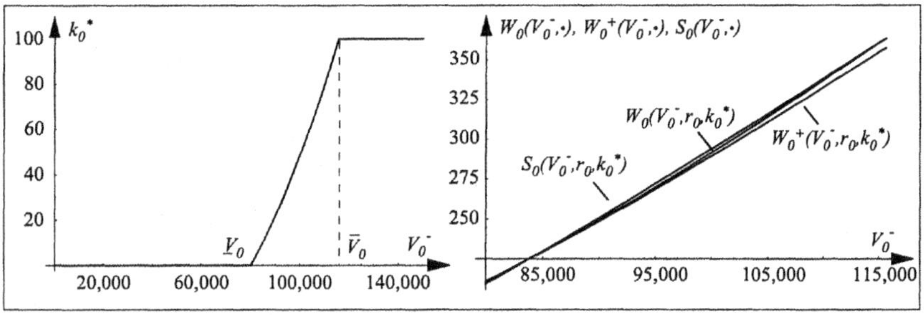

However, the optimal conversion volume k_0^* need not be continuous in V_0^-. This is due to the fact that the objective function $m \cdot W_0(V_0^-, r_0, k_0)$ can have both a local minimum and a local maximum in k_0. According to figure 5.12, for firm values V_0^- below 35,000, a conversion volume below that of the local maximum at $k_0^* = 26.5$ for $V_0^- = 35,000$ is optimal. However, for firm values higher than 35,000 a complete conversion is optimal. The local minimum, as argued at maturity, stems from the existence of additional debt. As at maturity, we assume $k_0^* = m$ in the case of indifference at $V_0^- = \overline{V}_0$.

The optimal conversion volume can have the following patterns similar to those in the unrestricted case:

- No conversion is optimal for all firm values V_0^- if the dividend rate δ is zero, as discussed at the beginning of this chapter.
- A complete conversion is optimal for all firm values V_0^-. This property occurs if

Figure 5.12: Value of the Outstanding Convertible Bonds before Maturity

The figure shows $m \cdot W_0\left(V_0^-, r_0, k_0\right)$, the value of the outstanding convertible bonds in the monopolistic case, as a function of the conversion volume k_0 for two firm values $V_0^- = 35{,}000$ and $V_0^- = 35{,}005$, respectively. The parameter values are $n = 100$, $m = 100$, $F = 100$, $FD = 10{,}000$, $c = 0$, $\delta = 0.0276$, $T = 1$, $TD = 2$, $r_0 = 0.05$, $\sigma = 0.25$, $\eta = 0.01097$, $\rho = -0.1$, $\kappa = 0.16643$, $\theta = 0.0639$.

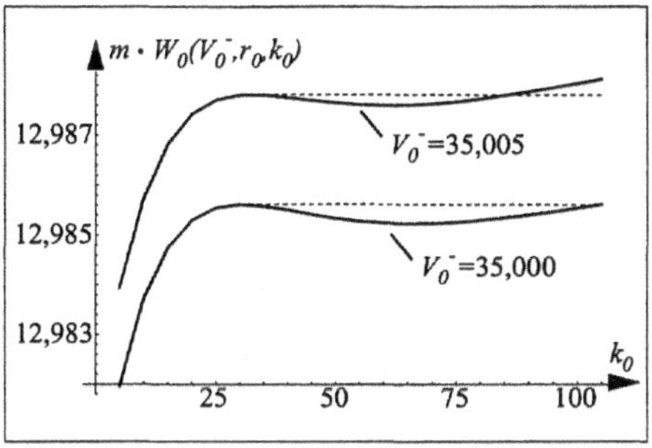

no coupon payment is made and δ equals one. In this case, the value of a non-converted convertible bond $W_0^+\left(V_0^-, r_0, k_0\right)$ is zero for all k_0, but the stock value $S_0\left(V_0^-, r_0, k_0\right)$ equals the prorated firm value $\frac{V_0^-}{n+k_0}$. Therefore, it is optimal to have as high a stake in the firm value as possible, i.e. $k_0^* = m$.

- When these two cases do not occur, a critical $\overline{V}_0$ exists that triggers a complete conversion, because a complete conversion is optimal if the firm value V_0^- is sufficiently high. This assertion results from the fact that for high firm values the value of a stock $S_0\left(V_0^-, r_0, k_0\right)$ is approximately equal to the convertible bond value $W_0^+\left(V_0^-, r_0, k_0\right)$ corrected by the dividend and coupon payments, i.e. $-c + \delta\frac{V_0^- - (m-k_0)\cdot c}{n+k_0}$. In other words, for high firm values the convertible bond offers no advantages at maturity to its holder compared to a stock. Therefore, a complete conversion is optimal to participate in the dividend payment $\delta\frac{V_0^- - (m-k_0)\cdot c}{n+k_0}$ which is much higher than the coupon payment for sufficiently high firm values.

- If the coupon c is positive, no conversion is optimal for low firm values, as for the other two conversion variants. Therefore, given a positive coupon and dividend rate, two finite critical firm values $\underline{V}_0$ and $\overline{V}_0$ exist that have the following properties. $\underline{V}_0$ is the highest firm value such that no conversion takes place for lower firm values, but $\overline{V}_0$ denotes the lowest firm value such that a complete conversion occurs for all firm values above $\overline{V}_0$. In figure 5.11, we find that the conversion volume k_0^* is zero for firm values below a critical value $\underline{V}_0$, then it continuously increases with V_0^-, and for high firm values exceeding a second critical value $\overline{V}_0$, a complete conversion occurs. However, we were not able to show that k_0^* is an increasing function of V_0^- or demonstrate the uniqueness of the critical firm values.

However, a critical $\underline{V}_0$ need not exist, even though $\overline{V}_0$ exists. If $c = 0$ and the dividend rate is sufficiently high but below one, a partial conversion can be optimal for low firm values and a complete conversion occurs for high firm values.

Values of the Convertible Bond and the Stock

The value of a *convertible bond* $W_0(V_0^-, r_0, k_0^*)$ immediately before maturity is a strictly and continuously increasing function of the firm value V_0^-. This property is a result of the fact that the objective function $m \cdot W_0(V_0^-, r_0, k_0)$ is continuous in V_0^- and k_0 and strictly increases with V_0^- for all k_0. The fact that $m \cdot W_0(V_0^-, r_0, k_0)$ increases with V_0^- follows from the property that the value obtained with the convertible bonds at maturity, i.e. the value of the objective function at maturity, increases with V_T^- for every strategy k_0.

At this point, it is important to note that the convertible bond value is not necessarily continuous in time t. Given that no complete conversion occurs, the convertible bond value immediately after conversion is defined by $W_0^+(V_0^-, r_0, k_0^*)$.[7] Therefore, a discontinuity of the convertible bond value takes place whenever $W_0(V_0^-, r_0, k_0^*)$ differs from $W_0^+(V_0^-, r_0, k_0^*)$ for $k_0^* < m$. Due to the fact that $W_0(V_0^-, r_0, k_0^*)$ is a convex combination of $W_0^+(V_0^-, r_0, k_0^*)$ and $S_0(V_0^-, r_0, k_0^*)$, we can see that a discontinuity occurs if $W_0^+(V_0^-, r_0, k_0^*)$ differs from $S_0(V_0^-, r_0, k_0^*)$. An example in which the convertible bond value is not continuous is shown in figure 5.10. In this figure, the convertible bond value before conversion $W_0(V_0^-, r_0, k_0^*)$ lies at 291.7, but the corresponding value $W_0^+(V_0^-, r_0, k_0^*)$ after a conversion is 289.6.

The convertible bond value immediately after conversion $W_0^+(V_0^-, r_0, k_0^*)$ shows similar properties to the convertible bond value before conversion. If k_0^* is continuous in V_0^- for $k_0^* < m$, $W_0^+(V_0^-, r_0, k_0^*)$ is also continuous. Given the typical case in which $W_0^+(V_0^-, r_0, k_0)$ increases with k_0 and the optimal conversion volume k_0^* increases with

[7] In general, a previsible discontinuity of the value of a certain (non dividend or coupon paying) asset presents arbitrage opportunities. However, the strategy of buying (short selling) one unit of $W_0(V_0^-, r_0, k_0^*)$ before conversion and selling (buying) one unit of $W_0^+(V_0^-, r_0, k_0^*)$ after conversion to achieve a positive gain of $|W_0(V_0^-, r_0, k_0^*) - W_0^+(V_0^-, r_0, k_0^*)|$ is not feasible in this case. The reason is that a monopolist holds all the convertible bonds and thus a single investor cannot follow this arbitrage strategy. Even the monopolist does not exploit any arbitrage opportunities because the total value obtained with the convertible bonds is continuous in time at $t = 0$.

V_0^-, the convertible bond value $W_0^+ \left(V_0^-, r_0, k_0^*\right)$ also increases with V_0^-. However, we were not able to show that this monotonicity always holds.

The *stock* value $S_0 \left(V_0^-, r_0, k_0^*\right)$ can increase or decrease with V_0^-. The fact that the stock value does not always benefit from a higher firm value is because a higher firm value can lead to a higher conversion volume such that the advantages of the firm value increase are lower than the wealth transfer to the debt holders caused by the higher conversion volume. Moreover, $S_0 \left(V_0^-, r_0, k_0^*\right)$ can be discontinuous in V_0^- due to jumps of the optimal conversion volume in V_0^-. If, as shown in the example from figure 5.12, k_0^* jumps from 26.5 to m, the stock value drops as a result of the higher conversion volume. A comparison of the stock value and the convertible bond value in figure 5.10 shows that the stock value can be higher than both convertible bond values $W_0 \left(V_0^-, r_0, k_0^*\right)$ and $W_0^+ \left(V_0^-, r_0, k_0^*\right)$. Intuition tells us that the wealth transfer to the debt holders prevents the monopolist from converting a higher volume. Thus, a stock value above the convertible bond values together with a lower debt value can be more favorable for the monopolist than a stock value below the convertible bond values associated with a rather high debt value. The following result summarizes these findings.

Result 24 *The optimal conversion volume k_0^* can be continuous or discontinuous in the firm value. It is zero for all firm values if and only if the dividend rate δ is equal to zero. A complete conversion can be optimal for all firm values, if the coupon is zero and the dividend rate equals one. Otherwise, a critical firm value that triggers a complete conversion exists. If the coupon is positive, no conversion is optimal for low firm values and a second critical firm value exists that triggers a partial conversion. The value of a convertible bond $W_0 \left(V_0^-, r_0, k_0^*\right)$ immediately before conversion is continuous in V_0^-. However, the convertible bond value is not always continuous at time $t = 0$, as the convertible bond value before conversion $W_0 \left(V_0^-, r_0, k_0^*\right)$ can differ from the corresponding value $W_0^+ \left(V_0^-, r_0, k_0^*\right)$ after a conversion. The stock value $S_0 \left(V_0^-, r_0, k_0^*\right)$ is not necessarily continuous in the firm value V_0^- and it can continuously increase, decrease, or drop with V_0^-. Moreover, the stock value can lie above the convertible bond value.*

1b) Conversion Strategy and the Value of a Convertible Bond as a Function of the Stock Value

Again, we take the market view and represent both the conversion volume k_0^* and the convertible bond values before and after conversion as a function of the stock value $S_0 \left(V_0^-, r_0, k_0^*\right)$. According to figure 5.13, the optimal *conversion volume* k_0^* is zero for low stock values $S_0 \left(V_0^-, r_0, k_0^*\right)$. Then, it continuously and strictly increases with $S_0 \left(V_0^-, r_0, k_0^*\right)$. In other examples, k_0^* might not be unique in the stock value. This

Figure 5.13: Optimal Conversion Strategy and Value of a Convertible Bond before Maturity under Monopolistic Conversion

The left diagram shows the optimal conversion volume k_0^* in the monopolistic case before maturity as a function of the stock value $S_0\left(V_0^-, r_0, k_0^*\right)$. The right diagram shows the related value of a convertible bond $W_0\left(V_0^-, r_0, k_0^*\right)$. The parameter values are $n = 100$, $m = 100$, $F = 100$, $FD = 50{,}000$, $c = 5$, $\delta = 0.03$, $T = 1$, $TD = 2$, $r_0 = 0.05$, $\sigma = 0.5$, $\eta = 0.01097$, $\rho = -0.1$, $\kappa = 0.16643$, $\theta = 0.0639$.

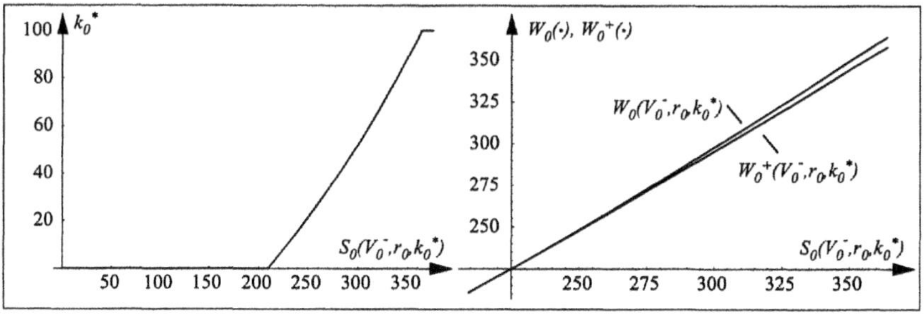

non-uniqueness stems from the fact that the stock value can continuously decrease with intermediate firm values and then increase, but the conversion volume always increases with V_0^-. Thus, three different conversion volumes can be associated with one particular stock value. Therefore, a unique representation of k_0^* as a function of the stock value does not always exist. Regarding that high (low) firm values are also associated with rather high (low) stock values, we can adapt the structure of k_0^* as a function of V_0^- given in subsection 1a) to determine the properties of k_0^* as a function of the stock value.

- No conversion is optimal for all stock values $S_0\left(V_0^-, r_0, k_0^*\right)$ if the dividend rate δ is zero.

- If no coupon payment is made, a conversion can be optimal for all stock values $S_0\left(V_0^-, r_0, k_0^*\right)$.

- A complete conversion is optimal if the stock value $S_0\left(V_0^-, r_0, k_0^*\right)$ is sufficiently high, given a positive dividend rate $\delta > 0$.

- If the coupon c is positive, no conversion is optimal for low stock values. For $c = 0$, a partial but no complete conversion can be optimal even for sufficiently low stock values.

The *convertible bond value* $W_0(V_0^-, r_0, k_0^*)$ immediately before and $W_0^+(V_0^-, r_0, k_0^*)$ immediately after conversion are shown in figure 5.13. If the firm value is not sufficient for the coupon payment, both $W_0(V_0^-, r_0, k_0^*)$ and $W_0^+(V_0^-, r_0, k_0^*)$ are equal to the prorated firm value $\frac{V_0^-}{m}$ and the stock value is zero. Thus, convertible bond values from zero to c are related to a stock value of zero. In general, the convertible bond value is unique in the stock value if the conversion volume is also unique. However, if the conversion volume is not unique in the stock value, the values of the convertible bond are not unique either. In particular, one stock value can be associated with three different convertible bond values $W_0(V_0^-, r_0, k_0^*)$ and $W_0^+(V_0^-, r_0, k_0^*)$. These considerations lead us to the following result.

Result 25 *The optimal conversion volume k_0^* is not necessarily unique in the stock value. It can equal either zero or m for all stock values. Otherwise, k_0^* is zero or at least below m for low stock values and is equal to m for high stock values. The convertible bond values $W_0(V_0^-, r_0, k_0^*)$ and $W_0^+(V_0^-, r_0, k_0^*)$ are non-unique for a stock value equal to zero as long as the coupon c is positive and for higher stock values for which the conversion volume is not unique either.*

2) Conversion Strategy and the Values of a Convertible Bond and Stock as a Function of the Short Rate

Conversion Strategy

First, we discuss the effect of the short rate on the *conversion volume* intuitively. The short rate r_0 affects both the value of a converted convertible bond $S_0(V_0^-, r_0, k_0)$ and the value of a non-converted convertible bond $W_0^+(V_0^-, r_0, k_0)$. The general direction of the effect of r_0 on $S_0(V_0^-, r_0, k_0)$ and $W_0^+(V_0^-, r_0, k_0)$ for an exogenous conversion volume k_0 is analogous to the block and unrestricted case. This is because $W_0^+(V_0^-, r_0, k_0)$ generally decreases with r_0, but it can also increase if the wealth transfer from the debt holders is sufficiently high. Conversely, $S_0(V_0^-, r_0, k_0)$ generally increases with r_0 and this increase is more severe than that of $W_0^+(V_0^-, r_0, k_0)$. These effects provide us with an intuition as to why the optimal *conversion volume* k_0^* increases with r_0. The higher k_0, the higher the number of those securities that more sharply increase with r_0. However, this argument is an intuition, but it was not possible to find a proof for this monotonicity. Figure 5.14 shows the optimal conversion volume as a function of the short rate r_0. In this figure the optimal conversion volume is zero for short rates below a critical value of $\underline{r}_0$, then it increases with r_0, and it equals m for short rates higher than a second critical short rate $\overline{r}_0$. In this example the optimal conversion volume is continuous in the short rate r_0. In other examples, however, k_0^* can have jumps in r_0. A jump occurs — as seen at maturity — if the objective function $m \cdot W_0(V_0^-, r_0, k_0)$ has both a local minimum and

Figure 5.14: Optimal Conversion Strategy before Maturity and Values of a Convertible Bond before and after Conversion and a Stock under Monopolistic Conversion

The left diagram shows the optimal conversion volume k_0^* in the monopolistic case before maturity as a function of the short rate r_0. The right diagram shows the related values of a stock $S_0\left(V_0^-, r_0, k_0^*\right)$ and a convertible bond before conversion $W_0\left(V_0^-, r_0, k_0^*\right)$ and after conversion $W_0^+\left(V_0^-, r_0, k_0^*\right)$. The parameter values are $n = 100$, $m = 100$, $F = 100$, $FD = 50,000$, $c = 5$, $\delta = 0.03$, $T = 1$, $TD = 2$, $V_0^- = 100,000$, $\sigma = 0.5$, $\eta = 0.01097$, $\rho = -0.1$, $\kappa = 0.16643$, $\theta = 0.0639$. The critical short rates $\underline{r}_0$ and $\overline{r}_0$ result in -0.1287 and 0.1605, respectively.

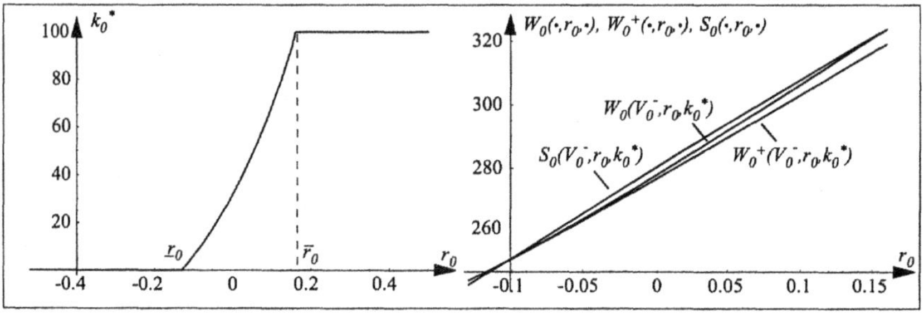

a maximum in k_0. Then, $m \cdot W_0\left(V_0^-, r_0, k_0\right)$ is at a maximum for two different values of k_0, one inner solution $0 < k_0^* < m$ and the corner solution $k_0^* = m$. If r_0 is below $\overline{r}_0$, the optimal conversion volume is close to k_0^*, the inner solution. However, for r_0 higher than $\overline{r}_0$, a complete conversion m is optimal. Thus in this case, the optimal conversion volume k_0^* has a jump in r_0 at $\overline{r}_0$. If the objective function does not have a local minimum, the derivative of k_0^* for r_0 given that $k_0^* \in (0, m)$ follows analogously from the implicit function theorem as in subsection 1a). In what follows, we discuss the general properties of k_0^* depending on r_0 for a given firm value V_0^-. The properties are:

- No conversion is optimal for all short rates, if δ is not above $\frac{c \cdot n^2}{V_0^-(n+m) - c \cdot m(2n+m)} > 0$ or the firm value is below $\frac{c \cdot m(2n+m)}{n+m}$. To illustrate this assertion, we argue that the conversion incentive is highest if the short rate converges to infinity. The reason is that in this case, the current value of the protection that a convertible bond provides over a stock at maturity is zero and the debt value is zero. Thus, after the coupon and dividend payment, there is no reason to hold the convertible bonds anymore.

  Thus, in this limit the value of a non-converted convertible bond $W_0^+\left(V_0^-, r_0, k_0\right)$ and a stock $S_0\left(V_0^-, r_0, k_0\right)$ converge to $\frac{V_0^- - (m-k_0) \cdot c}{n+m}(1-\delta) + c$ and $\frac{V_0^- - (m-k_0) \cdot c}{n+m}(1-\delta) + \delta\frac{V_0^- - (m-k_0) \cdot c}{n+k_0}$, respectively. Since in the limit the derivative

$$m\frac{\partial W_0\left(V_0^-,r_0,k_0\right)}{\partial k_0}=\frac{\partial\left((m-k_0)\cdot W_0^+\left(V_0^-,r_0,k_0\right)+k_0\cdot S_0\left(V_0^-,r_0,k_0\right)\right)}{\partial k_0}$$
$$=\frac{\delta V_0^-\cdot n}{(n+k_0)^2}-\frac{c\cdot n\left((n+k_0)^2+\delta\cdot(m-k_0)(m+k_0+2n)\right)}{(n+k_0)^2(n+m)}$$

of the monopolist's objective function is non-positive for all k_0 if $\delta \leq \frac{c\cdot n^2}{V_0^-(n+m)-c\cdot m(2n+m)}$ or $V_0^- \leq \frac{c\cdot m(2n+m)}{n+m}$, we can see why no conversion is optimal for all r_0 in the case of low dividends.

- A complete conversion can be optimal for all short rates. This particular case clearly occurs for $\delta = 1$ and a sufficiently low coupon.
- Next, we consider a higher dividend rate $\delta > \frac{c\cdot n^2}{V_0^-(n+m)-c\cdot m(2n+m)} > 0$ for which a conversion might occur. If the short rate is sufficiently high, a conversion but not necessarily a complete conversion occurs. This is because the derivative $m\frac{\partial W_0\left(V_0^-,r_0,k_0\right)}{\partial k_0}$ of the monopolist's objective function in the limit $r_0 \to \infty$, is positive for $k_0 = 0$. A complete conversion for high short rates requires a higher dividend rate δ above $c\frac{n+m}{V_0^-}$, because under this condition the derivative $m\frac{\partial W_0\left(V_0^-,r_0,k_0\right)}{\partial k_0}$ is positive for all k_0.
- If the short rate tends to minus infinity, a conversion occurs for a dividend rate δ above $\frac{c\cdot n}{V_0^- -(n+m)\cdot c} > 0$. However, a complete conversion only takes place, if δ exceeds $\frac{c(n+m)^2}{nV_0^- - c\cdot n(n+m)}$. Analogous to the case for $r_0 \to \infty$, these critical values arise from the approximations of the asset values when r_0 becomes arbitrarily small as presented in remark (4).

  As in the unrestricted case, the existence of a finite critical short rate $\overline{r}_0\left(\underline{r}_0\right)$ does not necessarily imply that a corresponding finite $\underline{r}_0\left(\overline{r}_0\right)$ also exists. This statement means that for every short rate either a sequential or a complete conversion but not no conversion (either no conversion or a sequential conversion but not a complete conversion) occurs. Moreover, no finite critical short rates exist, if a partial conversion is optimal for all short rates.

Values of the Convertible Bond and the Stock

The value of a *convertible bond* $W_0\left(V_0^-,r_0,k_0^*\right)$ immediately before conversion is continuous in r_0 and can increase or decrease. The continuity of r_0 — like the continuity of V_0^- — is a consequence of the fact that the objective function $m\cdot W_0\left(V_0^-,r_0,k_0\right)$ is continuous in r_0 and k_0. $W_0\left(V_0^-,r_0,k_0^*\right)$ generally decreases as a higher short rate is associated with a lower value of the bond component. However, $W_0\left(V_0^-,r_0,k_0^*\right)$ can also increase if the wealth transfer from the debt holders caused by a higher short rate is sufficiently high.

Accordingly, the value of a convertible bond $W_0^+(V_0^-, r_0, k_0^*)$ after conversion can also increase or decrease with r_0. As long as k_0^* is continuous in r_0 for $k_0^* < m$, $W_0^+(V_0^-, r_0, k_0^*)$ is also continuous.

The *stock* value $S_0(V_0^-, r_0, k_0^*)$ can continuously increase, continuously decrease, or drop with r_0. In typical cases, $S_0(V_0^-, r_0, k_0^*)$ continuously increases with r_0. It is also possible that the optimal conversion volume k_0^* rises so severely with r_0 that the loss from the higher conversion volume exceeds the benefits from the higher short rate and $S_0(V_0^-, r_0, k_0^*)$ decreases. Only if the optimal conversion volume k_0^* has an upward jump, does the stock value drop. These considerations give the following result.

Result 26 *The optimal conversion volume k_0^* for a fixed firm value V_0^- is zero for all short rates if and only if the dividend rate δ is not higher than $\frac{c \cdot n^2}{V_0^-(n+m) - c \cdot m(2n+m)} > 0$ or the firm value is not higher than $\frac{c \cdot m(2n+m)}{n+m}$. A complete conversion can be optimal if the dividend rate is equal to one. Otherwise, a critical short rate that triggers a partial or a complete conversion can but need not exist. The value of a convertible bond $W_0(V_0^-, r_0, k_0^*)$ immediately before conversion is a continuous function of r_0 that can increase or decrease. The value of a convertible bond $W_0^+(V_0^-, r_0, k_0^*)$ after conversion can also increase or decrease. The stock value $S_0(V_0^-, r_0, k_0^*)$ can continuously increase, continuously decrease, or drop with r_0.*

3) Conversion Strategy and the Values of a Convertible Bond and Stock as a Function of the Dividend Rate and the Debt Face Value

First, we regard the dividend rate. The higher the dividend rate δ, the higher the stock value $S_0(V_0^-, r_0, k_0)$ and the lower the value of a non-converted convertible bond $W_0^+(V_0^-, r_0, k_0)$. This effect supports the assertion that the optimal *conversion volume* k_0^* increases with the dividend rate, because a conversion becomes more attractive but the value of the non-converted convertible bonds suffers. Nevertheless, this reason is just an intuition but no proof.[8]

Figure 5.15 shows a typical case for the optimal conversion volume k_0^* as a function of the dividend rate δ. According to this figure, no conversion is optimal for dividend rates below a critical level of $\underline{\delta}$, then, a partial conversion is optimal for dividend rates below $\overline{\delta}$, and a complete conversion occurs for higher dividend rates. We note that k_0^* is not

[8] In particular, even if $S_0(V_0^-, r_0, k_0)$ increases with δ, but $W_0^+(V_0^-, r_0, k_0)$ decreases, a lower conversion volume caused by a higher dividend rate δ could be optimal. This effect would occur, if $W_0^+(V_0^-, r_0, k_0)$ suffered from a higher δ much more than $S_0(V_0^-, r_0, k_0)$ benefited. However, we could not find such a case.

Figure 5.15: Optimal Conversion Strategy before Maturity and Values of a Convertible Bond before and after Conversion and a Stock under Monopolistic Conversion

The left diagram shows the optimal conversion volume k_0^* in the monopolistic case before maturity as a function of the dividend rate δ. The right diagram shows the related values of a stock $S_0\left(V_0^-, r_0, k_0^*\right)$ and a convertible bond before conversion $W_0\left(V_0^-, r_0, k_0^*\right)$ and after conversion $W_0^+\left(V_0^-, r_0, k_0^*\right)$. The parameter values are $n = 100$, $m = 100$, $F = 100$, $FD = 50{,}000$, $c = 5$, $T = 1$, $TD = 2$, $V_0^- = 100{,}000$, $r_0 = 0.05$, $\sigma = 0.5$, $\eta = 0.01097$, $\rho = -0.1$, $\kappa = 0.16643$, $\theta = 0.0639$. The critical dividend rates $\underline{\delta}$ and $\overline{\delta}$ result in 0.01306 and 0.0550, respectively.

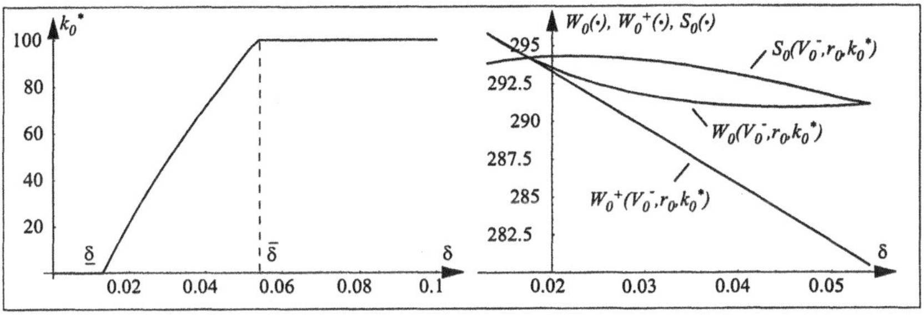

necessarily continuous in δ. For cases in which the objective function $m \cdot W_0\left(V_0^-, r_0, k_0\right)$ has both a local maximum and a local minimum in k_0, the optimal conversion volume k_0^* can have a jump to m. The reason for this jump is analogous to that for the jump with V_0^- which is illustrated in figure 5.12.

If V_0^- is below $(n+m) \cdot c$, no conversion occurs for any dividend rate. This is because in this case the stock value is below c, but the value of a non-converted convertible bond is at least c for any δ. In the opposite case $V_0^- > (n+m) \cdot c$, the stock value for the highest feasible dividend rate $\delta = 1$ is higher than c for all k_0 and a complete conversion is optimal, which we can see from the first order condition in this case. For the firm value $V_0^- = (n+m) \cdot c$, the values of both a non-converted convertible bond and a stock are equal to c for $\delta = 1$. Therefore, every conversion strategy is equally good for $\delta = 1$ and leads to the same value of the objective function namely $m \cdot c$. For lower dividend rates, the stock value is lower and therefore no conversion can occur.

Since no conversion is optimal for $\delta = 0$, two finite critical dividend rates $\underline{\delta}$ and $\overline{\delta}$ exist that trigger a positive conversion volume and a complete conversion, respectively, if the firm value is above $(n+m) \cdot c$.

The *value* of a *convertible bond* $W_0\left(V_0^-, r_0, k_0^*\right)$ before conversion is continuous in δ and can increase or decrease. Figure 5.15 illustrates this behavior. In general, $W_0\left(V_0^-, r_0, k_0^*\right)$ suffers from a higher dividend rate. However, since the debt holders also suffer from an increase of δ, the wealth transfer from the debt holders might be such that $W_0\left(V_0^-, r_0, k_0^*\right)$ can increase. The value of a convertible bond after conversion $W_0^+\left(V_0^-, r_0, k_0^*\right)$ that might differ from $W_0\left(V_0^-, r_0, k_0^*\right)$ if $0 < k_0^* < m$ can also increase or decrease with δ. An increase of $W_0^+\left(V_0^-, r_0, k_0^*\right)$ with δ can occur if $W_0\left(V_0^-, r_0, k_0\right)$ increases with k_0 and the increase of k_0^* with δ is especially severe.

The *stock value* $S_0\left(V_0^-, r_0, k_0^*\right)$ can continuously increase, decrease, and drop with δ. For $k_0^* = 0$, the stock value benefits from the higher dividend payment. If a sequential conversion occurs, the increase of k_0^* with δ can be such that $S_0\left(V_0^-, r_0, k_0^*\right)$ suffers from a higher δ. If the optimal conversion volume has a jump in δ, the stock value drops due to the wealth transfer to the debt holders.

Result 27 *The optimal conversion volume k_0^* is zero for all dividend rates if $V_0^- < (n+m) \cdot c$. For $V_0^- > (n+m) \cdot c$ two finite critical dividend rates exist that trigger a partial and a complete conversion. If $V_0^- = (n+m) \cdot c$ a conversion can only occur for $\delta = 1$. The value of a convertible bond $W_0\left(V_0^-, r_0, k_0^*\right)$ before conversion is continuous in δ. If δ rises, $W_0\left(V_0^-, r_0, k_0^*\right)$ can increase or decrease. Accordingly, the convertible bond value $W_0^+\left(V_0^-, r_0, k_0^*\right)$ after a conversion can also increase or decrease with δ. The stock value $S_0\left(V_0^-, r_0, k_0^*\right)$ can continuously increase, decrease, or drop with δ.*

An increase of the debt face value FD is generally associated with a less attractive conversion. This assertion is illustrated as follows. Since a higher debt face value FD leads to a lower total conversion volume $k_0 + k_T^*$ at maturity, the monopolist is supposed to account for this fact by selecting a lower premature conversion volume k_0^*. Otherwise, she or he would accept an unfavorable higher conversion volume at time T, because $k_0 + k_T^*$ increases with k_0 as explained in remark (2). We note that these considerations are a reasonable illustration for this assertion but we cannot provide a proof.

Therefore, in some cases the optimal conversion volume can continuously decrease for all FD. However in other cases, the optimal conversion volume might jump in FD in a similar way as at maturity.

Although the optimal conversion volume in the monopolistic case can deviate from that in the unrestricted case, the patterns of the optimal monopolistic conversion strategy in FD are analogous to those under unrestricted conversion.

In particular, it can be optimal not to convert for all FD, as no conversion can be optimal even for $FD = 0$. If the value of the dividend payment is sufficiently high, it is optimal for the monopolist to fully convert for all FD to participate in this high dividend.

Moreover, there can be two critical debt face values, $\underline{FD}'$ and $\overline{FD}'$, that trigger a sequential and a complete conversion, respectively. As seen in the unrestricted case, a finite $\underline{FD}'$ exists even though $\overline{FD}'$ does not exist, if either a sequential conversion or no conversion is optimal for all FD. The opposite case, that no finite $\underline{FD}'$ exists but $\overline{FD}'$ is finite occurs when either a complete conversion or a sequential conversion takes place for all FD. In the case that a partial conversion is optimal for all FD, finite critical values for both $\underline{FD}'$ and $\overline{FD}'$ do not exist.

The *convertible bond value* $W_0\left(V_0^-, r_0, k_0^*\right)$ before conversion continuously decreases with the debt face value FD. The reason is that the wealth a monopolist obtains at maturity is lower for every conversion volume k_0 when FD rises. Thus, the present value at time zero must also be lower. Analogously, the value of a convertible bond $W_0^+\left(V_0^-, r_0, k_0^*\right)$ after conversion is supposed to decrease with FD, but we cannot prove this assertion.

The *stock value* $S_0\left(V_0^-, r_0, k_0^*\right)$, however, can continuously increase, decrease, and jump with FD. Generally, the stock value $S_0\left(V_0^-, r_0, k_0^*\right)$ continuously decreases with FD. If a lower debt face value is associated with a lower conversion volume, the stock value might benefit from the lower conversion volume such that $S_0\left(V_0^-, r_0, k_0^*\right)$ continuously increases. In case that k_0^* has a drop with FD, the stock value jumps due to the wealth transfer from the debt holders. The following result summarizes our findings.

Result 28 *The optimal conversion volume k_0^* for a fixed firm value V_0^- continuously decreases with FD. It can be zero for all debt face values or a complete conversion can be optimal for all FD. Otherwise, a critical debt face value that triggers a partial or a complete conversion can exist but does not have to. The value of a convertible bond $W_0\left(V_0^-, r_0, k_0^*\right)$ before conversion is continuously decreasing in FD. The stock value $S_0\left(V_0^-, r_0, k_0^*\right)$ can continuously increase, decrease, or jump with FD.*

The analysis before maturity of the convertible bond shows several parallels to the findings at maturity. The optimal conversion volume k_0^* continuously or discontinuously benefits from a higher firm value, a higher short rate, and a lower debt face value. In contrast to the behavior at maturity, we were unable to rule out other effects.

The value of a convertible bond $W_0\left(V_0^-, r_0, k_0^*\right)$ before conversion is continuous in all considered parameters except for the stock value. It increases with a higher total firm value V_0^- and a lower debt face value FD. However, $W_0\left(V_0^-, r_0, k_0^*\right)$ is not uniquely determined by the stock value $S_0\left(V_0^-, r_0, k_0^*\right)$.

The value of a non-converted convertible bond $W_0^+\left(V_0^-, r_0, k_0^*\right)$ can differ from that of a convertible bond before conversion. Nevertheless, $W_0^+\left(V_0^-, r_0, k_0^*\right)$ shows similar properties, but we were unable to prove that $W_0^+\left(V_0^-, r_0, k_0^*\right)$ is continuous, which is equivalent to the assertion that k_0^* is continuous for $k_0^* < m$.[9]

The value of a stock can increase or decrease with all the considered parameters V_0^-, r_0, and FD, as at maturity.

The differences between the behavior before and at maturity are basically analogous to those which we have already seen in the unrestricted case. In particular, the optimal conversion volume before maturity can attain more patterns in the firm value, the short rate, and the debt face value and the convertible bond value might increase or decrease with the short rate.

In addition to these variations, we can also consider a variation of the dividend rate. If δ changes, the convertible bond value, like the value of a stock, can increase or decrease.

5.4 Analysis without additional Debt

In the general analysis, several findings have been derived under the assumption of outstanding additional debt. To see whether these effects require outstanding additional debt or not, we conduct the following analysis without debt. In the absence of additional debt, we will find some different properties of the optimal conversion volume and the values of a convertible bond and a stock. Moreover, we will be able to prove certain assertions which were intuitive but unsubstantiated when regarding additional debt.

A main difference in the block case in the absence of debt is that the stock value $S_0\left(V_0^-, r_0, k_0^*\right)$ cannot lie above the convertible bond value $W_0\left(V_0^-, r_0, k_0^*\right)$ if no conversion, $k_0^* = 0$, is optimal. In this case, a conversion would result in a conversion value that lies between $S_0\left(V_0^-, r_0, 0\right)$ and $W_0\left(V_0^-, r_0, 0\right)$, which would be higher than $W_0\left(V_0^-, r_0, k_0^*\right) = W_0\left(V_0^-, r_0, 0\right)$. As a consequence $\overline{V}_0$ and $\underline{V}_0$ must coincide, as the two critical short and dividend rates.

We can prove that the values of $\overline{V}_0$ and $\overline{r}_0$ are unique if the firm has no additional debt. As a consequence, the conversion volume cannot decrease with V_0^- or r_0 without additional debt. However, it was not possible to prove these statements in the case with additional debt. The proof for $\overline{r}_0$ is straightforward. Since $S_0\left(V_0^-, r_0, m\right) = \frac{V_0^-}{n+m}$ is independent of r_0, but $W_0\left(V_0^-, r_0, 0\right)$ decreases with r_0, the equation $W_0\left(V_0^-, r_0, 0\right) = S_0\left(V_0^-, r_0, m\right)$

9 In our examples k_0^* can only attain a jump towards m, but not to a level below. If this was a general property of k_0^*, $W_0^+\left(V_0^-, r_0, k_0^*\right)$ would be continuous.

cannot have more than one solution.[10]

The proof that $\overline{V}_0$ is unique is more demanding. It results from the fact that equation (5.1) equals zero for at most one critical firm value. This is a consequence of the fact that $dif_0\left(V_0^-, r_0\right)$ is a continuous function of V_0^- that is zero at $V_0^- = 0$, might attain a local maximum at a higher firm value, and tends to a non-positive constant afterwards. In particular, $dif_0\left(V_0^-, r_0\right)$ has one turning point such that it cannot have a local minimum or more than one local maximum. Therefore, the equation $dif_0\left(V_0^-, r_0\right) + c - \delta\frac{V_0^-}{n+m} = 0$ cannot be satisfied for more than one $\overline{V}_0$. To show that $dif_0\left(V_0^-, r_0\right)$ has one turning point, we can determine the second derivative of $dif_0\left(V_0^-, r_0\right)$ for V_0^- to show that this derivative cannot have more than one root.

The value of a *convertible bond* is decreasing with r_0 and δ and equals a constant conversion value $\frac{V_0^-}{n+m}$ if $r_0 \geq \overline{r}_0$ or $\delta \geq \overline{\delta}$. Thus, without additional debt $W_0\left(V_0^-, r_0, k_0^*\right)$ cannot increase with r_0 or δ, unlike in the case with additional debt.

The *value* of a *stock* is a continuous function in all arguments. In correspondence to the properties of the convertible bonds, the value of a stock increases with r_0 and δ if no conversion is optimal. Otherwise, it is equal to the constant conversion value $\frac{V_0^-}{n+m}$. With additional debt, we have seen that $S\left(V_0^-, r_0, k_0^*\right)$ can decrease with r_0 and δ and can be discontinuous.

As a result of the monotonicity of the stock value, the optimal conversion volume and the value of a convertible bond are unique in the stock value if the stock value is positive.

In the unrestricted case, we can show that k_0^* cannot decrease with V_0^- or r_0, even though we were unable to do so in the general case with additional debt. For this purpose we can show that $W_0\left(V_0^-, r_0, k_0\right) - S_0\left(V_0^-, r_0, k_0\right)$ in equation (5.4) cannot have more than one root in V_0^- and r_0. The derivation of these two proofs in detail is analogous to the corresponding ones in the block case.

By equation (5.6) the *value* of a *convertible bond* equals $\frac{V_0^-}{n+m}$ when a conversion occurs. Thus, $W_0\left(V_0^-, r_0, k_0^*\right)$ is decreasing with r_0 and δ if $r_0 < \underline{r}_0$ and $\delta < \underline{\delta}$ and remains constant, otherwise. Without additional debt, it is not possible that $W_0\left(V_0^-, r_0, k_0^*\right)$ increases with r_0 or δ.

As a consequence, the *value* of a *stock* increases with r_0 and δ if no conversion is optimal. If a conversion occurs, the stock value is $\frac{V_0^-}{n+m}$ as is the value of a convertible bond.

Under monopolistic conversion without additional debt, we find that the optimal *con-*

[10] To verify the fact that $W_0\left(V_0^-, r_0, 0\right)$ decreases with r_0, we can represent $W_0\left(V_0^-, r_0, 0\right)$ by the values of a put option short, a default-free zero bond, and a call option long. Then, the derivative of this portfolio value for r_0 is always negative.

version volume k_0^* is a continuous function of all arguments. Thus, k_0^* cannot jump as is possible with additional debt. The reason for this finding is that the objective function $m \cdot W_0(V_0^-, r_0, k_0)$ has at most one local maximum in k_0 and cannot have a local minimum. Therefore, a conversion volume $0 < k_0 < m$ cannot exist such that $m \cdot W_0(V_0^-, r_0, k_0) = m \cdot W_0(V_0^-, r_0, m)$ holds. This condition is the basis for a jump of k_0^* from $k_0 < m$ to m.

To show that the objective function $m \cdot W_0(V_0^-, r_0, k_0)$ has at most one local maximum, we can argue that the second derivative of $m \cdot W_0(V_0^-, r_0, k_0)$ for k_0 is negative given that $m \cdot \frac{\partial W_0(V_0^-, r_0, k_0)}{\partial k_0} = 0$ is satisfied. Consequently, every local optimum must be a maximum.

To recognize the properties of the asset values, it is useful to note that the objective function $\max m \cdot W_0(V_0^-, r_0, k_0)$ is equivalent to the goal $\min S_0(V_0^-, r_0, k_0)$. This equivalence follows from a sum $m \cdot W_0(V_0^-, r_0, k_0) + n \cdot S_0(V_0^-, r_0, k_0)$ being equal to V_0^- which does not depend on k_0. This objective function reveals that the value of a convertible bond $W_0(V_0^-, r_0, k_0^*)$ before conversion or $W_0^+(V_0^-, r_0, k_0^*)$ after conversion cannot lie below the stock value, as is possible with additional debt. If $W_0(V_0^-, r_0, k_0^*) < S_0(V_0^-, r_0, k_0^*)$ or equivalently $W_0^+(V_0^-, r_0, k_0^*) < S_0(V_0^-, r_0, k_0^*)$ held, then a different strategy such like a complete conversion would result in a higher convertible bond value between $W_0(V_0^-, r_0, k_0^*)$ and $S_0(V_0^-, r_0, k_0^*)$.

The *value* of a *convertible bond* $W_0(V_0^-, r_0, k_0^*)$ before conversion cannot increase with the short rate r_0 or the dividend rate δ, as is possible with additional debt. This property is a result of the objective function $\min S_0(V_0^-, r_0, k_0)$, because the stock value increases with r_0 and δ for all k_0. Since the firm has only stocks and convertible bonds outstanding, a higher stock value implies a lower convertible bond value for a given firm value. In particular, $W_0(V_0^-, r_0, k_0^*)$ is decreasing with r_0 and δ if no complete conversion is optimal or otherwise $W_0(V_0^-, r_0, k_0^*)$ is equal to $\frac{V_0^-}{n+m}$.

The value of a convertible bond immediately after conversion can still differ from the convertible bond value immediately before conversion. Since the optimal conversion volume is continuous in all arguments, $W_0^+(V_0^-, r_0, k_0^*)$ is also a continuous function in all the considered variables.[11]

The *stock value* $S_0(V_0^-, r_0, k_0^*)$ is a continuously increasing function of the firm value. The monotonicity holds, because $S_0(V_0^-, r_0, k_0)$ continuously increases with V_0^- for all k_0. The continuity results from the continuity of $S_0(V_0^-, r_0, k_0)$ in V_0^- and k_0 and of k_0^* in V_0^-. Furthermore, the stock value continuously increases with r_0 and δ. Again, the reason

[11] However, the value of a convertible bond $W_0^+(V_0^-, r_0, k_0^*)$ after conversion can still increase or decrease with δ. An increase of $W_0^+(V_0^-, r_0, k_0^*)$ occurs if the increase of the conversion volume k_0^* caused by a higher dividend rate δ is particularly sharp.

for this property is that $S_0(V_0^-, r_0, k_0)$ increases with r_0 or δ for all k_0. Consequently, $S_0(V_0^-, r_0, k_0^*) = \min S_0(V_0^-, r_0, k_0)$ must also increase as long as k_0^* is below m. For $k_0^* = m$, $S_0(V_0^-, r_0, k_0^*)$ is $\frac{V_0^-}{n+m}$. Unlike in the case with additional debt, $S_0(V_0^-, r_0, k_0^*)$ is a continuous function that cannot decrease with r_0 and δ.

Therefore, the optimal conversion volume and the value of a convertible bond before and after conversion are unique in the stock value as long as the stock value is positive.

The main differences without additional debt compared to the case with additional debt are summarized in the next result.

Result 29 *If the considered firm has no additional debt outstanding, the conversion volume before maturity is increasing in the firm value V_0^- and the short rate r_0 in the block and the unrestricted case. For the block case the optimal conversion volume jumps, but it is a continuous and unique function of V_0^- and r_0 under unrestricted or monopolistic conversion. The values of a convertible bond before conversion cannot increase with the short rate r_0 or the dividend rate δ for all three conversion variants. Accordingly, the stock value cannot decrease with the short rate r_0 or the dividend rate δ in all three conversion cases. Even in the block and the monopolistic case, the stock value is a continuous function in all considered arguments and it is increasing with the firm value. If no default occurs, the value of a convertible bond is uniquely determined by the stock value for all conversion variants. Moreover, the stock value can never lie above the convertible bond value.*

Chapter 6

Comparison of the Results for the three Conversion Variants

According to the findings in the previous chapters, the properties of the optimal conversion volume and the values of a convertible bond and a stock primarily depend on the underlying conversion variant. As a consequence, the magnitude of the conversion volume and the corresponding values can differ substantially if another conversion variant is assumed. In this section, we first *qualitatively* compare the different properties of both the conversion volume and the values of a convertible bond and a stock resulting from the three conversion variants block, unrestricted, and monopolistic conversion. This comparison allows us to identify fundamental differences in the behavior of the conversion volume and the asset values, which arise from the underlying conversion variant. Then, we focus on the magnitude of the conversion volume and the asset values to ascertain whether the conversion volume and the asset values are higher for a particular conversion variant than for another one. As for the previous analysis, we distinguish between the point in time at maturity of the convertible bond and before maturity.

6.1 Analysis at Maturity of the Convertible Bond

The properties of the optimal *conversion volume* at maturity are qualitatively the same for the three conversion variants. In all three cases, the conversion volume increases with V_T^-, r_T, and decreases with FD. However, a difference is that the conversion volume in the block case increases discontinuously as a result of the restricted strategy set, but is continuous in the unrestricted case. The conversion volume in the monopolistic case shows properties of both other variants, i.e. it can change continuously and discontinuously in each parameter.

The properties of the *convertible bond value* for the three conversion variants share the common characteristics that the convertible bond value $W_T(V_T^-, r_T, K_T, k_T^*)$ continuously increases with V_T^-, and r_T, and continuously decreases with FD for every variant if $K_T = 0$. If $0 < K_T \leq m$, the convertible bond value can jump under monopolistic conversion, but it is always continuous under the other two conversion variants.

The *stock value* in the unrestricted case continuously increases with V_T^-, and r_T, and continuously decreases with FD. In the block case, the stock value can drop when V_T^- and r_T rise and FD declines. The stock value under monopolistic conversion can continuously increase or decrease with V_T^-, r_T, and FD and — as does the stock value in the block case — drop when V_T^- and r_T rise and FD declines. Thus, the underlying conversion variant results in fundamentally different properties of the stock value.

The fact that the stock value under block and monopolistic conversion can decline with the firm value, but the conversion volume and the related convertible bond value increase, prevents a unique representation of the conversion volume and the convertible bond value as a function of the stock value. For stock values of a certain interval neither the conversion volume nor the convertible bond value are uniquely determined. On the contrary, the convertible bond value under unrestricted conversion is uniquely given for a positive stock value. The conversion volume in the unrestricted case is unique as long as the stock value does not equal the face value of the convertible bond.

In the next step, we regard the *quantitative* differences between both the conversion volumes and the asset values for the three conversion variants. The *conversion strategy* for every conversion variant is basically characterized by the critical firm values. In the unrestricted case as well as in the monopolistic one, a partial conversion is optimal for firm values V_T^- between $\underline{V}_T(K_T)$ and $\overline{V}_T$, but a complete (no) conversion occurs for higher (lower) firm values. In the block case a conversion is optimal if V_T^- exceeds $\overline{V}_T$.

To compare the values to the corresponding conversion variant, we extend our notation by adding (bc) for block conversion, (uc) for unrestricted conversion, and (mc) for monopolistic conversion to the critical values. We obtain the following relations for the *lower critical firm values*

$$\begin{aligned} \underline{V}_T(bc) = \underline{V}_T(K_T)(uc) &= \underline{V}_T(K_T)(mc), \text{ if } K_T = 0, \\ \underline{V}_T(K_T)(uc) &< \underline{V}_T(K_T)(mc), \text{ if } 0 < K_T < m. \end{aligned} \tag{6.1}$$

The equality of the critical values for $K_T = 0$ is an immediate consequence of the fact that $\underline{V}_T$ is characterized by a stock value given no conversion equal to F for every conversion variant. After a premature conversion, $0 < K_T < m$, the stock value also equals F for $\underline{V}_T(K_T)(uc)$ but is strictly above F at $\underline{V}_T(K_T)(mc)$. Therefore, we can conclude in this case that $\underline{V}_T(K_T)(uc) < \underline{V}_T(K_T)(mc)$ must hold such that a conversion in the unrestricted case can occur and no conversion is optimal in the monopolistic case.

The corresponding relations of the upper *critical firm values* are

$$\overline{V}_T\,(bc) = \overline{V}_T\,(uc) < \overline{V}_T\,(K_T)\,(mc)\,. \tag{6.2}$$

The equality of $\overline{V}_T\,(bc)$ and $\overline{V}_T\,(uc)$ holds because for this critical firm value, the stock value after a complete conversion is equal to F by definition. To verify $\overline{V}_T\,(uc) < \overline{V}_T\,(K_T)\,(mc)$, we note that $k_T = m - K_T$ results in $S_T\left(V_T^-, r_T, K_T, m - K_T\right) = F$ for $V_T^- = \overline{V}_T\,(uc)$ and the objective function of the monopolist would equal $m \cdot S_T\left(V_T^-, r_T, K_T, m - K_T\right) + 0 \cdot F = m \cdot F$. Since every lower conversion volume results in a higher stock value, the objective function is strictly above $m \cdot F$ for every $0 < k_T < m - K_T$. Thus, the monopolist can increase the value of her or his objective function by not converting all convertible bonds even though a complete conversion occurs in the unrestricted case, and therefore the critical level $\overline{V}_T\,(K_T)\,(mc)$ that leads to a complete conversion is higher than $\overline{V}_T\,(uc)$.

These relations immediately imply whether a partial or a complete conversion under a certain conversion variant is also associated with a conversion under another variant. For a firm value V_T^- below $\underline{V}_T\,(bc) = \underline{V}_T\,(0)\,(uc) = \underline{V}_T\,(0)\,(mc)$, no conversion is optimal for any conversion variant. Then, for a higher firm value, a partial conversion in the unrestricted case can occur, although no conversion is optimal in the block and monopolistic case. Conversely, if the monopolist converts at least a certain part of the convertible bond holdings, the conversion volume in the unrestricted case is positive but a conversion does not have to take place in the block case. If a conversion is optimal in the block case, then the conversion volume under unrestricted conversion is positive but it can be positive or equal to zero in the monopolistic case.

To illustrate the case, that the monopolist does not convert, even though a complete block conversion is optimal, we consider a premature conversion volume K_T sufficiently close to m. In this case, the monopolist does not convert for certain firm values slightly above $\overline{V}_T\,(bc)$ to prevent a decrease of the value of her or his substantial stock holdings, which would be caused by a conversion.

As $\overline{V}_T\,(bc) = \overline{V}_T\,(uc)$, a conversion in the block case is optimal if and only if a complete conversion in the unrestricted case takes place. A complete monopolistic conversion is always associated with a complete conversion under the other two variants. This effect is an immediate consequence of $\overline{V}_T\,(bc) = \overline{V}_T\,(uc) < \overline{V}_T\,(K_T)\,(mc)$. The delayed complete conversion in the monopolistic case restricts the wealth transfer to the debt holders in favor of a higher stock value.

Moreover, we find the following relations for the *optimal conversion volume*

$$
\begin{aligned}
k_T^*(bc) &\leq k_T^*(uc) + K_T(uc), \\
k_T^*(uc) &\geq k_T^*(mc) \\
k_T^*(bc) &\lesseqgtr k_T^*(mc).
\end{aligned}
\tag{6.3}
$$

The first inequality, $k_T^*(bc) \leq k_T^*(uc) + K_T(uc)$, follows from the above made considerations that a partial conversion, $0 < k_T^*(uc) < m - K_T(uc)$, under unrestricted conversion implies no conversion in the block case, but $k_T^*(bc) = m$ in the block case is always associated with a complete conversion in the unrestricted case.

The second inequality, $k_T^*(uc) \geq k_T^*(mc)$, is less obvious. To show this relation, we refer to the argument from chapter 4 that a partial monopolistic conversion must result in a convertible bond value $W_T(V_T^-, r_T, K_T, k_T^*)$ and a stock value $S_T(V_T^-, r_T, K_T, k_T^*)$ higher than the redemption value F. Since in the unrestricted case, $W_T(V_T^-, r_T, K_T, k_T^*)$ and $S_T(V_T^-, r_T, K_T, k_T^*)$ equal F if a partial conversion occurs, the stock value in the monopolistic case is higher for those firm values for which a partial conversion is optimal under both conversion variants. Therefore, a higher conversion volume with a higher wealth transfer from stock to debt holders is required in the unrestricted case to obtain a lower stock value than in the monopolistic case.

The indeterminate relation between $k_T^*(bc)$ and $k_T^*(mc)$ is again a consequence of the relation between the critical firm values. If a complete block conversion is optimal, a partial monopolistic conversion might be optimal. Conversely, for firm values below $\overline{V}_T(bc)$, $k_T^*(mc)$ can be positive, but $k_T^*(bc)$ is zero.

We could also regard the critical values of the short rate r_T or the debt face value FD as long as they exist. The corresponding relations result from the following consideration. The higher the critical firm value $\underline{V}_T$ $(\overline{V}_T)$ of a certain conversion variant, the less likely a (complete) conversion. Since a higher r_T and a lower FD (as is a higher firm value) are associated with a higher conversion incentive, we can find the same relations for the critical short rates and the opposite inequalities for the critical debt face values. As a result of these considerations, we do not write these relations explicitly.

For the *values* of a *convertible bond* at maturity, we obtain:

$$
\begin{aligned}
W_T(V_T^-, r_T, 0, k_T^*)(bc) &= W_T(V_T^-, r_T, K_T, k_T^*)(uc) \\
&\leq W_T(V_T^-, r_T, K_T, k_T^*)(mc), \text{ if } K_T = 0, \\
W_T(V_T^-, r_T, 0, k_T^*)(bc) &\leq W_T(V_T^-, r_T, K_T, k_T^*)(uc) \lesseqgtr W_T(V_T^-, r_T, K_T, k_T^*)(mc), \\
W_T(V_T^-, r_T, 0, k_T^*)(bc) &\lesseqgtr W_T(V_T^-, r_T, K_T, k_T^*)(mc), \text{ if } 0 < K_T < m
\end{aligned}
\tag{6.4}
$$

The fact that the convertible bond value $W_T(V_T^-, r_T, 0, k_T^*)(mc)$ under monopolistic conversion for $K_T = 0$ is either as high or even higher as under the other two variants is a consequence of the way $k_T^*(mc)$ is obtained. Since under monopolistic conversion, it is the goal to maximize the value of $W_T\left(V_T^-, r_T, 0, k_T^*\right)$, where the full scope of conversion volumes $k_T^* \in [0; m]$ is available, $W_T\left(V_T^-, r_T, 0, k_T^*\right)(mc)$ is higher whenever the conversion volume $k_T^*(mc)$ differs from $k_T^*(bc)$ or $k_T^*(uc)$. This effect occurs for firm values between $\underline{V}_T(0)(mc)$ and $\overline{V}_T(0)(mc)$. For the other firm values, the block strategy is also optimal under monopolistic conversion and the value of a convertible bond does not depend on the conversion variant.

The corresponding value under block conversion is always the same as under unrestricted conversion for $K_T = 0$, even though the conversion strategy k_T^* can differ at maturity. The reason why $W_T\left(V_T^-, r_T, 0, k_T^*\right)(bc)$ and $W_T\left(V_T^-, r_T, 0, k_T^*\right)(uc)$ coincide is nevertheless that in the case of a partial conversion $k_T^*(uc) < m$, a convertible bond value above its face value cannot occur. As the critical firm value that triggers a complete conversion is the same for both variants, $W_T\left(V_T^-, r_T, 0, k_T^*\right)(bc) = W_T\left(V_T^-, r_T, 0, k_T^*\right)(uc)$ always holds.

If a default occurs, the convertible bond value $W_T\left(V_T^-, r_T, K_T, k_T^*\right)(uc)$ increases with the premature conversion volume K_T. This property is because the prorated bankruptcy payment of a convertible bond $\frac{V_0^-}{m-K_T}$ is higher, the fewer the number of convertible bonds still outstanding at maturity. However, $W_T\left(V_T^-, r_T, K_T, k_T^*\right)(uc)$ does not depend on K_T, if the firm does not default. Therefore, $W_T\left(V_T^-, r_T, K_T, k_T^*\right)(uc)$ can lie above $W_T\left(V_T^-, r_T, 0, k_T^*\right)(bc)$.

For $K_T > 0$, the convertible bond value in the monopolistic case can be higher or lower than for the other two variants. We find the relation $W_T\left(V_T^-, r_T, 0, k_T^*\right)(bc), W_T\left(V_T^-, r_T, K_T, k_T^*\right)(uc) > W_T\left(V_T^-, r_T, K_T, k_T^*\right)(mc)$ if the critical firm value $\underline{V}_T(K_T)(mc)$ is higher than $\overline{V}_T(bc) = \overline{V}_T(uc)$. Then, for firm values slightly above $\overline{V}_T(bc) = \overline{V}_T(uc)$, the convertible bond values for block and unrestricted conversion are above F, where in the monopolistic case it is possible that $k_T^*(mc) = 0$, and therefore, the corresponding convertible bond value $W_T\left(V_T^-, r_T, K_T, k_T^*\right)(mc)$ equals F.

The relations between the *stock values* are characterized as follows:

$$\begin{aligned}
S_T\left(V_T^-, r_T, 0, k_T^*\right)(bc) &\geq S_T\left(V_T^-, r_T, K_T, k_T^*\right)(uc), \text{ if } K_T = 0 \\
S_T\left(V_T^-, r_T, 0, k_T^*\right)(bc) &\lesseqgtr S_T\left(V_T^-, r_T, K_T, k_T^*\right)(uc), \text{ if } K_T > 0 \\
S_T\left(V_T^-, r_T, K_T, k_T^*\right)(uc) &\leq S_T\left(V_T^-, r_T, K_T, k_T^*\right)(mc) \\
S_T\left(V_T^-, r_T, 0, k_T^*\right)(bc) &\lesseqgtr S_T\left(V_T^-, r_T, K_T, k_T^*\right)(mc), \text{ for all } K_T
\end{aligned} \tag{6.5}$$

If $K_T = 0$ for all variants or if K_T is the same under unrestricted and monopolistic conversion, the differences between the corresponding stock values at maturity for the conversion variants can only result from different optimal conversion volumes. In particular, for those firm values for which a partial conversion is optimal, the stock value $S_T\left(V_T^-, r_T, 0, k_T\right)$

decreases with the conversion volume, as a conversion represents a wealth transfer to the debt holders. Therefore, the relations between the stock values are just a reversed representation of those for the optimal conversion volume given in (6.3).

For $K_T > 0$, the stock value in the block case can be higher or lower than in the unrestricted case. For example $S_T\left(V_T^-, r_T, 0, k_T^*\right)(bc)$ can be zero in the case of default, but $S_T\left(V_T^-, r_T, K_T, k_T^*\right)(uc)$ might be positive. A default in the unrestricted case might not occur due to the lower number of outstanding convertible bonds and the lower total redemption value at maturity. The opposite case that $S_T\left(V_T^-, r_T, K_T, k_T^*\right)(uc)$ is lower than $S_T\left(V_T^-, r_T, 0, k_T^*\right)(bc)$ occurs if a partial conversion takes place in the unrestricted case, $S_T\left(V_T^-, r_T, K_T, k_T^*\right)(uc) = F$, and no conversion is optimal in the block case, $S_T\left(V_T^-, r_T, 0, k_T^*\right)(bc) > F$. The same argumentation can be applied to show the relation between block and monopolistic conversion.

These considerations provide us with the following result.

Result 30 *The critical firm values triggering a partial or a complete conversion, the optimal conversion volumes, and the values of both a stock and a convertible bond can differ depending on the assumed conversion variant. A complete conversion in the block case occurs if and only if a complete conversion in the unrestricted case is optimal but does not necessarily lead to a complete monopolistic conversion. Conversely, a complete monopolistic conversion results in a complete conversion under the other two conversion variants. A conversion in the monopolistic case implies a conversion in the unrestricted case but not vice versa. The optimal conversion volume under unrestricted conversion at maturity is higher than for the other two variants. The convertible bond value at maturity is the same for the unrestricted and the block case and is higher in the monopolistic case if* $K_T = 0$ *holds. For* $K_T > 0$*, the convertible bond value in the unrestricted case dominates the convertible bond value in the block case. The value under monopolistic conversion can be higher or lower than under the other two variants. The stock value under unrestricted conversion at maturity is lower than under monopolistic conversion for all* K_T *and under block conversion for* $K_T = 0$*. In the block case, the stock value can be higher or lower than in the monopolistic case for all* K_T *and in the unrestricted case if* $K_T > 0$*.*

6.2 Analysis before Maturity of the Convertible Bond

The *qualitative* properties of the optimal *conversion volume* before maturity have a similar structure for all three conversion variants. k_0^* can increase with the firm value V_0^-, the short rate r_0, the dividend rate δ, and decrease with the debt face value FD. However, we could only provide a proof for the monotonicity of k_0^* in δ and FD in the block and unrestricted case, but not in the monopolistic case or for the other parameters. Moreover, k_0^* under unrestricted conversion is always continuous (for $\delta < 1$), but it can show jumps in the block and monopolistic case.

The *convertible bond value* $W_0\left(V_0^-, r_0, k_0^*\right)$ before conversion is a continuous function that increases with V_0^-, decreases with FD, and that can increase or decrease with r_0 and δ for all three variants. The convertible bond value $W_0^+\left(V_0^-, r_0, k_0^*\right)$ after conversion can differ from the corresponding value before conversion in the monopolistic case. However, under unrestricted and block conversion, the convertible bond value does not exhibit this jump in time. Like $W_0\left(V_0^-, r_0, k_0^*\right)$ does, the value $W_0^+\left(V_0^-, r_0, k_0^*\right)$ in the monopolistic case after conversion can increase with V_0^-, decrease with FD, and is both increasing or decreasing with r_0 and δ. However, we were unable to prove whether $W_0^+\left(V_0^-, r_0, k_0^*\right)$ is necessarily increasing (decreasing) with V_0^- (FD).

The *stock value* in the unrestricted case has the same structural properties as the convertible bond value before conversion. It is a continuous function that increases with V_0^-, decreases with FD, and that can both increase or decrease with r_0 and δ. The differences compared to the block and monopolistic conversion are that the stock value under these two conversion variants can also continuously and discontinuously decrease with V_0^- and increase with FD. Moreover, the stock value can drop in the short rate and the dividend rate for the block and monopolistic conversion.

A unique representation for the optimal conversion volume and the convertible bond value as a function of the stock value exists in the unrestricted case for positive stock values, but not in the block and monopolistic case. This property is analogous to that at maturity of a convertible bond.

After regarding the structural differences between the properties of both the optimal conversion volume and the asset values for the three conversion variants, we next look at the relations between the magnitude of the optimal conversion volumes and the values of a convertible bond and a stock.

To examine whether the conversion volume is higher or lower for a certain conversion variant, we first analyze the relation between the upper *critical firm values* $\overline{V}_0$. Whenever the three critical firm values exist,[1] the following relation holds for these values:[2]

$$\overline{V}_0(bc) \leq \overline{V}_0(uc) \leq \overline{V}_0(mc) \tag{6.6}$$

To show the first inequality, we note that the values of both a non-converted convertible bond $W_0^+(V_0^-, r_0, 0)$ and a stock $S_0(V_0^-, r_0, m)$ after a conversion coincide under the block and unrestricted case. This finding is due to the fact that the related values at maturity also coincide. We regard the conversion conditions that determine these critical values; i.e. $W_0^+(\overline{V}_0(bc), r_0, 0) = S_0(\overline{V}_0(bc), r_0, m)$ in the block case and $W_0^+(\overline{V}_0(uc), r_0, m) = S_0(\overline{V}_0(uc), r_0, m)$ in the unrestricted case. Since the value of a non-converted convertible bond $W_0^+(V_0^-, r_0, k_0)$ strictly increases with k_0, $W_0^+(V_0^-, r_0, 0)(bc) < W_0^+(V_0^-, r_0, m)(uc)$ holds. Consequently, if the conversion condition in the block case $W_0^+(\overline{V}_0(bc), r_0, 0) = S_0(\overline{V}_0(bc), r_0, m)$ is satisfied, the corresponding convertible bond value $W_0^+(\overline{V}_0(bc), r_0, m)(uc)$ is above the stock value $S_0(\overline{V}_0(bc), r_0, m)$. Thus, a higher critical firm value $\overline{V}_0(uc) \geq \overline{V}_0(bc)$ is required to satisfy the condition under unrestricted conversion.

The second inequality is an immediate result of a negative derivative of the objective function $m \cdot \frac{\partial W_0(V_0^-, r_0, k_0)}{\partial k_0}$ at $V_0^- = \overline{V}_0(uc)$ and $k_0 = m$. The derivative $m \cdot \left.\frac{W_0(\overline{V}_0(uc), r_0, k_0)}{\partial k_0}\right|_{k_0=m}$ equals $S_0(\overline{V}_0(uc), r_0, m) - W_0^+(\overline{V}_0(uc), r_0, m)(mc) + m \left.\frac{\partial S_0(\overline{V}_0(uc), r_0, k_0)}{\partial k_0}\right|_{k_0=m}$. The negative sign results from the fact that the first term $S_0(\overline{V}_0(uc), r_0, m) - W_0^+(\overline{V}_0(uc), r_0, m)(mc)$ is zero and $m \left.\frac{\partial S_0(\overline{V}_0(uc), r_0, k_0)}{\partial k_0}\right|_{k_0=m}$ is negative. $S_0(\overline{V}_0(uc), r_0, m) - W_0^+(\overline{V}_0(uc), r_0, m)(mc) = 0$ is valid, because after a complete conversion $k_0 = m$, the values of a stock and a convertible bond under monopolistic conversion are the same as in the unrestricted case. The fact that $\left.\frac{\partial S_0(\overline{V}_0(uc), r_0, k_0)}{\partial k_0}\right|_{k_0=m}$ is negative stems from the well-known wealth transfer from the stockholders to the debt holders caused by a conversion. Since $m \cdot \left.\frac{\partial W_0(\overline{V}_0(uc), r_0, k_0)}{\partial k_0}\right|_{k_0=m}$ is negative, a complete conversion in the unrestricted case at $V_0^- = \overline{V}_0(uc)$ is always associated with a lower

---

1 We can still interpret the relation $a \leq b$, even if one of the two critical firm values does not exist. If a does not exist in contrast to b, then a is infinitely small, i.e. all firm values $V_0^- \geq 0$ are above a and a complete conversion occurs independent of the firm value. The case that b does not exist in contrast to a, cannot occur. The reason is that the existence of one critical firm value implies $\delta > 1$. Thus, b is either finite or "infinitely small". From the argumentations below, we will see that b cannot be infinitely low, because it must exceed a.

2 In an analogous way as at maturity, we can argue that the relations for the corresponding critical values of the short and dividend rates are the same as for the firm values. Accordingly, the relation between the critical debt face values is opposite to that of the critical firm values.

monopolistic conversion and therefore $\overline{V}_0(uc) \leq \overline{V}_0(mc)$ holds.

The corresponding results for the lower *critical firm values*, given that they all exist,[3] read:

$$\underline{V}_0(bc) \leq \underline{V}_0(uc), \qquad (6.7)$$
$$\underline{V}_0(bc) \lesseqgtr \underline{V}_0(mc),$$

In addition, we found for all numerical examples

$$\underline{V}_0(mc) \leq \underline{V}_0(uc)$$

but we were unable to prove this relation.

The first relation in (6.7) is a result of the fact that the stock value $S_0\left(V_0^-, r_0, 0\right)(bc)$ in the case of no conversion in the block case is higher than $S_0\left(V_0^-, r_0, 0\right)(uc)$. This property is due to the fact that the stock value in the block case at maturity dominates that in the unrestricted case. As the convertible bond values $W_0^+\left(V_0^-, r_0, 0\right)(bc)$ and $W_0^+\left(V_0^-, r_0, 0\right)(uc)$ coincide, the conversion condition in the unrestricted case $W_0^+\left(\underline{V}_0(uc), r_0, 0\right) = S_0\left(\underline{V}_0(uc), r_0, 0\right)(uc)$ implies $W_0^+\left(\underline{V}_0(uc), r_0, 0\right) < S_0\left(\underline{V}_0(uc), r_0, 0\right)(bc)$. Consequently, a lower critical value $\underline{V}_0(bc) \leq \underline{V}_0(uc)$ satisfies the condition $W_0^+\left(\underline{V}_0(bc), r_0, 0\right) = S_0\left(\underline{V}_0(bc), r_0, 0\right)(bc)$ in the block case.

Regarding the critical values in the block and monopolistic case, we do not find a unique relation. Exemplary computations verify this assertion. The intuition for the fact that $\underline{V}_0(bc)$ can be higher or lower than $\underline{V}_0(mc)$ is that the stock value $S_0\left(\underline{V}_0(bc), r_0, 0\right)(bc)$ can be higher or lower than $S_0\left(\underline{V}_0(bc), r_0, 0\right)(mc)$ in the monopolistic case. Consequently, the condition $W_0^+\left(\underline{V}_0(bc), r_0, 0\right) = S_0\left(\underline{V}_0(bc), r_0, 0\right)(bc)$ can be associated with a positive difference $W_0^+\left(\underline{V}_0(bc), r_0, 0\right)(mc) - S_0\left(\underline{V}_0(bc), r_0, 0\right)(mc)$ for which no conversion might be optimal in the monopolistic case and with a negative difference $W_0^+\left(\underline{V}_0(bc), r_0, 0\right)(mc) - S_0\left(\underline{V}_0(bc), r_0, 0\right)(mc)$ for which a conversion can occur.

To give an intuition for $\underline{V}_0(mc) \leq \underline{V}_0(uc)$, which we were unable to prove, we argue that the conversion condition in the unrestricted case $W_0^+\left(\underline{V}_0(uc), r_0, 0\right)(uc) = S_0\left(\underline{V}_0(uc), r_0, 0\right)(uc)$ corresponds to a stock value $S_0\left(\underline{V}_0(uc), r_0, 0\right)(mc)$ that is higher

---

[3] Analogously to the upper critical firm values, we can also interpret the relation $a \leq b$, even if one of the two critical firm values does not exist. If a does not exist in contrast to b, then a is infinitely small, i.e. all firm values $V_0^- \geq 0$ are above a. In the opposite case that b does not exist, then b is "infinitely high" such that no conversion occurs for all firm values.

than the value of the convertible bond $W_0^+(\underline{V}_0(uc), r_0, 0)(mc)$.[4] As the stock value is above the convertible bond value, it seems reasonable that for a small conversion volume ε the wealth of the monopolist, $\varepsilon \cdot S_0(V_0^-, r_0, \varepsilon) + (m - \varepsilon) \cdot W_0^+(V_0^-, r_0, \varepsilon)$, results in a higher value, which lies between $m \cdot W_0^+(\underline{V}_0(uc), r_0, 0)(mc)$ and $m \cdot S_0(\underline{V}_0(uc), r_0, 0)(mc)$.[5]

If the critical firm values that trigger a conversion in the block and unrestricted case exist, a further useful relation is as follows:

$$\overline{V}_0(bc) \geq \underline{V}_0(uc) \tag{6.8}$$

If this relation did not hold, a complete conversion in the block case could be associated with no conversion in the unrestricted case. To show relation (6.8), we consider the firm value $\overline{V}_0(bc)$ for which $W_0^+(\overline{V}_0(bc), r_0, 0)(bc) = S_0(\overline{V}_0(bc), r_0, m)$ holds. Hence, $S_0(\overline{V}_0(bc), r_0, m) = \frac{\overline{V}_0(bc) - D_0(\overline{V}_0(bc), r_0, m)}{n+m} < \frac{\overline{V}_0(bc) - D_0(\overline{V}_0(bc), r_0, 0)(uc)}{n+m}$ and $W_0^+(\overline{V}_0(bc), r_0, 0)(uc) = W_0^+(\overline{V}_0(bc), r_0, 0)(bc)$ are valid, because the debt value benefits from a conversion and the convertible bond value is the same for block and unrestricted conversion. As $\frac{\overline{V}_0(bc) - D_0(\overline{V}_0(bc), r_0, 0)(uc)}{n+m}$ always lies between $S_0(\overline{V}_0(bc), r_0, 0)(uc)$ and $W_0^+(\overline{V}_0(bc), r_0, 0)(uc)$,[6] the relation $W_0^+(\overline{V}_0(bc), r_0, 0)(uc)\ (= S_0(\overline{V}_0(bc), r_0, m)) < \frac{V_0^- - D_0(\overline{V}_0(bc), r_0, 0)(uc)}{n+m}$ implies $S_0(\overline{V}_0(bc), r_0, 0)(uc) > W_0^+(\overline{V}_0(bc), r_0, 0)$. Since for $\overline{V}_0(bc)$ the stock value given no conversion is above the corresponding convertible bond value, a conversion is optimal and therefore $\underline{V}_0(uc) \leq \overline{V}_0(bc)$ must hold.

To derive the relations between the conversion volumes for the three conversion variants, we can employ formulae (6.6), (6.7), and (6.8). These representations allow us to conclude that the optimal *conversion volume* for every conversion variant can be higher or lower

---

4 We can show the relation $S_0(\underline{V}_0(uc), r_0, 0)(mc) > W_0^+(\underline{V}_0(uc), r_0, 0)(mc)$ by representing the values of a stock and a convertible bond at maturity by the corresponding values in the unrestricted case plus a non-negative spread. Since this spread for the stock is higher than for the convertible bond, the difference $S_0(\underline{V}_0(uc), r_0, 0)(mc) - W_0^+(\underline{V}_0(uc), r_0, 0)(mc)$ of the asset values before maturity is also non-negative, but $S_0(\underline{V}_0(uc), r_0, 0)(uc) - W_0^+(\underline{V}_0(uc), r_0, 0)(uc)$ equals zero by definition.

5 The complete proof requires that $\frac{\partial W_0^+(\underline{V}_0(uc), r_0, k_0)(mc)}{\partial k_0} > -\frac{S_0(\underline{V}_0(uc), r_0, k_0)(mc) - W_0^+(\underline{V}_0(uc), r_0, k_0)(mc)}{m}$ holds for $k_0 = 0$ which we cannot show.

6 The fact that $\frac{\overline{V}_0(bc) - D_0(\overline{V}_0(bc), r_0, 0)(uc)}{n+m}$ always lies between $W_0^+(\overline{V}_0(bc), r_0, 0)(uc)$ and $S_0(\overline{V}_0(bc), r_0, 0)(uc)$ follows from the analogous representation of $\frac{\overline{V}_0(bc) - D_0(\overline{V}_0(bc), r_0, 0)(uc)}{n+m}$ as $\frac{n}{n+m} S_0(\overline{V}_0(bc), r_0, 0)(uc) + \frac{m}{n+m} W_0^+(\overline{V}_0(bc), r_0, 0)(uc)$. This representation arises from equation (3.8).

than for every other variant, i.e.:

$$\begin{aligned} k_0^*(uc) &\lesseqqgtr k_0^*(bc), \\ k_0^*(bc) &\lesseqqgtr k_0^*(mc), \\ k_0^*(mc) &\lesseqqgtr k_0^*(uc) \end{aligned} \tag{6.9}$$

It follows from (6.6) that a complete conversion under monopolistic conversion implies a complete conversion under unrestricted conversion. Accordingly, $k_0^*(uc) = m$ results in a complete conversion under the block assumption. Therefore, a complete conversion occurs less often in the monopolistic case. On the contrary, the opposite is the case for a partial conversion. A conversion under the block assumption requires a positive conversion volume under unrestricted conversion by equation (6.8). If the hypothesized relation $\underline{V}_0(mc) \leq \underline{V}_0(uc)$ is valid, then a positive conversion volume under unrestricted conversion results in a positive conversion volume under monopolistic conversion. Thus, a conversion in the block case requires a conversion under the other two variants.

Although there is no clear relationship between the optimal conversion volumes for the three conversion variants, we can nevertheless rank the *values* of the *convertible bonds* before conversion as follows:

$$W_0(V_0^-, r_0, k_0^*)(bc) \leq W_0(V_0^-, r_0, k_0^*)(uc) \leq W_0(V_0^-, r_0, k_0^*)(mc) \tag{6.10}$$

The property that the value of a convertible bond is most valuable under monopolistic conversion holds on account of the fact that the monopolist maximizes $W_0(V_0^-, r_0, k_0)(mc)$.[7]

To show the relation between block and unrestricted conversion, we distinguish between three possible cases. In the first case in which the conversion volume is the same for both variants, $W_0(V_0^-, r_0, k_0^*)(bc)$ and $W_0(V_0^-, r_0, k_0^*)(uc)$ obviously coincide. In the second case, in that a sequential conversion occurs under unrestricted conversion and no conversion in the block case, the convertible bond value under unrestricted conversion $W_0(V_0^-, r_0, k_0^*)(uc)$ is higher than $W_0(V_0^-, r_0, 0)(bc)$. This effect occurs because for $k_0 = 0$, the values of $W_0(V_0^-, r_0, 0)(bc)$ and $W_0(V_0^-, r_0, 0)(uc)$ coincide, but $W_0(V_0^-, r_0, k_0^*)(uc) > W_0(V_0^-, r_0, 0)(uc)$ benefits additionally from a higher conversion volume by the note at the beginning of section 5.2. In the third case, a complete conversion occurs in the block case and a sequential conversion in the unrestricted case. Then, $W_0(V_0^-, r_0, k_0^*)(bc)$ equals $\frac{V_0^- - D_0(V_0, r_0, m)}{n+m}$, but $W_0(V_0^-, r_0, k_0^*)(uc)$ is $\frac{V_0^- - D_0(V_0, r_0, k_0^*)(uc)}{n+m}$ according to equation (5.5). Since the debt value in the unrestricted case $D_0(V_0, r_0, k_0^*)(uc)$

[7] In the case that a conversion had taken place before time zero (which is not feasible in our two period model), the value of the convertible bonds might be lower than for the other two variants. We will discuss this point in more detail in chapter 7.

is lower than $D_0(V_0, r_0, m)$ due to the lower conversion volume, $W_0(V_0^-, r_0, k_0^*)(uc)$ is above $W_0(V_0^-, r_0, k_0^*)(bc)$. Other cases than those considered here cannot occur according to equation (6.8).

We recall that the value of a convertible bond $W_0^+(V_0^-, r_0, k_0^*)$ after a sequential conversion in the monopolistic case can deviate from the convertible bond value $W_0(V_0^-, r_0, k_0^*)$ before conversion. Regarding the convertible bond values after a conversion, we find that a relation like (6.10) does not hold for the values after a conversion. For the values after a conversion, given that not all convertible bonds are converted, the corresponding findings are

$$W_0^+(V_0^-, r_0, k_0^*)(bc) \leq W_0^+(V_0^-, r_0, k_0^*)(uc)$$
$$W_0^+(V_0^-, r_0, k_0^*)(uc) \lesseqgtr W_0^+(V_0^-, r_0, k_0^*)(mc).$$

Furthermore, we hypothesize

$$W_0^+(V_0^-, r_0, k_0^*)(bc) \leq W_0^+(V_0^-, r_0, k_0^*)(mc).$$

The value of a non-converted convertible bond $W_0^+(V_0^-, r_0, k_0^*)(bc)$ in the block case only exists when $k_0^*(bc)$ is equal to zero. Therefore, the value of $W_0^+(V_0^-, r_0, 0)(bc)$ is not larger than $W_0^+(V_0^-, r_0, k_0^*)(uc)$ and can also lie below $W_0^+(V_0^-, r_0, k_0^*)(mc)$.

The convertible bond value after a conversion in the unrestricted case can be higher or lower than that in the monopolistic case. For $k_0^* = 0$, the value in the monopolistic case is obviously higher. If the conversion volume $k_0^*(mc)$ under monopolistic conversion is lower than $k_0^*(uc)$, the convertible bond value under monopolistic conversion can be lower. This effect occurs because the values of $W_0^+(V_0^-, r_0, k_0)$ for the two conversion variants do not necessarily deviate severely, but $W_0^+(V_0^-, r_0, k_0^*)(uc)$ benefits from the higher conversion volume.

However, we were unable to rule out that $W_0^+(V_0^-, r_0, k_0^*)(bc)$ lies above $W_0^+(V_0^-, r_0, k_0^*)(mc)$. Of course, as long as no conversion is optimal under both variants, the value under monopolistic conversion is higher by as shown by (6.10). Therefore, a positive conversion in the monopolistic case, $k_0^*(mc) > 0$ and no conversion in the block case, $k_0^*(bc) = 0$, is a necessary condition for $W_0^+(V_0^-, r_0, k_0^*)(bc) > W_0^+(V_0^-, r_0, k_0^*)(mc)$. In all considered examples, however, $W_0^+(V_0^-, r_0, k_0)(mc)$ was either increasing with k_0 such that $W_0^+(V_0^-, r_0, k_0^*)(bc) < W_0^+(V_0^-, r_0, k_0^*)(mc)$ is valid or a complete conversion was optimal in the block case for which $W_0^+(V_0^-, r_0, k_0^*)(bc)$ is not reasonably defined.

For the *stock values*, the relations are indeterministic:

$$\begin{aligned} S_0\left(V_0^-, r_0, k_0^*\right)(uc) &\lesseqgtr S_0\left(V_0^-, r_0, k_0^*\right)(bc), \\ S_0\left(V_0^-, r_0, k_0^*\right)(bc) &\lesseqgtr S_0\left(V_0^-, r_0, k_0^*\right)(mc), \\ S_0\left(V_0^-, r_0, k_0^*\right)(mc) &\lesseqgtr S_0\left(V_0^-, r_0, k_0^*\right)(uc) \end{aligned} \tag{6.11}$$

In the next chapter, several examples will be introduced in which the stock value for every conversion variant is higher or lower than for the other two variants. The intuition for these relations is that the stock value generally suffers from a higher conversion volume. Although the stock values might differ for the three conversion variants given the same conversion volume, the effect from the different strategy can be such strong that the stock value differences for the same exogenous conversion volume can have a minor effect on the stock value differences under the optimal conversion strategies. Thus, if the conversion volume differs considerably for two conversion variants, the stock value is generally lower for the variant associated with the higher conversion volume. As a result of the indeterministic relations for the optimal conversion volumes (6.9), we obtain (6.11). In other words, as the conversion volume for every conversion variant can be considerably higher or lower than that for any different variant, the same indeterministic relations as for the conversion volumes also hold for the stock values.

These considerations give us the next result.

Result 31 *A complete conversion under monopolistic conversion implies a complete conversion under unrestricted conversion, and the complete conversion in the unrestricted case results in a complete conversion in the block case. If a conversion in the block case occurs, a conversion is also optimal under unrestricted conversion. The conversion volume for any conversion variant can be higher or lower than for a different variant. The convertible bond value before maturity in the monopolistic case is higher than under unrestricted conversion, which is again higher than in the block case. However, the convertible bond value in the monopolistic case after conversion can be higher or lower than for the unrestricted conversion. The stock value for a certain conversion variant can be higher or lower than for any other conversion variant.*

6.3 Analysis without additional Debt

Again, we do the same analysis for the much simpler case without additional debt to ascertain the relations that stem exclusively from the existence of additional debt and those that are also valid even in this simple setting.

According to our findings presented in section 4.4, the block strategy at maturity is also an equilibrium strategy for the other two conversion variants, unrestricted and monopolistic conversion. In particular, the conversion volume under a certain conversion variant can only differ from that under another variant if the firm value V_T^- is equal to $(n+m) \cdot F$. As a consequence, we obtain the following relations for the critical firm values

$$\begin{aligned} \underline{V}_T\,(bc) &= \underline{V}_T\,(uc) = \underline{V}_T\,(mc) \\ &= \overline{V}_T\,(bc) = \overline{V}_T\,(uc) = \overline{V}_T\,(mc) \\ &= (n+m) \cdot F. \end{aligned}$$

Therefore, the values of a convertible bond and a stock at maturity do not depend on the assumption about the conversion variant but rather on the number of prematurely converted bonds K_T. In particular, we obtain

$$\begin{aligned} W_T\,(V_T, r_T, 0, k_T^*)\,(bc) &= W_T\,(V_T, r_T, K_T, k_T^*)\,(uc) \\ &= W_T\,(V_T, r_T, K_T, k_T^*)\,(mc)\,, \text{ if } K_T = 0 \\ W_T\,(V_T, r_T, 0, k_T^*)\,(bc) &\leq W_T\,(V_T, r_T, K_T, k_T^*)\,(uc) \\ W_T\,(V_T, r_T, K_T, k_T^*)\,(uc) &= W_T\,(V_T, r_T, K_T, k_T^*)\,(mc)\,, \text{ if } 0 < K_T < m \\ S_T\,(V_T, r_T, 0, k_T^*)\,(bc) &= S_T\,(V_T, r_T, K_T, k_T^*)\,(uc) \\ &= S_T\,(V_T, r_T, K_T, k_T^*)\,(mc)\,, \text{ if } K_T = 0 \\ S_T\,(V_T, r_T, 0, k_T^*)\,(bc) &\leq S_T\,(V_T, r_T, K_T, k_T^*)\,(uc) \\ S_T\,(V_T, r_T, K_T, k_T^*)\,(uc) &= S_T\,(V_T, r_T, 0, k_T^*)\,(mc)\,, \text{ if } 0 < K_T < m. \end{aligned}$$

Clearly, the asset values for all three conversion variants coincide for $K_T = 0$. Accordingly, the values under unrestricted and monopolistic conversion are also the same, even for a positive prior conversion. To visualize the other relations, we consider a positive premature conversion volume $K_T > 0$. If a default occurs in the block case but not in the other two cases, $V_T^- \in ((m - K_T) \cdot F, m \cdot F)$, the value of a convertible bond and a stock in the block case are lower than for the other two variants. Since the convertible bond value benefits from a premature conversion, the opposite effect that the convertible bond value in the monopolistic or unrestricted case is lower than in the block case cannot occur. Accordingly, the stock value benefits if no conversion is optimal but a premature conversion has taken place. The intuition for this property is that the stockholders benefit from a too high conversion volume at the cost of the convertible bond holders. Thus, $S_T\,(V_T, r_T, K_T, k_T^*)$ cannot decrease with K_T in the unrestricted or monopolistic case. If a complete conversion is optimal, $k_T^* = m - K_T$, $S_T\,(V_T, r_T, K_T, k_T^*) = \frac{V_T^-}{n+m}$ is independent of K_T and otherwise, it benefits from a higher K_T.

In contrast to the case with additional debt, we can see that without additional debt it is not possible for the monopolist to follow a superior strategy at maturity. Therefore, higher convertible bond and stock values cannot occur in the monopolistic case. As a consequence, different values of convertible bonds and stocks for these two conversion variants at maturity result from additional debt and the advantage of the monopolist rests on the fact that she or he can exploit the debt holders more severely than the investors in the unrestricted case. In addition, the effects that the stock value in the block case can be highest and that the convertible bond value in the monopolistic case is lowest also requires the existence of additional debt.

At time $t = 0$, we can conclude that the values of a convertible bond $W_0\left(V_0^-, r_0, k_0\right)$ and a stock $S_0\left(V_0^-, r_0, k_0\right)$ under unrestricted conversion coincide with those under monopolistic conversion due to the accordance at maturity. This is also the reason why the value of a convertible bond $W_0\left(V_0^-, r_0, 0\right)$ in the block case equals the values under the other two variants. Furthermore, $S_0\left(V_0^-, r_0, m\right)$ is independent of the conversion variant. As a consequence, the relevant values of a convertible bond and a stock for a given feasible conversion volume are the same for every conversion variant.

Therefore, we obtain the following relation for the lower *critical firm values* in the absence of additional debt, given that these exist:

$$\underline{V}_0\,(bc)\ \left(=\overline{V}_0\,(bc)\right) = \underline{V}_0\,(uc) \geq \underline{V}_0\,(mc)$$

Since without additional debt, the stock value cannot be higher than the convertible bond value as seen in section 5.4, the two critical firm values $\underline{V}_0\,(bc)$ and $\overline{V}_0\,(bc)$ coincide.

The property that $\underline{V}_0\,(uc) = \overline{V}_0\,(bc)$ is a finding by Constantinides (1984) which we briefly outlined in section 2.3. It simply says that the critical firm value for which the convertible bond value hits the conversion value is the same for both variants. As a result, a conversion in the block case occurs if and only if any conversions occur in the unrestricted case. Thus, a partial conversion in the unrestricted case cannot occur, if no conversion is optimal in the block case.

A conversion in the monopolistic case can occur, even though no conversion takes place under the other two variants. This property coincides with that for the case with additional debt. To show that $\underline{V}_0\,(uc) \geq \underline{V}_0\,(mc)$ holds, we determine the derivative of the monopolist's objective function, $m \cdot W_0\left(V_0^-, r_0, k_0\right)$ for $k_0 = 0$, $V_0^- = \underline{V}_0\,(uc)$, and use the equality $W_0\left(\underline{V}_0\,(uc), r_0, 0\right) = S_0\left(\underline{V}_0\,(uc), r_0, 0\right)$. Then, we find that $m \cdot \frac{\partial W_0\left(V_0^-, r_0, k_0\right)}{\partial k_0}$ is strictly positive and that $k_0^*\,(mc)$ must be strictly positive at $\underline{V}_0\,(uc)$. Consequently, $\underline{V}_0\,(mc)$ is lower than $\underline{V}_0\,(uc)$.

The relation between the upper *critical firm values* — in the case they exist — is as follows:

$$\overline{V}_0\,(bc) \leq \overline{V}_0\,(uc) = \overline{V}_0\,(mc)$$

The first inequality indicates that for certain firm values a partial conversion in the unrestricted case occurs, but a complete conversion is optimal in the block case. To show $\overline{V}_0(bc) \leq \overline{V}_0(uc)$ we regard the conversion condition $W_0\left(\overline{V}_0(bc), r_0, 0\right) = S_0\left(\overline{V}_0(bc), r_0, m\right)$ and that $W_0\left(V_0^-, r_0, k_0\right)$ strictly increases with k_0. Therefore, $W_0\left(\overline{V}_0(bc), r_0, m\right) > S_0\left(\overline{V}_0(bc), r_0, m\right)$ holds such that the firm value $\overline{V}_0(bc)$ is not high enough for a complete conversion in the unrestricted case.

The second relation demonstrates that a complete conversion under unrestricted conversion is optimal if and only if a complete conversion occurs under monopolistic conversion. We prove this equality by contradiction. If $\overline{V}_0(uc) < \overline{V}_0(mc)$ held, $k_0^*(mc)$ would be below m for some $V_0^- \geq \overline{V}_0(uc)$. Then, the stock value $S_0\left(V_0^-, r_0, k_0^*\right)$ for this firm value would be higher than the convertible bond value $W_0\left(V_0^-, r_0, k_0^*\right)$. The reason is that $S_0\left(V_0^-, r_0, k_0\right) > W_0\left(V_0^-, r_0, k_0\right)$ for all $k_0 < m$ if a complete conversion is optimal in the unrestricted case. However, according to section 5.4, a stock value above the convertible bond value cannot occur without debt. Supposing the opposite case that $\overline{V}_0(uc) > \overline{V}_0(mc)$ holds for $V_0^- = \overline{V}_0(mc)$, no conversion or a partial conversion $0 < k_0^*(uc) < m$ would occur in the unrestricted case, but $k_0^* = m$ is the optimal strategy in the monopolistic case. These conditions result in convertible bond value in the unrestricted case above the stock value or the convertible bond and stock values equal $\frac{V_0^-}{n+m}$ for both variants. Thus, $k_0^*(uc)$ would either result in a strictly better strategy for the monopolist or it would be as good as the monopolist's strategy. However, this second equally good strategy is a contradiction to the uniqueness of the optimal conversion volume presented in section 5.4.

For the optimal *conversion volumes*, we get the following relations:

$$k_0^*(uc) \leq k_0^*(bc), k_0^*(mc),$$
$$k_0^*(bc) \lesseqgtr k_0^*(mc)$$

The relation $k_0^*(uc) \leq k_0^*(bc)$ and the indeterministic one $k_0^*(bc) \lesseqgtr k_0^*(mc)$ are an immediate consequence of the relations of the critical firm values.

The property $k_0^*(uc) \leq k_0^*(mc)$ results from the fact that an optimal sequential conversion in the monopolistic case results in a stock value $S_0\left(V_0^-, r_0, k_0^*\right)$ which is strictly below the value of a convertible bond $W_0\left(V_0^-, r_0, k_0^*\right)$ and $W_0^+\left(V_0^-, r_0, k_0^*\right)$, but in the unrestricted case the convertible bond and stock value must coincide. Since $W_0\left(V_0^-, r_0, k_0\right)$ increases with k_0, a higher conversion volume is required in the monopolistic case.

The values of a *convertible bond* before conversion are related as follows:

$$W_0\left(V_0^-, r_0, k_0^*\right)(bc) = W_0\left(V_0^-, r_0, k_0^*\right)(uc) \leq W_0\left(V_0^-, r_0, k_0^*\right)(mc)$$

Since the monopolistic conversion strategy is to maximize $m \cdot W_0\left(V_0^-, r_0, k_0\right)$, it is clear that this strategy can result in a higher but not in a lower convertible bond value than under the other conversion variants.

The fact that the convertible bond value in the block case coincides with the corresponding one under unrestricted conversion is a result presented by Constantinides (1984). The idea behind this equality is that the convertible bond values are obviously the same if no conversion occurs. Moreover, the convertible bond values equal $\frac{V_0^-}{n+m}$ if a conversion in the unrestricted or in the block case occurs. Since according to the relation $\overline{V}_0\,(bc) = \underline{V}_0\,(uc)$, a conversion in the block case is optimal if and only if a conversion in the unrestricted case occurs, the convertible bond values $W_0\left(V_0^-, r_0, k_0^*\right)(bc)$ and $W_0\left(V_0^-, r_0, k_0^*\right)(uc)$ are always the same.

Thus, the fact that the convertible bond value in the unrestricted case is higher than that in the block case can only occur with additional debt. By preventing a stock value above the convertible bond value in the unrestricted case, the convertible bond holders in the unrestricted case with additional debt obtain a higher value than the investors in the block case.

We obtain the same relation for the values of a convertible bond after conversion:

$$W_0^+\left(V_0^-, r_0, k_0^*\right)(bc) = W_0^+\left(V_0^-, r_0, k_0^*\right)(uc) \leq W_0^+\left(V_0^-, r_0, k_0^*\right)(mc)$$

If k_0^* equals zero for all conversion variants, the values of $W_0^+\left(V_0^-, r_0, k_0^*\right)$ coincide for all conversion variants, because the value of $W_0^+\left(V_0^-, r_0, k_0\right)$ does not depend on the conversion variant. However, if a partial conversion occurs in the monopolistic case, $W_0^+\left(V_0^-, r_0, k_0^*\right)(mc)$ is strictly larger due to the higher conversion volume in the monopolistic case than under unrestricted conversion.

Thus, without additional debt, the monopolist has no incentive to choose a conversion strategy that results in a lower convertible bond value after conversion in favor of higher stock values.

Without additional debt, the total firm value only consists of convertible bonds and stocks. Therefore, a higher convertible bond value $W_0\left(V_0^-, r_0, k_0^*\right)$ necessarily results in a lower stock value $S_0\left(V_0^-, r_0, k_0^*\right)$ for a fixed firm value V_0^-. As a consequence, the corresponding relations of the stock values are a reversed version of the convertible bond values:

$$S_0\left(V_0^-, r_0, k_0^*\right)(bc) = S_0\left(V_0^-, r_0, k_0^*\right)(uc) \geq S_0\left(V_0^-, r_0, k_0^*\right)(mc)$$

Comparing these findings to those with additional debt, we can summarize the following effects. Without additional debt, the monopolist always selects a non-lower conversion volume than in the unrestricted case. Thus, the only reason why a monopolist might convert a lower volume than the investors in the unrestricted case, is to prevent a wealth transfer to the debt holders. This effect also explains why the block holders do not convert, even though a conversion is optimal under unrestricted conversion. Moreover, we can see that additional debt is required to attain a higher convertible bond value in the unrestricted case than in the block case. Without debt, these values, same as the stock values under block and unrestricted conversion, coincide. In addition, the fact that the convertible bond value $W_0^+ \left(V_0^-, r_0, k_0^*\right)(mc)$ after conversion in the monopolistic case is not lower than under unrestricted conversion can only occur without additional debt. Finally, a monopolist only accepts higher stock values than under block or unrestricted conversion, if the firm has debt outstanding and if this debt value suffers considerably from the higher stock value.

As a result, we obtain:

Result 32 *At maturity, a block conversion is also optimal for the other two conversion variants and the related asset values are the same if no prior conversion takes place. Even if a premature conversion is allowed, the asset values in the unrestricted case are always the same as in the monopolistic case. At a point in time before maturity, the conversion volume under monopolistic conversion is higher than in the unrestricted case. A conversion in the unrestricted case occurs if and only if a block conversion is optimal. The asset values in the block and unrestricted case coincide. The convertible bond values immediately before and after conversion in the monopolistic case are higher than for the other two variants and the corresponding stock values are lower.*

Chapter 7

Optimal Conversion Strategies and Valuation of Convertible Bonds in a Multi Period Framework

The analysis of the previous chapters provided us with the basic properties of the conversion strategy and the asset values at maturity and at the last premature conversion date. In this chapter, we employ the general multi period framework presented in chapter 3 to analyze the properties of the conversion strategy and the values of a convertible bond and a stock for the three conversion variants. This extension will not only allow us to analyze convertible bonds in a *static* way but also *dynamically* in the course of the convertible bond's maturity.

The following analysis consists of three steps. First, we examine in how far the properties of the conversion volume and the asset values, which we have derived for the last premature conversion date, are still valid at an arbitrary premature conversion date. A main difference at an arbitrary conversion date is that we must allow for a positive premature conversion volume $K_t > 0$, where in our two period model K_0 is zero. This effect especially impacts the conversion decision of the monopolist. Second, we regard the relations between the conversion strategies and between the associated asset values for the different conversion variants. This analysis generalizes the analysis in chapter 6, for an arbitrary point in time. In the third step, we present examples for the differences between the conversion strategies and between the asset values of the different conversion variants over time.

Analogous to the properties presented at the beginning of chapter 5, no conversion is optimal at any premature conversion date t if the firm is liquidated $V_t^- \leq m \cdot c$ or the dividend is zero, $\delta = 0$. Thus, consistent with the analysis in the previous chapters, we can focus on the more interesting case that the firm survives and a conversion can possibly occur.

7.1 Optimal Conversion Strategies and Valuation of Convertible Bonds at an Arbitrary Point in Time

In this section, we discuss the main effects that can occur at an arbitrary conversion date and focus on the outcomes that differ from those occurring at the last premature conversion date $t = t_N$.

Block Conversion

The optimal conversion decision in the block case at an arbitrary conversion date results from a comparison of the value of a non-converted convertible bond $W_t^+(V_t^-, r_t, 0, 0)$ with the conversion value $S_t(V_t^-, r_t, 0, m)$. The stock value after conversion equals the value of an European call option and therefore has the same properties as at the last premature conversion date t_N. The behavior of $W_t^+(V_t^-, r_t, 0, 0)$ at an arbitrary conversion date t is such that the properties derived for t_N in chapter 5 also hold at an arbitrary conversion date. These properties are that the optimal conversion volume is increasing in δ and decreasing in FD, because the increase (decrease) of $W_t^+(V_t^-, r_t, 0, 0)$ in δ (FD) is not as strong as the one associated with $S_t(V_t^-, r_t, 0, m)$. The convertible bond value is continuous in all arguments and strictly increasing with the firm value, decreasing with FD, but not monotonous in the short rate and the dividend rate. The stock value is not continuous and not monotonous in all of these considered parameters as is the case at time t_N. All these properties can be shown using a proof by complete induction. The primary challenge of these proofs are the induction steps, which, however, require analogous arguments as used in chapter 5 to show the corresponding properties for time t_N.

To give an example for the proof by complete induction, we show the property that $W_{t_1}(V_{t_1}^-, r_{t_1}, 0, k_{t_1}^*)$ is a continuous and strictly increasing function of $V_{t_1}^-$ for the case with more than one coupon date $N > 1$. The *induction base*, that this statement holds for $t = t_N$, follows from chapter 5. The *induction hypothesis* is that $W_{t_i}(V_{t_i}^-, r_{t_i}, 0, k_{t_i}^*)$ is a continuous and strictly increasing function in $V_{t_i}^-$ for all $i = x, x+1, ..., N$, where x is a fixed natural number. The *induction step* is to show that the induction hypothesis implies this statement for $i = x - 1$. Since $W_{t_i}(V_{t_i}^-, r_{t_i}, 0, k_{t_i}^*)$ is strictly increasing in the firm value for $i = x$, the convertible bond value $W_{t_i}(V_{t_i}^-, r_{t_i}, 0, 0)$, given no conversion for $i = x - 1$, must also be a continuous and strictly increasing function. In addition, the conversion value $S_{t_i}(V_{t_i}^-, r_{t_i}, 0, m)$ for $i = x - 1$ is the value of a call option and therefore also continuous and strictly increasing in the firm value. Since

$W_{t_i}\left(V_{t_i}^-, r_{t_i}, 0, k_{t_i}^*\right) = \max\left(W_{t_i}\left(V_{t_i}^-, r_{t_i}, 0, 0\right), S_{t_i}\left(V_{t_i}^-, r_{t_i}, 0, m\right)\right)$, we see that the convertible bond value, $W_{t_i}\left(V_{t_i}^-, r_{t_i}, 0, k_{t_i}^*\right)$ at $t = t_{x-1}$, is continuous and strictly increasing in $V_{t_{x-1}}^-$. Therefore, this statement holds for all $i = 1, ..., N$.

Unrestricted Conversion

There is a major difference when conducting the analysis at an arbitrary conversion date t rather than at the last premature conversion date t_N as in chapter 5. At an arbitrary point in time we have to account for a premature conversion $K_t > 0$ in the unrestricted case. In the block case, $0 < K_t < m$ cannot occur due to the block condition.

In the unrestricted case, the conversion condition is $S_t\left(V_t^-, r_t, K_t, k_t^*\right) = W_t^+\left(V_t^-, r_t, K_t, k_t^*\right)$ for $k_t^* < m - K_T$. Otherwise, k_t^* is zero if the convertible bond value is always higher than the related stock value or a complete conversion is optimal when the stock value exceeds the convertible bond value. This conversion condition in the unrestricted case indicates that the optimal conversion volume k_t^* is independent of whether K_t stocks are created by conversion or whether $n + K_t$ stocks have been initially outstanding and the prior conversion volume is set to zero. This invariance is due to the fact that the values of $S_t\left(V_t^-, r_t, K_t, k_t\right)$ and $W_t\left(V_t^-, r_t, K_t, k_t\right)$ are the same as those of an identical firm with $m - K_t$ convertible bonds and $n + K_t$ stocks outstanding.

In our numerical computations, the conversion volume in the unrestricted case is always unique and continuously increasing with the firm value. Under this assumption, we can prove by complete induction the primary properties, namely that $W_t^+\left(V_t^-, r_t, K_t, k_t\right)$ increases in V_t^- and k_t, $S_t\left(V_t^-, r_t, K_t, k_t\right)$ increases in V_t^-, and $D_t\left(V_t^-, r_t, K_t, k_t\right)$ increases in k_t, which were used in chapter 5 to derive the results for time t_N. In the case of a positive coupon, $c > 0$, we cannot show these properties without such an assumption.[1] In what follows, we indicate the assumption of a monotonous conversion volume in the unrestricted case by an asterisk.

Under this assumption, the results we obtain at an arbitrary conversion date correspond to those at the last premature conversion date. The conversion volume is increasing in the dividend rate and decreasing in the debt face value, because the convertible bond value $W_t^+\left(V_t^-, r_t, K_t, k_t\right)$ increases less strongly in δ (decreases less strongly in FD) than the stock value $S_t\left(V_t^-, r_t, K_t, k_t\right)$ does. Moreover, the values of a convertible bond and a stock are continuous and increasing in the firm value and decreasing in the debt face value. All these properties can be verified using a proof by complete induction for which an example was presented in the block case.

---

[1] For $c > 0$, we cannot rule out the case that a higher conversion volume k_t at time t, that leads to a higher firm value V_t after coupon payment due to the lower coupon payment, can result in a lower conversion volume k_{t+1} in the future and therefore in a lower current convertible bond value.

The other results found for the unrestricted conversion at time $t = t_N$, i.e. that the values of a convertible bond and a stock are not monotonous in the short rate and the dividend rate, are also valid at an arbitrary conversion date.

Monopolistic Conversion

A possibly premature conversion K_t especially affects the conversion strategy of a monopolist. While under unrestricted conversion the conversion strategy depends on the current number of outstanding stocks $n + K_t$ and convertible bonds $m - K_t$ but not explicitly on K_t, the prior conversion volume K_t is additionally required in the monopolistic case to determine the optimal conversion volume. The reason is that the monopolist's objective function

$$\max_{0 \leq k_t \leq m-K_t} (K_t + k_t) \cdot S_t \left(V_t^-, r_t, K_t, k_t\right) + (m - K_t - k_t) \cdot W_t^+ \left(V_t^-, r_t, K_t, k_t\right)$$

and the maximization of the convertible bond value

$$\max_{0 \leq k_t \leq m-K_t} W_t \left(V_t^-, r_t, K_t, k_t\right)$$

$$= \max_{0 \leq k_t \leq m-K_t} k_t \cdot S_t \left(V_t^-, r_t, K_t, k_t\right) + (m - K_t - k_t) \cdot W_t^+ \left(V_t^-, r_t, K_t, k_t\right)$$

differ, respectively. In the first case the stock component has a stronger effect on the conversion decision than in the second case. If $m - K_t$ is close to one, the monopolist is seen more as a large stockholder who also holds a few convertible bonds, whereas in the second case she or he is a "small" monopolist in convertible bonds. Hence, unlike the case of unrestricted conversion, the knowledge of the number of outstanding convertible bonds $m - K_t$ and stocks $n + K_t$ is not sufficient to determine the optimal conversion policy if K_t is unknown.

In the monopolistic case, the properties of the conversion strategy and the asset values still hold if no prior conversion $K_t = 0$ has taken place. The optimal conversion volume can be but does not need to be continuous in every parameter. The convertible bond value is continuous in every considered parameter and strictly increasing with the firm value, decreasing with FD, but not monotonous in the short rate and the dividend rate. The stock value is not continuous and not monotonous in all of these considered parameters. We can verify these properties for an arbitrary conversion date by complete induction.

In the other case with a prior conversion $K_t > 0$, some differences occur. The reason is that it is no longer the goal of the monopolist to maximize the value of outstanding convertible bonds but instead to maximize the value of his or her portfolio that additionally contains stocks from conversion. As a consequence, we cannot show that the value of a convertible bond $W_t \left(V_t^-, r_t, K_t, k_t^*\right)$ increases with the firm value and decreases with the debt face value. However, the wealth of the monopolist

$K_t \cdot S_t(V_t^-, r_t, K_t, k_t^*) + (m - K_t) \cdot W_t(V_t^-, r_t, K_t, k_t^*)$, consisting of stocks from prior conversion and the outstanding convertible bonds, increases with the firm value and decreases with the debt face value. This property follows from the fact that the monopolist's objective function $K_t \cdot S_t(V_t^-, r_t, K_t, k_t) + (m - K_t) \cdot W_t(V_t^-, r_t, K_t, k_t)$ increases with V_t^- and decreases with FD for all conversion volumes k_t as a result of a proof by complete induction, which is similar to that demonstrated in the block case. This objective function for the optimal conversion strategy k_t^* must then also be increasing in the firm value and decreasing in the debt face value.

If K_t is positive, contrary to the results in chapter 5, the convertible bond value $W_t(V_t^-, r_t, K_t, k_t^*)$ can have jumps in all considered parameters. Strictly speaking, whenever the stock value has a drop, the convertible bond value $W_t(V_t^-, r_t, K_t, k_t^*)$ jumps in the opposite direction. The reason for this finding is that the wealth of the monopolist $K_t \cdot S_t(V_t^-, r_t, K_t, k_t^*) + (m - K_t) \cdot W_t(V_t^-, r_t, K_t, k_t^*)$ is continuous.[2] Therefore, a discontinuity of $S_t(V_t^-, r_t, K_t, k_t^*)$ implies a discontinuity of the convertible bond value $W_t(V_t^-, r_t, K_t, k_t^*)$. Hence, we obtain the following result.

Result 33 *In the block case, the properties of the conversion volume and the asset values correspond to those at the last premature conversion date. In the unrestricted case, we can also obtain the same properties as found for the last premature conversion date if the conversion volume is increasing in the firm value. In the monopolistic case, it is important whether or not a premature conversion K_t has occurred. If $K_t = 0$, the properties of the conversion volume and the asset values are analogous to those at the last premature conversion date. However, for $K_t > 0$, the convertible bond value before conversion exhibits a jump in V_t^-, r_t, δ, and FD, whenever the stock value is discontinuous.*

Analysis without Additional Debt

As in the preceding chapters, we now consider the case without additional debt.

First, we start with the *block conversion*. Although we always see in our examples that the conversion volume in the block case increases in the firm value, we cannot prove this assertion, which holds at time t_N, for an arbitrary conversion date. Nevertheless, we can show that the conversion volume k_t^* in the block case increases with the short rate r_t, because the convertible bond value $W_t^+(V_t^-, r_t, 0, 0)$ is decreasing with r_t and $S_t(V_t^-, r_t, 0, m) = \frac{V_t^-}{n+m}$ does not depend on r_t. Therefore, the critical short rate $\overline{r}_t$ is uniquely given by $W_t^+(V_t^-, r_t, 0, 0) = S_t(V_t^-, r_t, 0, m)$ or it does not exist. The behavior

[2] The continuity of $K_t \cdot S_t(V_t^-, r_t, K_t, k_t^*) + (m - K_t) \cdot W_t(V_t^-, r_t, K_t, k_t^*)$ is a result of the fact that the objective function $K_t \cdot S_t(V_t^-, r_t, K_t, k_t) + (m - K_t) \cdot W_t(V_t^-, r_t, K_t, k_t)$ is continuous in all considered parameters.

of $W_t^+\left(V_t^-, r_t, 0, 0\right)$ in r_t is a result of a complete induction. Like with additional debt, k_t^* increases with the dividend rate δ.

The convertible bond value $W_t\left(V_t^-, r_t, 0, k_t^*\right)$ under block conversion continuously and strictly increases in V_t^- as with additional debt. The same arguments as for time $t = t_N$ reveal that $W_t\left(V_t^-, r_t, 0, k_t^*\right)$ is decreasing with r_t and δ. Since the total convertible bond value can never increase with the firm value more sharply than the firm value itself, an increase of the firm value results in both an increase of the convertible bond and the stock value $S_t\left(V_t^-, r_t, 0, k_t^*\right)$. Due to the continuity of the convertible bond value and the identity

$$V_t^- = m \cdot W_t\left(V_t^-, r_t, 0, k_t^*\right) + n \cdot S_t\left(V_t^-, r_t, 0, k_t^*\right),$$

$S_t\left(V_t^-, r_t, 0, k_t^*\right)$ is also continuous in V_t^-. From this identity it also follows that the stock value is an increasing function of the short rate r_t and the dividend rate δ, as the convertible bond value exhibits the opposite properties.

In the *unrestricted case*, we can show that the same properties exist at an arbitrary conversion date t as in the block case. Since $W_t^+\left(V_t^-, r_t, K_t, k_t\right)$ decreases with r_t and δ but the stock value $S_t\left(V_t^-, r_t, K_t, k_t\right)$ increases with r_t and δ, we see that a conversion becomes more attractive with r_t and δ and therefore k_t^* increases. Analogous to the block case, the convertible bond value $W_t\left(V_t^-, r_t, K_t, k_t^*\right)$ increases with V_t^- and decreases with r_t and δ, where the stock value $S_t\left(V_t^-, r_t, K_t, k_t^*\right)$ increases in V_t^-, r_t, and δ. However, we cannot prove the monotonicity of the conversion volume k_t^* in the firm value V_t^-.

In the *monopolistic case*, a major difference without debt compared to the case with debt is that even in the case of a premature conversion $K_t > 0$, the monopolist does not account for the value of her or his stock holdings, but instead only maximizes the value of outstanding convertible bonds. The reason is that the objective function of the monopolist

$$K_t \cdot S_t\left(V_t^-, r_t, K_t, k_t\right) + (m - K_t) \cdot W_t\left(V_t^-, r_t, K_t, k_t\right)$$

is maximal if $W_t\left(V_t^-, r_t, K_t, k_t\right)$ is maximal and simultaneously $S_t\left(V_t^-, r_t, K_t, k_t\right)$ is minimal. We can see from the identity

$$V_t^- = (m - K_t) \cdot W_t\left(V_t^-, r_t, K_t, k_t^*\right) + (n + K_t) \cdot S_t\left(V_t^-, r_t, K_t, k_t^*\right)$$

that

$$\arg \max_{0 \le k_t \le m - K_t} K_t \cdot S_t\left(V_t^-, r_t, K_t, k_t\right) + (m - K_t) \cdot W_t\left(V_t^-, r_t, K_t, k_t\right)$$

corresponds to

$$\arg \max_{0 \le k_t \le m - K_t} V_t^- - n \cdot S_t\left(V_t^-, r_t, K_t, k_t\right)$$

which is equal to

$$\arg \min_{0 \le k_t \le m - K_t} S_t\left(V_t^-, r_t, K_t, k_t\right).$$

Obviously, we obtain the lowest stock value if the value of an outstanding convertible bond $W_t(V_t^-, r_t, K_t, k_t)$ is maximal. Thus, it is sufficient to focus on $W_t(V_t^-, r_t, K_t, k_t)$ for the optimal conversion decision as k_t^* in the case with additional debt was primarily driven by the goal to attain a rather high stock value at the cost of a low debt value.

At the last premature conversion date, the uniqueness of k_t^* was the only property of the optimal conversion volume that could be shown. However, at an arbitrary conversion date, we cannot prove this uniqueness.

The values $W_t(V_t^-, r_t, K_t, k_t^*)$ and $S_t(V_t^-, r_t, K_t, k_t^*)$ are continuously increasing with V_t^-, because both the convertible bond value before conversion $W_t(V_t^-, r_t, K_t, k_t)$ and the stock value $S_t(V_t^-, r_t, K_t, k_t)$ continuously increase with V_t^- for any k_t and are continuous in k_t. Similarly, as the stock value $S_t(V_t^-, r_t, K_t, k_t)$ is an increasing function of r_t and δ for all k_t, $W_t(V_t^-, r_t, K_t, k_t^*)$ must decrease with r_t and δ, but $S_t(V_t^-, r_t, K_t, k_t^*)$ increases. Moreover, the convertible bond value after conversion $W_t^+(V_t^-, r_t, K_t, k_t^*)$ can still deviate from the value before conversion $W_t(V_t^-, r_t, K_t, k_t^*) = \frac{k_t^*}{m-K_t} \cdot S_t(V_t^-, r_t, K_t, k_t^*) + \frac{m-K_t-k_t^*}{m-K_t} \cdot W_t^+(V_t^-, r_t, K_t, k_t^*)$. This effect happens if the optimal conversion volume is positive and the value of a non-converted convertible bond differs from the stock value. If the optimal conversion volume is continuous in the firm value, the short rate, and the dividend rate, $W_t^+(V_t^-, r_t, K_t, k_t^*)$ is also continuous in these arguments.

As a result, we can write:

Result 34 *In the block and unrestricted case without additional debt, the optimal conversion volume is increasing with the short rate and the dividend rate. The properties of the asset values are the same as at the last conversion date before maturity for all three conversion variants. In particular, the convertible bond value in the monopolistic case is continuous and monotonous in the firm value, the short rate, and the dividend rate, even if a premature conversion $K_t > 0$ has already taken place.*

7.2 Comparison of the Results for the three Conversion Variants at an arbitrary Point in Time

Next, we compare the relations between the optimal conversion strategy and between the values of a convertible bond and a stock for the three conversion variants at an arbitrary conversion date. Several relations and their derivations are analogous to those found at the last premature conversion date.

Critical Firm Values and Conversion Volume

The relations between the upper *critical firm values* that trigger a complete conversion, given their existence, are

$$\overline{V}_t(bc) \leq^* \overline{V}_t(uc) \leq^* \overline{V}_t(K_t)(mc).$$

An asterisk indicates that this particular relation is based on the assumption that the optimal conversion volume is monotonous in the firm value under unrestricted conversion. As at maturity, the critical value $\overline{V}_t(K_t)(mc)$ in the monopolistic case can depend on the prior conversion volume K_t.

The illustration of these two relations is similar to that in section 6.2 for $t = t_N$. For the first relation $\overline{V}_t(bc) \leq^* \overline{V}_t(uc)$, we need the property that $W_t(V_t^-, r_t, K_t, k_t)(uc)$ increases with k_t and K_t which holds under the asterisk assumption. For $V_t^- = \overline{V}_t(bc)$, the stock value $S_t(V_t^-, r_t, 0, m)$ is equal to $W_t(V_t^-, r_t, 0, 0)(bc)$. Due to the fact that $W_t(V_t^-, r_t, K_t, k_t)(uc)$ strictly increases with K_t and k_t and that the value of a convertible bond $W_t(V_t^-, r_t, 0, 0)(bc)$ in the block case cannot be higher than $W_t(V_t^-, r_t, 0, 0)(uc)$ in the unrestricted case, we obtain $W_t(V_t^-, r_t, K_t, m - K_t)(uc) > S_t(V_t^-, r_t, K_t, m - K_t) = S_t(V_t^-, r_t, 0, m)$. Thus, no complete conversion is optimal in the unrestricted case. The reason why $W_t(V_t^-, r_t, 0, 0)(bc)$ lies below $W_t(V_t^-, r_t, 0, 0)(uc)$ will become clear below.

The rationale for the second relation $\overline{V}_t(uc) \leq^* \overline{V}_t(K_t)(mc)$ is, like at time $t = t_N$, that for $V_t^- = \overline{V}_t(uc)$ the monopolist can reduce the wealth transfer in favor of the stock value and obtain a portfolio value higher than $m \cdot S_t(V_t^-, r_t, 0, m)$ by not converting the entire holdings. If no complete conversion was optimal in the unrestricted case but a complete conversion was optimal under monopolistic conversion, the value of the monopolist's objective function

$$K_t \cdot S_t(V_t^-, r_t, K_t, k_t^*)(uc) + (m - K_t) \cdot W_t(V_t^-, r_t, K_t, k_t^*)(uc)$$

following the unrestricted conversion strategies would be higher than the value from a complete conversion

$$m \cdot S_t(V_t^-, r_t, K_t, m - K_t).$$

This property follows from $S_t(V_t^-, r_t, K_t, k_t^*)(uc) = W_t(V_t^-, r_t, K_t, k_t^*)(uc) = \frac{V_t^- - D_t(V_t^-, r_t, K_t, k_t^*)(uc)}{n+m} > S_t(V_t^-, r_t, K_t, m - K_t) = \frac{V_t^- - D_t(V_t^-, r_t, K_t, m - K_t)}{n+m}$. To show this inequality, we can apply the asterisk condition which implies that $D_t(V_t^-, r_t, K_t, k_t)(uc)$ increases with the conversion volume k_t. Therefore, the monopolist would be better off by following a sequential conversion and switching to the unrestricted strategy.

The relations to the lower *critical firm values*, as long as they exist, are indeterministic:

$$\begin{aligned} \underline{V}_t(bc) &\lesseqgtr \underline{V}_t(K_t)(uc), \\ \underline{V}_t(K_t)(mc) &\lesseqgtr \underline{V}_t(K_t)(uc), \\ \underline{V}_t(bc) &\lesseqgtr \underline{V}_t(K_t)(mc). \end{aligned} \tag{7.1}$$

At an arbitrary point in time, $\underline{V}_t(bc)$ is not necessarily below $\underline{V}_t(K_t)(uc)$ as it is the case at time $t = t_N$. This is a result of the fact that the stock value, given no conversion in the block case, can be higher or lower than in the unrestricted case.

If $K_t = 0$ holds, we find in our examples in section 7.3 that $\underline{V}_t(0)(mc)$ is below $\underline{V}_t(0)(uc)$. The intuition is that the non-converted convertible bonds benefit from a conversion and therefore a conversion can occur in the monopolistic case even if the stock value is below the convertible bond value and no conversion is optimal in the unrestricted case. On the contrary, for $K_t > 0$ no conversion can be optimal under monopolistic conversion but in the unrestricted case a conversion is optimal, because the potential loss of the value of the monopolist's stock holdings $K_t \cdot S_t\left(V_t^-, K_t, k_t^*\right)(mc)$ prevents her or him from converting.

Since there is no unique relation between $\underline{V}_t(bc)$ and $\underline{V}_t(mc)$ at time $t = t_N$, there is also no unique relation at an arbitrary conversion date.

As a result, we find under the monotonicity assumption of k_t^* that a complete conversion in the monopolistic case implies a complete unrestricted conversion which again results in a complete block conversion. On the contrary, we cannot conclude that a (partial) conversion under one variant implies a conversion under one of the two other variants. In particular, we cannot show at an arbitrary conversion date that $\underline{V}_t(0)(uc)$ is lower than $\overline{V}_t(bc)$, though due to relation (6.8), this is true at time $t = t_N$. However, if the prior conversion volume K_t is high, $\underline{V}_t(K_t)(uc)$ can obviously be higher than $\overline{V}_t(bc)$ such that no conversions in the unrestricted can be associated with a complete conversion in the block case.

As a result of the relations between the critical firm values, we see that the relations between the optimal *conversion volumes* are indeterministic as was the case at time $t = t_N$, i.e. for every conversion variant the optimal conversion volume can be higher or lower than for a different variant:

$$\begin{aligned} k_t^*(uc) &\lesseqgtr k_t^*(bc), \\ k_t^*(bc) &\lesseqgtr k_t^*(mc), \\ k_t^*(mc) &\lesseqgtr k_t^*(uc) \end{aligned}$$

Convertible Bond Values

For the *convertible bond values*, we find:

$$
\begin{aligned}
W_t\left(V_t^-, r_t, 0, k_t^*\right)(bc) &\leq^* W_t\left(V_t^-, r_t, K_t, k_t^*\right)(uc) \\
W_t\left(V_t^-, r_t, K_t, k_t^*\right)(uc) &\leq W_t\left(V_t^-, r_t, K_t, k_t^*\right)(mc)\,, \text{ for } K_t = 0 \\
W_t\left(V_t^-, r_t, K_t, k_t^*\right)(mc) &\lesseqgtr W_t\left(V_t^-, r_t, 0, k_t^*\right)(bc) \\
W_t\left(V_t^-, r_t, K_t, k_t^*\right)(uc) &\lesseqgtr W_t\left(V_t^-, r_t, K_t, k_t^*\right)(mc)\,, \text{ for } 0 < K_t < m
\end{aligned}
\tag{7.2}
$$

The argumentation for the relation between the block and unrestricted case is similar to section 6.2. The complete proof that requires the assumption of a monotonous k_t^* in the firm value, which is indicated by an asterisk, can be done by complete induction. The idea behind the induction is that if the conversion volume is the same for both variants, the dominance of the convertible bond value in the unrestricted case follows from the assumption of the induction. When a positive conversion volume is optimal in the unrestricted case but not in the block case, $W_t\left(V_t^-, r_t, K_t, k_t^*\right)(uc)$ is higher, because the convertible bond value increases in the conversion volume in the asterisk case. If the conversion volume under block conversion is higher, the convertible bond value $W_t\left(V_t^-, r_t, K_t, k_t^*\right)(uc) = \frac{V_t^- - D_t\left(V_t^-, r_t, K_t, k_t^*\right)(uc)}{n+m} > \frac{V_t^- - D_t\left(V_t^-, r_t, 0, m\right)}{n+m} = S_t\left(V_t^-, r_t, 0, m\right)$ benefits from the lower wealth transfer to the debt holders. This again holds if the asterisk condition is satisfied.

Figure 7.1 shows an example for the difference between the convertible bond values under unrestricted and block conversion over the firm value. For low firm values for which no conversions are optimal the difference is low. Then, it increases with the firm value especially if the conversion volume in the unrestricted case exceeds that under block conversion. In this case, the value in the unrestricted case additionally benefits from the conversion. At the critical firm value $\overline{V}_t(bc)$, the difference attains its maximum because afterwards $W_t\left(V_t^-, r_t, 0, k_t^*\right)(uc)$ approaches $S_t\left(V_t^-, r_t, 0, m\right)$ when the firm value tends to $\overline{V}_t(uc)$. For firm values larger than $\overline{V}_t(uc)$, $W_t\left(V_t^-, r_t, 0, k_t^*\right)(uc)$ equals the conversion value $S_t\left(V_t^-, r_t, 0, m\right)$, which is the same as under block conversion and therefore the difference is zero.

The qualitative difference between the convertible bond value under monopolistic conversion and under block conversion is similar to that between unrestricted and block conversion as a comparison of figures 7.1 and 7.2 shows. However, the absolute differences in figure 7.2 are higher, especially for firm values around the two critical firm values of the unrestricted case.

The value of the convertible bond $W_t\left(V_t^-, r_t, K_t, k_t^*\right)(mc)$ under monopolistic conversion obviously dominates $W_t\left(V_t^-, r_t, K_t, k_t^*\right)(uc)$ as long as no prior conversion has taken place. This dominance is because the monopolist follows the strategy that results in the highest possible value of $W_t\left(V_t^-, r_t, K_t, k_t^*\right)$.

Figure 7.1: Differences between the Convertible Bond Values under Block and Unrestricted Conversion

The diagram shows the difference $W_t\left(V_t^-, r_t, 0, k_t^*\right)(uc) - W_t\left(V_t^-, r_t, 0, k_t^*\right)(bc)$ *as a function of the firm value* V_t^-. *The parameter values are* $n = 100$, $m = 100$, $K_t = 0$, $F = 100$, $FD = 50,000$, $c = 5$, $\delta = 0.03$, $T = 8$, $TD = 9$, $t = t_1 = 0$, $t_i = i - 1$, $N = 8$, $r_0 = 0.05$, $\sigma = 0.5$, $\eta = 0.01097$, $\rho = -0.1$, $\kappa = 0.16643$, $\theta = 0.0639$. *The critical firm values are* $\underline{V}_t^-(uc) = 51,991.1$, $\overline{V}_t(bc) = 83,861.2$, *and* $\overline{V}_t(uc) = 104,968.0$.

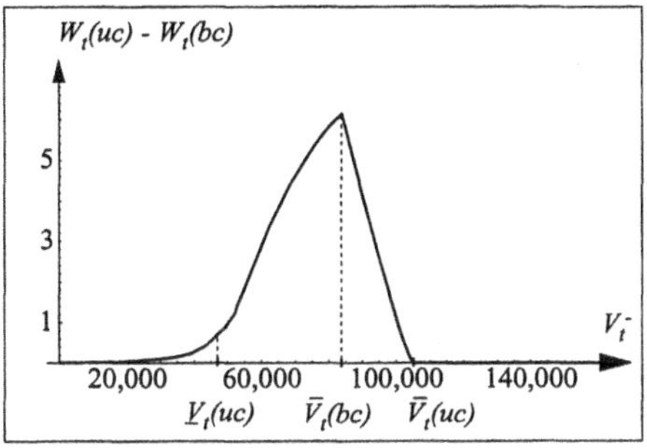

Figure 7.3 shows the difference between the convertible bond values under monopolistic and unrestricted conversion. For low firm values, no conversion occurs in both cases and the difference only slightly increases with the firm value starting at a level of zero. Then, a conversion occurs under monopolistic but not under unrestricted conversion. Therefore, the difference increases very sharply because the convertible bond value in the monopolistic case benefits additionally from the increased conversion volume. When the firm value increases further, a conversion also occurs in the unrestricted case. The difference of the convertible bond values declines as the conversion volumes of the two variants approach each other. In particular, the difference attains a local minimum at a point at which the two conversion volumes are especially close to each other. Then, the difference increases again, as the convertible bond value in the monopolistic case benefits from a lower conversion volume that mitigates the wealth transfer from the stockholders. The second local maximum is reached at $\overline{V}_t(uc)$. For higher firm values, the difference decreases because the conversion strategy of the monopolist tends to complete conversion. When the firm value exceeds $\overline{V}_t(K_t)(mc)$, a complete conversion is optimal in both cases and the difference is zero. Thus, the difference is a non-negative function with two peaks. In general we can see that a higher difference between the optimal conversion volumes under the two conversion variants is related to a higher difference of the corresponding convertible bond values.

Figure 7.2: Differences between the Convertible Bond Values under Block and Monopolistic Conversion

The diagram shows the difference $W_t(V_t^-, r_t, 0, k_t^*)(mc) - W_t(V_t^-, r_t, 0, k_t^*)(bc)$ *as a function of the firm value* V_t^-. *The parameter values are* $n = 100$, $m = 100$, $K_t = 0$, $F = 100$, $FD = 50{,}000$, $c = 5$, $\delta = 0.03$, $T = 8$, $TD = 9$, $t = t_1 = 0$, $t_i = i - 1$, $N = 8$, $r_0 = 0.05$, $\sigma = 0.5$, $\eta = 0.01097$, $\rho = -0.1$, $\kappa = 0.16643$, $\theta = 0.0639$. *The critical firm values are* $\underline{V}_t(mc) = 31{,}947.6$, $\overline{V}_t(bc) = 83{,}861.2$, *and* $\overline{V}_t(mc) = 114{,}572.0$.

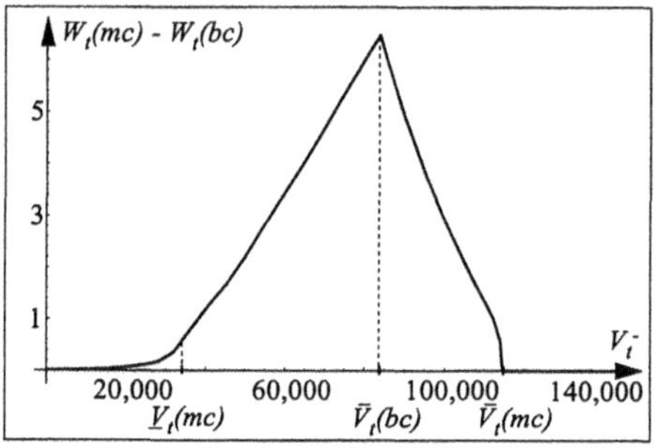

However, a prior conversion $K_t > 0$ can result in a convertible bond value under monopolistic conversion $W_t(V_t^-, r_t, K_t, k_t^*)(mc)$ that is lower than $W_t(V_t^-, r_t, K_t, k_t^*)$ in the block or unrestricted case. This effect can occur when K_t is such high that no conversion occurs in the monopolistic case but a complete conversion occurs under the other two variants. Then, the convertible bond value in the block and unrestricted case benefits from the higher conversion volume relative to $W_t(V_t^-, r_t, K_t, k_t^*)(mc)$. The reason for the monopolist not to convert is that the portfolio value $K_t \cdot S_t(V_t^-, r_t, K_t, k_t^*) + (m - K_t) W_t(V_t^-, r_t, K_t, k_t^*)$ is higher than $m \cdot S_t(V_t^-, r_t, K_t, m - K_t)$, because the stock value is protected against a higher wealth transfer to the debt holders by the monopolist.

Next, we regard the *convertible bond value* $W_t^+(V_t^-, r_t, K_t, k_t^*)$ *after conversion* for those firm values for which it is reasonably defined and obtain the following:

$$W_t^+(V_t^-, r_t, 0, k_t^*)(bc) \leq^* W_t^+(V_t^-, r_t, K_t, k_t^*)(uc), \text{ for all } K_t$$
$$W_t^+(V_t^-, r_t, 0, k_t^*)(bc) \lesseqgtr W_t^+(V_t^-, r_t, K_t, k_t^*)(mc), \text{ for all } K_t$$
$$W_t^+(V_t^-, r_t, K_t, k_t^*)(uc) \lesseqgtr W_t^+(V_t^-, r_t, K_t, k_t^*)(mc), \text{ for all } K_t$$

The values of $W_t^+(V_t^-, r_t, 0, k_t^*)(bc)$ and $W_t^+(V_t^-, r_t, K_t, k_t^*)(uc)$, which are defined for $\min(k_t^*(bc), K_t + k_t^*(uc)) < m$, coincide with the corresponding values, $W_t(V_t^-, r_t, 0, k_t^*)(bc)$ and $W_t(V_t^-, r_t, K_t, k_t^*)(uc)$, before conversion. Thus, like in relation (7.2), the convertible bond value in the unrestricted case dominates that in the block

Figure 7.3: Differences between the Convertible Bond Values under Unrestricted and Monopolistic Conversion

The diagram shows the difference $W_t\left(V_t^-, r_t, 0, k_t^*\right)(mc) - W_t\left(V_t^-, r_t, 0, k_t^*\right)(uc)$ as a function of the firm value V_t^-. The parameter values are $n = 100$, $m = 100$, $K_t = 0$, $F = 100$, $FD = 50{,}000$, $c = 5$, $\delta = 0.03$, $T = 8$, $TD = 9$, $t = t_1 = 0$, $t_i = i - 1$, $N = 8$, $r_0 = 0.05$, $\sigma = 0.5$, $\eta = 0.01097$, $\rho = -0.1$, $\kappa = 0.16643$, $\theta = 0.0639$. The critical firm values are $\underline{V}_t(mc) = 31{,}947.6$, $\underline{V}_t(uc) = 51{,}991.1$, $\overline{V}_t(uc) = 104{,}968.0$, and $\overline{V}_t(mc) = 114{,}572.0$.

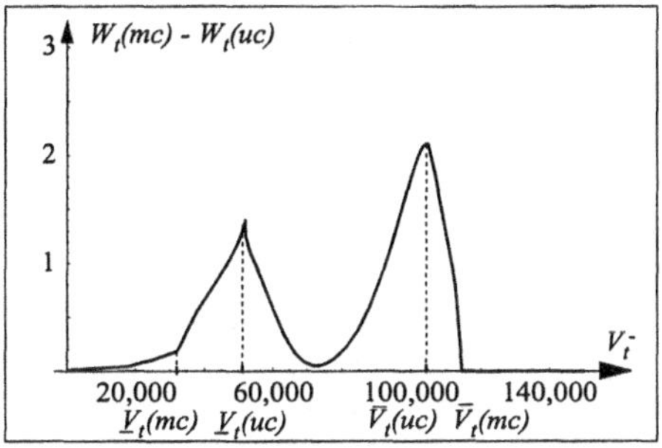

case and the difference is the same as in figure 7.1 for $\min\left(k_t^*(bc), K_t + k_t^*(uc)\right) < m$.

In some but not all cases, the value of a non-converted convertible bond $W_t^+\left(V_t^-, r_t, K_t, k_t^*\right)(mc)$ in the monopolistic case is higher than $W_t^+\left(V_t^-, r_t, 0, k_t^*\right)(bc)$ in the block case. Figure 7.4 shows a typical example in which this difference is positive and increases with the firm value.

The reason for this shape is as follows. For firm values below $\underline{V}_t(K_t)(mc)$, no conversion takes place and the difference is equal to $W_t\left(V_t^-, r_t, 0, k_t^*\right)(mc) - W_t\left(V_t^-, r_t, 0, k_t^*\right)(uc)$. Then, the difference increases strongly because the convertible bond value in the monopolistic case benefits from a higher conversion volume unlike in the block case.

The opposite case that $W_t^+\left(V_t^-, r_t, 0, k_t^*\right)(bc)$ is higher than $W_t^+\left(V_t^-, r_t, K_t, k_t^*\right)(mc)$ occurs if the convertible bond value $W_t\left(V_t^-, r_t, K_t, k_t^*\right)(mc)$ before conversion is lower than $W_t\left(V_t^-, r_t, 0, k_t^*\right)(bc)$ and no conversion is optimal for both variants. Then, the convertible bond values immediately before and after the conversion date coincide and $W_t^+\left(V_t^-, r_t, K_t, k_t^*\right)(mc)$ is lower than $W_t^+\left(V_t^-, r_t, 0, k_t^*\right)(bc)$. A negative difference can occur for all feasible V_t^-, if K_t is sufficiently high that $\underline{V}_t(K_t)(mc) > \overline{V}_t(bc)$ holds. Since $W_t^+\left(V_t^-, r_t, 0, k_t^*\right)(bc)$ is only defined for those V_t^- for which no conversion is optimal under both conversion variants, the convertible bond value under block conversion is higher than under monopolistic conversion as explained above.

Figure 7.4: Differences between the Convertible Bond Values after Conversion under Block and Monopolistic Conversion

The diagram shows the difference $W_t^+ (V_t^-, r_t, 0, k_t^*) (mc) - W_t^+ (V_t^-, r_t, 0, k_t^*) (bc)$ *as a function of the firm value* V_t^-*. The parameter values are* $n = 100$, $m = 100$, $K_t = 0$, $F = 100$, $FD = 50,000$, $c = 5$, $\delta = 0.03$, $T = 8$, $TD = 9$, $t = t_1 = 0$, $t_i = i - 1$, $N = 8$, $r_0 = 0.05$, $\sigma = 0.5$, $\eta = 0.01097$, $\rho = -0.1$, $\kappa = 0.16643$, $\theta = 0.0639$. *The critical firm values are* $\underline{V}_t (mc) = 31,947.6$*, and* $\overline{V}_t (bc) = 83,861.2$.

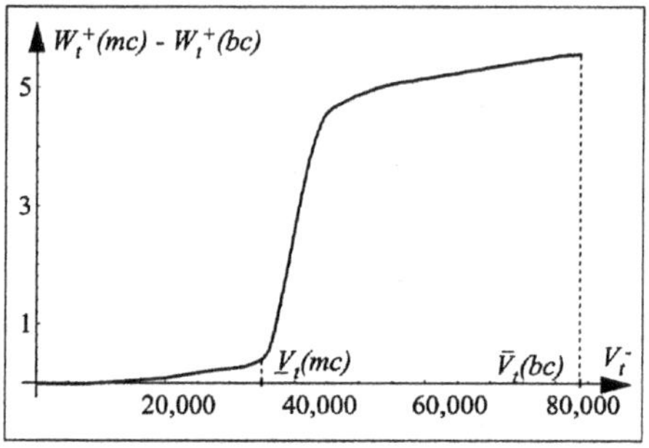

Finally, we compare the convertible bond values after conversion for the unrestricted and monopolistic conversion. The difference between $W_t^+ (V_t^-, r_t, K_t, k_t^*) (mc)$ and $W_t^+ (V_t^-, r_t, K_t, k_t^*) (uc)$ depends on two effects, namely the difference between these two functions for identical parameters and the different conversion strategies followed in the monopolistic and unrestricted case. As a rule of thumb, the differences between the convertible bond values for identical parameters are essentially less important for the difference $W_t^+ (V_t^-, r_t, K_t, k_t^*) (mc) - W_t^+ (V_t^-, r_t, K_t, k_t^*) (uc)$ than the different conversion strategies. Since in many but not all cases, the values of $W_t^+ (V_t^-, r_t, K_t, k_t) (uc)$ and $W_t^+ (V_t^-, r_t, K_t, k_t) (mc)$ benefit from a higher conversion volume, we typically find that the convertible bond value after conversion is higher for that variant under which the conversion volume is higher. Figure 7.5 shows this effect. For low firm values with no conversion under both variants, the convertible bond values after conversion are the same as before conversion and therefore the difference slightly increases with V_t^- as in figure 7.3. When a conversion occurs in the monopolistic case but not in the unrestricted case, the difference exhibits an even greater increase than in figure 7.3, because $W_t^+ (V_t^-, r_t, K_t, k_t^*) (mc) > W_t (V_t^-, r_t, K_t, k_t^*) (mc)$ holds for low conversion volumes. When the firm value increases further, a conversion is optimal under both variants and the difference between the two conversion volumes tends to zero. Thus, the difference $W_t^+ (V_t^-, r_t, K_t, k_t^*) (mc) - W_t^+ (V_t^-, r_t, K_t, k_t^*) (uc)$ also declines. For higher firm values,

Figure 7.5: Differences between the Convertible Bond Values after Conversion under Unrestricted and Monopolistic Conversion

The diagram shows the difference $W_t^+(V_t^-, r_t, 0, k_t^*)(mc) - W_t^+(V_t^-, r_t, 0, k_t^*)(uc)$ as a function of the firm value V_t^-. The parameter values are $n = 100$, $m = 100$, $K_t = 0$, $F = 100$, $FD = 50{,}000$, $c = 5$, $\delta = 0.03$, $T = 8$, $TD = 9$, $t = t_1 = 0$, $t_i = i - 1$, $N = 8$, $r_0 = 0.05$, $\sigma = 0.5$, $\eta = 0.01097$, $\rho = -0.1$, $\kappa = 0.16643$, $\theta = 0.0639$. The critical firm values are $\underline{V}_t(mc) = 31{,}947.6$, $\underline{V}_t(uc) = 51{,}991.1$, and $\overline{V}_t(uc) = 104{,}968.0$.

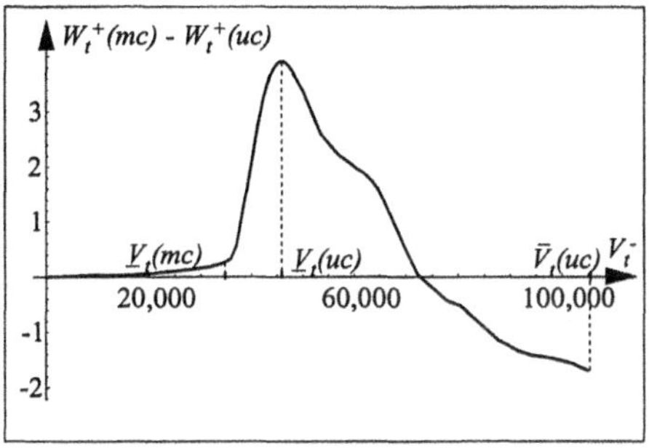

the conversion volume in the unrestricted case is higher and the difference of the two conversion volumes becomes negative. This is the reason why the difference further declines until $V_t^- = \overline{V}_t(uc)$, the critical firm value below which the difference is defined.

Stock Values

The relations between the *stock values* are indeterministic:

$$S_t(V_t^-, r_t, 0, k_t^*)(bc) \lesseqqgtr S_t(V_t^-, r_t, K_t, k_t^*)(uc), \text{ for all } K_t$$
$$S_t(V_t^-, r_t, 0, k_t^*)(bc) \lesseqqgtr S_t(V_t^-, r_t, K_t, k_t^*)(mc), \text{ for all } K_t$$
$$S_t(V_t^-, r_t, K_t, k_t^*)(uc) \lesseqqgtr S_t(V_t^-, r_t, K_t, k_t^*)(mc), \text{ for all } K_t$$

Similarly to the difference $W_t^+(V_t^-, r_t, K_t, k_t^*)(mc) - W_t^+(V_t^-, r_t, K_t, k_t^*)(uc)$, it is primarily the difference between the optimal conversion volumes that drives the difference between the stock values rather than the fact that the stock values differ for identical parameters. We have seen that for firm values close to those for which a conversion occurs, the stock value suffers from a higher conversion volume. Since the conversion volume for every conversion variant can be higher or lower than under a different variant, the relations between the stock values for different conversion variants are indeterministic. Figure 7.6 shows the differences of the stock values between the block and unrestricted case.

Figure 7.6: Differences between the Stock Values under Block and Unrestricted Conversion

The diagram shows the difference $S_t(V_t^-, r_t, 0, k_t^*)(uc) - S_t(V_t^-, r_t, 0, k_t^*)(bc)$ *as a function of the firm value* V_t^-. *The parameter values are* $n = 100$, $m = 100$, $K_t = 0$, $F = 100$, $FD = 50{,}000$, $c = 5$, $\delta = 0.03$, $T = 8$, $TD = 9$, $t = t_1 = 0$, $t_i = i - 1$, $N = 8$, $r_0 = 0.05$, $\sigma = 0.5$, $\eta = 0.01097$, $\rho = -0.1$, $\kappa = 0.16643$, $\theta = 0.0639$. *The critical firm values are* $\underline{V}_t(uc) = 51{,}991.1$, $\overline{V}_t(bc) = 83{,}861.2$, *and* $\overline{V}_t(uc) = 104{,}968.0$.

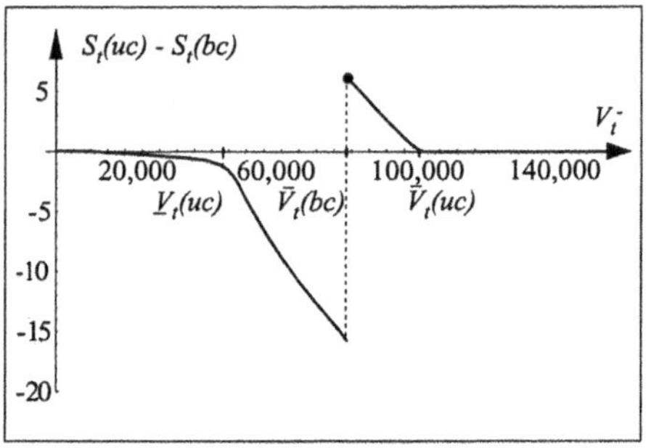

For low firm values, the stock value difference is negative but close to zero. Then, it decreases with the firm value especially when the stock value in the unrestricted case suffers additionally from a conversion. At $V_t^- = \overline{V}_t(bc)$, the stock value in the block case has a drop, but $S_t(V_t^-, r_t, K_t, k_t^*)(uc)$ is continuous. This effect results in the jump of the difference $S_t(V_t^-, r_t, 0, k_t^*)(uc) - S_t(V_t^-, r_t, 0, k_t^*)(bc)$ such that the difference is subsequently positive. Then, for higher firm values the difference $S_t(V_t^-, r_t, 0, k_t^*)(uc) - S_t(V_t^-, r_t, 0, k_t^*)(bc)$ decreases, because the total conversion volume in the unrestricted case tends to m. If it is optimal under both variants to convert the entire holdings, i.e. for $V_t^- > \overline{V}_t(uc)$, a complete conversion is optimal conversion is optimal for both variants and the stock values coincide. We note that for firm values above $\overline{V}_t(bc)$ both $S_t(V_t^-, r_t, 0, k_t^*)(bc)$ and $S_t(V_t^-, r_t, K_t, k_t^*)(uc)$ coincide with the corresponding convertible bond value such that the stock value difference is as high as the convertible bond value difference.

The structure of the stock value differences in the monopolistic and in the block case is the same as that between the block and unrestricted case. This difference is shown in figure 7.7.

We know that in our example the optimal conversion volume in the monopolistic case is higher than in the unrestricted case for low firm values and is lower for high firm values. In line with this property, figure 7.8 shows that the difference $S_t(V_t^-, r_t, K_t, k_t^*)(mc) -$

Figure 7.7: Differences between the Stock Values under Block and Monopolistic Conversion

The diagram shows the difference $S_t(V_t^-, r_t, 0, k_t^*)(mc) - S_t(V_t^-, r_t, 0, k_t^*)(bc)$ *as a function of the firm value* V_t^-. *The parameter values are* $n = 100$, $m = 100$, $K_t = 0$, $F = 100$, $FD = 50,000$, $c = 5$, $\delta = 0.03$, $T = 8$, $TD = 9$, $t = t_1 = 0$, $t_i = i - 1$, $N = 8$, $r_0 = 0.05$, $\sigma = 0.5$, $\eta = 0.01097$, $\rho = -0.1$, $\kappa = 0.16643$, $\theta = 0.0639$. *The critical firm values are* $\underline{V}_t(mc) = 31,947.6$, $\overline{V}_t(bc) = 83,861.2$, *and* $\overline{V}_t(mc) = 114,572.0$.

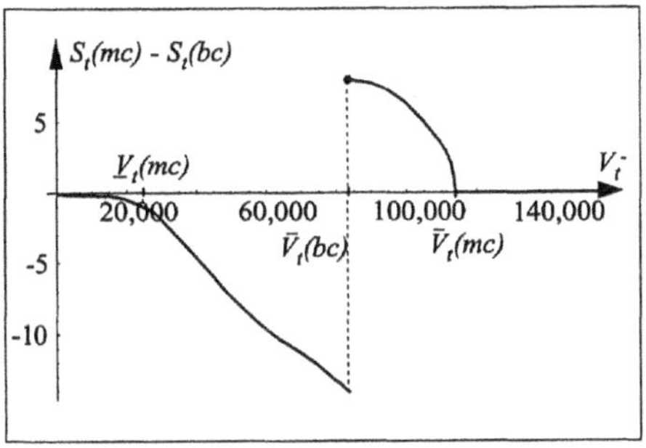

$S_t(V_t^-, r_t, K_t, k_t^*)(uc)$ decreases with V_t^- as long as $k_t^*(mc) > k_t^*(uc) = 0$ and the stock value $S_t(V_t^-, r_t, K_t, k_t^*)(mc)$ suffers from a conversion but $S_t(V_t^-, r_t, K_t, k_t^*)(uc)$ does not. After a local minimum, the difference rises until it reaches a positive local maximum. Then, the difference tends to zero, because for firm values above $\overline{V}_t(0)(mc)$, a complete conversion is optimal for both variants and therefore the stock values coincide.

At this point, we can see that the relations at an arbitrary point in time before conversion, derived under the assumption of a monotonous conversion volume in the firm value, are mostly similar to those at time $t = t_N$. For example, the convertible bond value is highest in the monopolistic case and lowest under block conversion for all firm values, given no prior conversion. In addition, the relations between the optimal conversion volumes and between the stock values are indeterministic as at time $t = t_N$. One major difference to the results at $t = t_N$ is a consequence of a positive prior conversion volume $K_t > 0$. After a high prior conversion volume, the monopolist focuses on her or his large stock holdings and therefore the convertible bond value in the monopolistic case can be lower than for the other two variants.

Next, we again consider the case *without additional debt* and concentrate on a comparison between the block and the unrestricted conversion variants. We know from section 6.3 that at the last premature conversion date t_N the values of a convertible bond and a

Figure 7.8: Differences between the Stock Values under Unrestricted and Monopolistic Conversion

The diagram shows the difference $S_t\left(V_t^-, r_t, 0, k_t^*\right)(mc) - S_t\left(V_t^-, r_t, 0, k_t^*\right)(uc)$ *as a function of the firm value* V_t^-. *The parameter values are* $n = 100$, $m = 100$, $K_t = 0$, $F = 100$, $FD = 50,000$, $c = 5$, $\delta = 0.03$, $T = 8$, $TD = 9$, $t = t_1 = 0$, $t_i = i - 1$, $N = 8$, $r_0 = 0.05$, $\sigma = 0.5$, $\eta = 0.01097$, $\rho = -0.1$, $\kappa = 0.16643$, $\theta = 0.0639$. *The critical firm values are* $\underline{V}_t(mc) = 31,947.6$, $\underline{V}_t(uc) = 51,991.1$, $\overline{V}_t(uc) = 104,968.0$, *and* $\overline{V}_t(mc) = 114,572.0$.

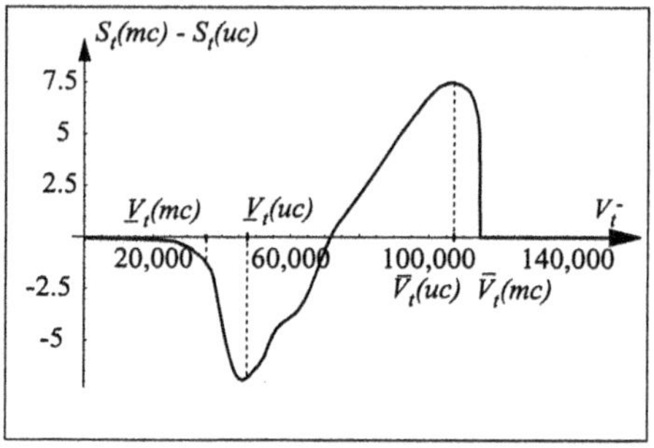

stock do not depend on which of these two conversion variants is used. This result goes back to Constantinides (1984) and holds for every arbitrary conversion date. It states that the asset values in the block and unrestricted case coincide if the firm has no debt outstanding and no prior conversions $K_t = 0$ have taken place. Moreover, a conversion in the block case is optimal if and only if conversions can occur in the unrestricted case, $\underline{V}_t(uc)(0) = \overline{V}(bc)$.

In the case of a prior conversion $K_t > 0$ in the unrestricted case, a conversion in the block case can occur without any conversions in the unrestricted case but not vice versa. If already K_t convertible bonds were converted before time t, a conversion in the unrestricted case only occurs, if the optimal conversion volume in the case with no prior conversion lies above K_t. Therefore, the relation $\underline{V}_t(uc)(K_t) > \overline{V}(bc)$ holds for $K_t > 0$.

Since the convertible bond value in the unrestricted case increases with the conversion volume k_t and K_t, we have $W_t\left(V_t^-, r_t, K_t, k_t^*\right)(uc) \geq W_t\left(V_t^-, r_t, 0, k_t^*\right)(uc) = W_t\left(V_t^-, r_t, 0, k_t^*\right)(bc)$ because without a prior conversion the values in the block and unrestricted case coincide. Conversely, the stock value $S_t\left(V_t^-, r_t, K_t, k_t^*\right)(uc)$ can be higher or lower than $S_t\left(V_t^-, r_t, 0, k_t^*\right)(bc)$. If K_t is positive and both $k_t^*(uc)$ and $k_t^*(bc)$ are zero, the default probability in the unrestricted case is lower than in the block case and $S_t\left(V_t^-, r_t, 0, k_t^*\right)(uc) > S_t\left(V_t^-, r_t, 0, k_t^*\right)(bc)$ can hold. On the contrary, if a conversion occurs in the block case but not in the unrestricted case, $S_t\left(V_t^-, r_t, 0, k_t^*\right)(bc)$ equals $\frac{V_t^-}{n+m}$, where $S_t(V_t^-, r_t, K_t, k_t^*)(uc)$ is below $\frac{V_t^-}{n+m}$ because $W_t(V_t^-, r_t, K_t, k_t^*)(uc)$ is above $\frac{V_t^-}{n+m}$. If we compare the *monopolistic* case with the *unrestricted conversion*, we find that a conversion in the monopolistic case already occurs for lower firm values. However, we can prove this relation only for the last premature conversion date $t = t_N$. Given that the considered critical firm values exist, the critical firm value $\overline{V}_t(mc)$ cannot be lower than $\overline{V}_t(uc)$ as with additional debt, but we cannot show whether $\overline{V}_t(mc)$ and $\overline{V}_t(uc)$ coincide or not even though they coincide for $t = t_N$. We have seen above that the monopolist's goal to maximize $W_t(V_t^-, r_t, K_t, k_t)(mc)$ and equivalently to minimize $S_t(V_t^-, r_t, K_t, k_t)(mc)$ independent of her or his stock holdings. Thus, the convertible bond value $W_t(V_t^-, r_t, K_t, k_t^*)(mc)$ must be higher in the monopolistic case than for the other two variants. This property is a major difference to the case with additional debt when a premature conversion $K_t > 0$ has already occurred.

In the monopolistic case without additional debt, the value of a non-converted convertible bond $W_t^+(V_t^-, r_t, K_t, k_t^*)$ cannot be lower than $W_t(V_t^-, r_t, K_t, k_t^*) = \frac{k_t^*}{m-K_t} \cdot S_t(V_t^-, r_t, K_t, k_t^*) + \frac{m-K_t-k_t^*}{m-K_t} \cdot W_t^+(V_t^-, r_t, K_t, k_t^*)$, the convertible bond value before conversion. This is a result of the fact that the monopolist would never allow for a stock value above the convertible bond value $\left(W_t(V_t^-, r_t, K_t, k_t^*) \geq S_t(V_t^-, r_t, K_t, k_t^*)\right)$, because it is the objective to maximize the convertible bond value. For the other two variants, the convertible bond values before and after conversion coincide. Therefore, the relation that the convertible bond value is highest in the monopolistic case and lowest in the block case also applies to the convertible bond values after conversion for those firm values for which they are defined.

Accordingly, the stock value in the monopolistic case $S_t(V_t^-, r_t, K_t, k_t^*)(mc)$ is lower than in the unrestricted case $S_t(V_t^-, r_t, K_t, k_t^*)(uc)$. However, the premature conversion in the monopolistic case can result in stock values $S_t(V_t^-, K_t, k_t^*)(mc)$ that are higher or lower than in the block case $S_t(V_t^-, r_t, 0, k_t^*)(bc)$. The reason is analogous to the one discussed when comparing the unrestricted and block case. Summing up, we obtain the following result.

Result 35 *Without additional debt, the critical firm values $\underline{V}_t(0)(uc)$ and $\overline{V}_t(bc)$ coincide. If K_t is positive, $\underline{V}_t(K_t)(uc)$ is above $\overline{V}_t(bc)$ as long as these critical values exist. The values of a convertible bond in the monopolistic case, $W_t(V_t^-, r_t, K_t, k_t^*)$ and $W_t^+(V_t^-, r_t, K_t, k_t^*)$, dominate those in the unrestricted case which are again above those in the block case. If $K_t = 0$, the values of a convertible bond in the block and unrestricted case coincide. The stock value in the unrestricted case is at least as high as in the monopolistic case for all K_t and it equals the stock value in the block case for $K_t = 0$. The stock value in the block case can be higher or lower than for the other two variants after* *a prior conversion* $K_t > 0$.

7.3 Relations between the Conversion Strategies and between the Asset Values over Time

According to the previous section, the optimal conversion strategies and the related values of a convertible bond and a stock can differ depending on the conversion variant. In this section, we analyze these differences by regarding a typical example. We conduct this analysis as follows.

First, we focus on the differences between the optimal conversion strategies. We derive these differences from the critical firm values $\underline{V}_t\,(uc)\,(0)$, $\underline{V}_t\,(mc)\,(0)$, $\overline{V}_t\,(bc)$, $\overline{V}_t\,(uc)$, and $\overline{V}_t\,(mc)$ that trigger a sequential and a complete conversion, respectively.[3] These parameters indicate two points. We can see for which firm values no conversion, a sequential conversion, and a complete conversion occurs. As a rule of thumb, the higher the critical firm values, the lower the optimal conversion volume for a fixed firm value.

Second, we consider — for a typical example — the difference between the convertible bond values before conversion. The difference between the unrestricted and the block case shown in figure 7.1 is especially characterized by the peak at a firm value equal to $\overline{V}_t\,(bc)$. Analogously, the difference of the convertible bond values in the monopolistic and the block case is also maximal at $\overline{V}_t\,(bc)$. Therefore, we regard the two differences

$$\max W_t\,(uc - bc) := W_t\left(\overline{V}_t\,(bc)\,, r_t, 0, k_t^*\right)(uc) - W_t\left(\overline{V}_t\,(bc)\,, r_t, 0, k_t^*\right)(bc)$$

and

$$\max W_t\,(mc - bc) := W_t\left(\overline{V}_t\,(bc)\,, r_t, 0, k_t^*\right)(mc) - W_t\left(\overline{V}_t\,(bc)\,, r_t, 0, k_t^*\right)(bc)\,,$$

for this particular critical firm value. Since the difference of $W_t\,(V_t, r_t, 0, k_t^*)\,(mc) - W_t\,(V_t, r_t, 0, k_t^*)\,(uc)$ between the monopolistic and the unrestricted case exhibits two peaks, we consider both of them. We will denote these two local maxima by $\max^{(1)} W_t\,(mc - uc)$ and $\max^{(2)} W_t\,(mc - uc)$.

The last step is the examination of the stock value differences. According to figures 7.6 and 7.7, the absolute differences between the stock value in the block case and one of the other two variants are maximal for a firm value of $\overline{V}_t\,(bc)$. Since the stock value in the

[3] The reason why we consider the case $K_t = 0$ is that this case allows for the best comparability. This is because under every conversion variant, the firm has the same number of convertible bonds and stocks outstanding.

block case has a drop at this particular firm value, but the stock values of the other two variants are continuous, we look at both differences, i.e. the difference between the stock value in the block and unrestricted case immediately before the drop

$$\min S_t (uc - bc) := \lim_{\substack{V_t^- \to \overline{V}_t(bc) \\ V_t^- < \overline{V}_t(bc)}} \left[S_t \left(V_t^-, r_t, 0, k_t^* \right) (uc) - S_t \left(V_t^-, r_t, 0, k_t^* \right) (bc) \right]$$

and immediately after the drop

$$\max S_t (uc - bc) := \lim_{\substack{V_t^- \to \overline{V}_t(bc) \\ V_t^- \geq \overline{V}_t(bc)}} \left[S_t \left(V_t^-, r_t, 0, k_t^* \right) (uc) - S_t \left(V_t^-, r_t, 0, k_t^* \right) (bc) \right].$$

Analogously, the relevant stock value differences between the monopolistic and the block case are given by

$$\min S_t (mc - bc) := \lim_{\substack{V_t^- \to \overline{V}_t(bc) \\ V_t^- < \overline{V}_t(bc)}} \left[S_t \left(V_t^-, r_t, 0, k_t^* \right) (mc) - S_t \left(V_t^-, r_t, 0, k_t^* \right) (bc) \right]$$

and

$$\max S_t (mc - bc) := \lim_{\substack{V_t^- \to \overline{V}_t(bc) \\ V_t^- \geq \overline{V}_t(bc)}} \left[S_t \left(V_t^-, r_t, 0, k_t^* \right) (mc) - S_t \left(V_t^-, r_t, 0, k_t^* \right) (bc) \right].$$

The difference between the monopolistic and the unrestricted case, as shown in figure 7.8, is essentially characterized by a local maximum and minimum in V_t^- which we denote by $\max S_t (mc - uc)$ and $\min S_t (mc - uc)$, respectively. We will report these relevant differences in absolute terms and in percent.

Figure 7.9 shows the evolution of the *critical firm values* $\underline{V}_t (uc) (0)$, $\underline{V}_t (mc) (0)$, $\overline{V}_t (bc), \overline{V}_t (uc)$, and $\overline{V}_t (0) (mc)$ over time. As shown above for all cases with a monotonous conversion volume in the firm value such as in this example, the critical upper firm values in the monopolistic case $\overline{V}_t (0) (mc)$ are always above $\overline{V}_t (uc)$ which are themselves higher than $\overline{V}_t (bc)$. Moreover, we find in our example that $\underline{V}_t (mc) (0)$ is always below $\underline{V}_t (uc) (0)$ and $\underline{V}_t (uc) (0)$ is always below $\overline{V}_t (bc)$. Thus, we can see that the intuition we gave for the relation $\underline{V}_t (mc) (0) \leq \underline{V}_t (uc) (0)$ at $t = t_N$ in section 6.2 — the convertible bonds are converted earlier in the monopolistic case as the convertible bond value benefits from a higher conversion volume — is supported for arbitrary conversion dates in this example. Furthermore, the inequality $\underline{V}_t (uc) (0) < \overline{V}_t (bc)$ that we have proven for $t = t_N$ is always satisfied in this example.

Thus, the firm value range with a sequential monopolistic conversion is broadest and it includes the firm value interval in which a sequential unrestricted conversion is optimal. Moreover, a block conversion occurs for a firm value for which a sequential but no complete conversion under the other two variants occurs.

Figure 7.9: Critical Firm Values over Time to Maturity

The diagram shows the critical firm values $\underline{V}_t(0)(uc)$, $\underline{V}_t(0)(mc)$, $\overline{V}_t(bc)$, $\overline{V}_t(uc)$, $\overline{V}_t(0)(mc)$ *of the three conversion variants as a function of time to maturity* $T-t$. *The parameter values are* $n = 100$, $m = 100$, $K_t = 0$, $F = 100$, $FD = 50{,}000$, $c = 5$, $\delta = 0.03$, $T = t_{N+1} = N$, $TD = N+1$, $t = t_1 = 0$, $t_i = i-1$, $r_0 = 0.05$, $\sigma = 0.5$, $\eta = 0.01097$, $\rho = -0.1$, $\kappa = 0.16643$, $\theta = 0.0639$.

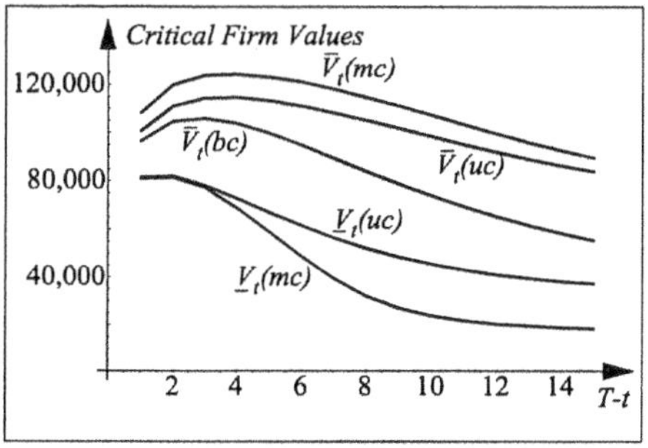

In this example, these five critical firm values all first increase with time to maturity $T-t$ and then decrease. We can explain this shape as follows. We have seen in chapters 4 and 5 that the conversion volume is high if the difference between the convertible bond value and the stock value is low and vice versa. This is due to the fact that a relatively high stock value $S_t\left(V_t^-, r_t, 0, k_t\right)$ documents a high incentive for conversion. Thus, we can use the time behavior of the difference $W_t^+\left(V_t^-, r_t, 0, k_t\right) - S_t\left(V_t^-, r_t, 0, k_t\right)$ to explain the shape of the critical firm values, because the higher the conversion incentive at a certain point in time, the lower the critical firm values.

The magnitude of this difference primarily consists of the value of the downside protection a convertible bond provides over a stock. By the value of the downside protection, we mean the current value of the difference between a convertible bond and a stock at maturity.[4] This value of the downside protection depends on both the value that the difference attains at maturity and its risk-neutral probability. Starting with a firm value V_t^- at time T above $\overline{V}_T$ for which this difference is zero, the risk-neutral probability for a positive difference at T increases when time to maturity $T-t$ rises. Therefore, the value of the downside protection also increases for a low time to maturity which can result in an increasing difference of $W_t^+\left(V_t^-, r_t, K_t, k_t\right) - S_t\left(V_t^-, r_t, K_t, k_t\right)$ for a higher time to maturity. This

[4] The idea behind this difference is analogous to the view we have taken in chapter 5 by defining dif_T for the block and unrestricted case.

effect illustrates why the conversion incentive first decreases and analogously the critical firm values increase.

The opposite effect that the critical firm values decrease for high maturities can be explained as follows. The amount by which the convertible bond value can exceed the stock value at maturity is not higher than its redemption value F. Therefore, the current value of the downside protection is at most as high as the value of the zero bond $F \cdot B_t(T)$. Since this value approaches zero as the time to maturity increases, the difference between $W_t^+\left(V_t^-, r_t, 0, k_t\right)$ and $S_t\left(V_t^-, r_t, 0, k_t\right)$ also decreases. As a consequence of this decrease, the critical firm values must decrease with time to maturity $T-t$, because the conversion incentive is high for a longer time to maturity.

This is a simple intuition to explain the behavior of the critical firm values in the example in figure 7.9. Strictly speaking, the current value of the difference by which a convertible bond at maturity exceeds the value of a stock is only one but an especially relevant component in the value of $W_t^+\left(V_t^-, r_t, K_t, k_t\right) - S_t\left(V_t^-, r_t, K_t, k_t\right)$.

Moreover, it is interesting to regard the differences between the critical firm values, because they do not remain constant over time. Since for an infinite time to maturity the debt value diminishes, the critical firm values converge to their corresponding values in the case without additional debt. According to our considerations in chapter 6 and in section 7.2, the critical firm value $\overline{V}_t(bc)$ equals $\overline{V}_t(uc)$ for $t = T$ and equals $\underline{V}_t(uc)(0)$ without additional debt. Therefore, $\overline{V}_t(bc)$ moves from $\overline{V}_t(uc)$ towards $\underline{V}_t(uc)(0)$ when time to maturity $T-t$ rises. Furthermore, in the example of figure 7.9, the distance between the two lower critical firm values $\underline{V}_t(0)(mc)$ and $\underline{V}_t(0)(uc)$ increases with time to maturity. This effect is consistent with the relation that $\underline{V}_t(0)(mc)$ is below $\underline{V}_t(0)(uc)$ without additional debt (at least at the last premature conversion date), but they coincide at maturity.

The critical lower firm values have a strictly positive limit for $T-t \to \infty$, because a positive coupon payment is made. No conversion is always optimal if the firm value does not exceed the promised coupon payment. Otherwise, for $c=0$, a complete conversion is always optimal if time to maturity is infinitely high and the dividend rate is positive. This assertion is due to the fact that a convertible bond does not provide its holder with any advantages compared to a stock but a conversion entitles its holder to receive dividends. Therefore, a complete conversion is required to participate in the dividend payment.

The difference $\max W_t(uc - bc)$ between the convertible bond value before conversion in the unrestricted and the block case is shown in figure 7.10. It increases first with time to maturity $T-t$, then it declines towards zero, but it is always positive as shown in section 7.2 under the assumption of a monotonous conversion volume in the firm value.

Figure 7.10: Differences between the Convertible Bond Values under Block and Unrestricted Conversion over Time to Maturity

The left diagram shows $\max W_t\,(uc - bc)$ *as a function of time to maturity* $T - t$. *The right diagram is the corresponding diagram of* $\max W_t\,(uc - bc)$ *as a percentage of the convertible bond value* $W_t\left(V_t^-, r_t, 0, k_t^*\right)(bc)$ *under the block conversion. The parameter values are* $n = 100$, $m = 100$, $K_t = 0$, $F = 100$, $FD = 50{,}000$, $c = 5$, $\delta = 0.03$, $T = t_{N+1} = N$, $TD = N + 1$, $t = t_1 = 0$, $t_i = i - 1$, $r_0 = 0.05$, $\sigma = 0.5$, $\eta = 0.01097$, $\rho = -0.1$, $\kappa = 0.16643$, $\theta = 0.0639$.

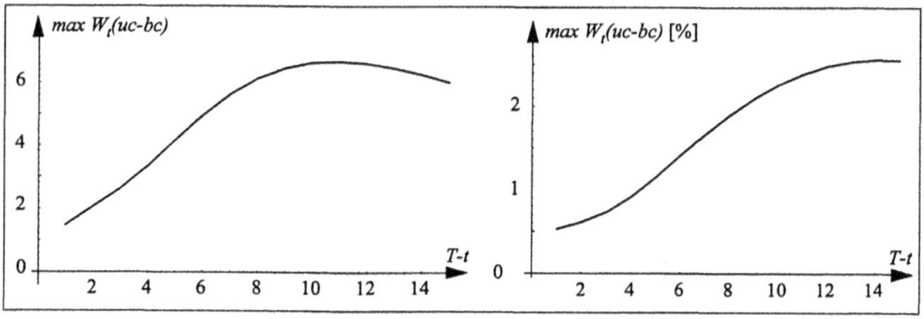

For maturities from one to 15 years, $\max W_t\,(uc - bc)$ varies between 1.8 Euros per 100 Euro redemption value and a maximum of 6.7 Euros or 2.5% at a maturity $T - t$ of eleven years.

The fact that $\max W_t\,(uc - bc)$ increases first can be illustrated as follows. According to our intuition, the greater the deviation of the optimal conversion volumes in the block and the unrestricted case at $\overline{V}_t\,(bc)$, the higher $\max W_t\,(uc - bc)$. Since in the block case $k_t^* = 0$ for firm values below $\overline{V}_t\,(bc)$ and $k_t^* = m$ for $V_t^- \geq \overline{V}_t\,(bc)$, the difference between the optimal conversion strategies in the block and unrestricted case is especially strong if $k_t^*\,(uc)$ is not close to zero or m for $V_t^- = \overline{V}_t\,(bc)$. Therefore, $\max W_t\,(uc - bc)$ is especially high if $\overline{V}_t\,(bc)$ is not close to $\underline{V}_t\,(0)\,(uc)$ and $\overline{V}_t\,(uc)$. Since $\overline{V}_t\,(bc)$ is close to $\overline{V}_t\,(uc)$ for low maturities, but the distance increases with $T - t$, the difference $\max W_t\,(uc - bc)$ rises first.

The difference $\max W_t\,(uc - bc)$ declines for two reasons. The first reason is that $\overline{V}_t\,(bc)$ approaches $\underline{V}_t\,(0)\,(uc)$. Therefore, the optimal conversion volume in the unrestricted case at $\overline{V}_t\,(bc)$ is close to zero like in the block case. The second reason is that the influence of the additional debt decreases and $\max W_t\,(uc - bc)$ approaches zero according to section 7.2. Although the difference in percent is increasing with time to maturity in figure 7.10, it must also decrease for a sufficiently high time to maturity, like the absolute difference.

Figure 7.11: Differences between the Convertible Bond Values under Block and Monopolistic Conversion over Time to Maturity

The left diagram shows $\max W_t\,(mc - bc)$ *as a function of time to maturity* $T-t$. *The right diagram is the corresponding diagram of* $\max W_t\,(mc - bc)$ *as a percentage of the convertible bond value* $W_t\,(V_t^-, r_t, 0, k_t^*)\,(bc)$ *under the block conversion. The parameter values are* $n = 100$, $m = 100$, $K_t = 0$, $F = 100$, $FD = 50{,}000$, $c = 5$, $\delta = 0.03$, $T = t_{N+1} = N$, $TD = N+1$, $t = t_1 = 0$, $t_i = i-1$, $r_0 = 0.05$, $\sigma = 0.5$, $\eta = 0.01097$, $\rho = -0.1$, $\kappa = 0.16643$, $\theta = 0.0639$.

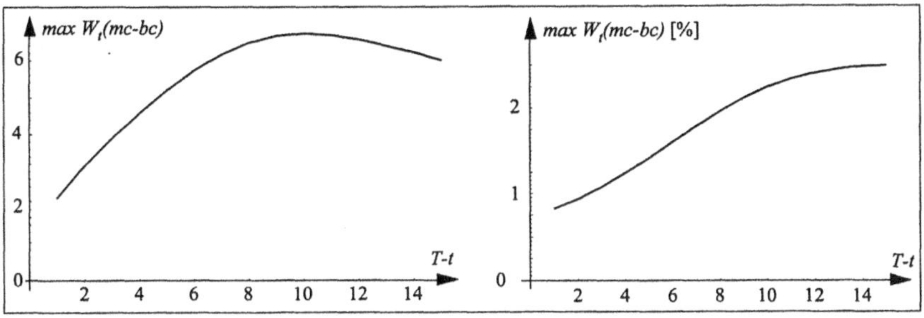

The value of $\max W_t\,(mc - bc)$ essentially behaves like $\max W_t\,(uc - bc)$. We can see in figure 7.11 that $\max W_t\,(mc - bc)$ attains very similar values. The reason is that for firm values at $\overline{V}_t\,(bc)$ the strategies in the monopolistic and the unrestricted case do not differ much for these maturities and therefore the convertible bond values are almost the same. A difference of $\max W_t\,(mc - bc)$ compared to $\max W_t\,(uc - bc)$ is that $\max W_t\,(mc - bc)$ does not necessarily converge to zero when $T - t$ tends to infinity but rather to a strictly positive limit. In those cases in which the strategy in the monopolistic case is different from the strategy in the unrestricted case, the convertible bond value in the monopolistic case must be higher. In the special case $c = 0$, all critical firm values $\overline{V}_t\,(bc)$, $\underline{V}_t\,(0)\,(mc)$, and $\overline{V}_t\,(mc)$ tend to zero for $T - t \to \infty$, and the difference $\max W_t\,(mc - bc)$ approaches zero.

The difference between the convertible bond values in the monopolistic and unrestricted case in our example can be characterized by two maxima. The maximum $\max^{(2)} W_t\,(mc - uc)$ that occurs at the higher firm value is a result of the fact that the monopolist selects a lower conversion volume than in the unrestricted case to protect the stock value at the cost of the debt value. This difference $\max^{(2)} W_t\,(mc - uc)$ qualitatively behaves like $\max W_t\,(uc - bc)$, as both differences have in common that they are primarily caused by the existence of additional debt. However, the magnitude of this difference is less strong than that of $\max W_t\,(uc - bc)$. The difference of $\max^{(2)} W_t\,(mc - uc)$

lies below one percent and attains its maximum of 2.5 Euros or 0.6% at $T-t=8$. The increase of $\max^{(2)} W_t\,(mc-uc)$ for low maturities is a result of different conversion strategies in the monopolistic and unrestricted case. Then, the debt value tends to zero and $\max^{(2)} W_t\,(mc-uc)$, whose size primarily depends on the existence of additional debt, diminishes for high maturities.

Figure 7.12: Differences between the Convertible Bond Values under Unrestricted and Monopolistic Conversion over Time to Maturity

The left diagram shows $\max W_t^{(1)}\,(mc-uc)$ *and* $\max W_t^{(2)}\,(mc-uc)$ *as a function of time to maturity* $T-t$. *The right diagram is the corresponding diagram of* $\max W_t^{(1)}\,(mc-uc)$ *and* $\max W_t^{(2)}\,(mc-uc)$ *as a percentage of the convertible bond value* $W_t\left(V_t^-, r_t, 0, k_t^*\right)(uc)$ *under the unrestricted conversion. The parameter values are* $n=100$, $m=100$, $K_t=0$, $F=100$, $FD=50{,}000$, $c=5$, $\delta=0.03$, $T=t_{N+1}=N$, $TD=N+1$, $t=t_1=0$, $t_i=i-1$, $r_0=0.05$, $\sigma=0.5$, $\eta=0.01097$, $\rho=-0.1$, $\kappa=0.16643$, $\theta=0.0639$.

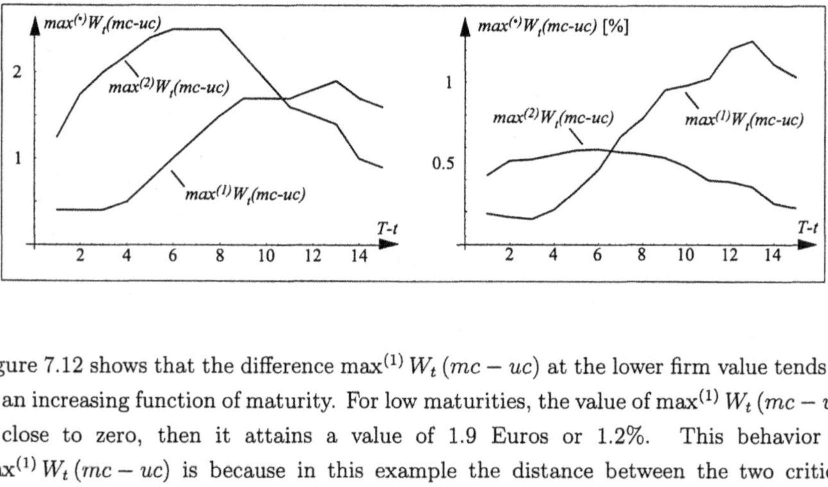

Figure 7.12 shows that the difference $\max^{(1)} W_t\,(mc-uc)$ at the lower firm value tends to be an increasing function of maturity. For low maturities, the value of $\max^{(1)} W_t\,(mc-uc)$ is close to zero, then it attains a value of 1.9 Euros or 1.2%. This behavior of $\max^{(1)} W_t\,(mc-uc)$ is because in this example the distance between the two critical values $\underline{V}_t\,(0)\,(uc)$ and $\underline{V}_t\,(0)\,(mc)$ increases over time. A high distance indicates that the conversion strategy in the monopolistic case is especially different from that in the unrestricted case. Since a higher difference of the optimal conversion volumes suggests a higher value of $\max^{(1)} W_t\,(mc-uc)$, the difference nearly increases with time to maturity $T-t$. In the special case without a coupon payment, the critical firm values for an infinitely long time to maturity are zero and the difference is also zero.

The difference between the *stock values* $\max S_t\,(uc-bc)$ in the unrestricted and the block case is identical with $\max W_t\,(uc-bc)$. The reason is that the value of a convertible bond is equal to that of a stock for both conversion variants at $\overline{V}_t\,(bc)$. Therefore,

$\max S_t\,(uc - bc)$ like $\max W_t\,(uc - bc)$ increases first with $T - t$ and then declines.

Figure 7.13: Differences between the Stock Values under Block and Unrestricted Conversion over Time to Maturity

The left diagram shows $\max S_t\,(uc - bc)$ *and* $\min S_t\,(uc - bc)$ *as a function of time to maturity* $T - t$. *The right diagram is the corresponding diagram of* $\max S_t\,(uc - bc)$ *and* $\min S_t\,(uc - bc)$ *as a percentage of the stock value* $S_t\left(V_t^-, r_t, 0, k_t^*\right)(uc)$ *under the unrestricted conversion. The parameter values are* $n = 100$, $m = 100$, $K_t = 0$, $F = 100$, $FD = 50{,}000$, $c = 5$, $\delta = 0.03$, $T = t_{N+1} = N$, $TD = N + 1$, $t = t_1 = 0$, $t_i = i - 1$, $r_0 = 0.05$, $\sigma = 0.5$, $\eta = 0.01097$, $\rho = -0.1$, $\kappa = 0.16643$, $\theta = 0.0639$.

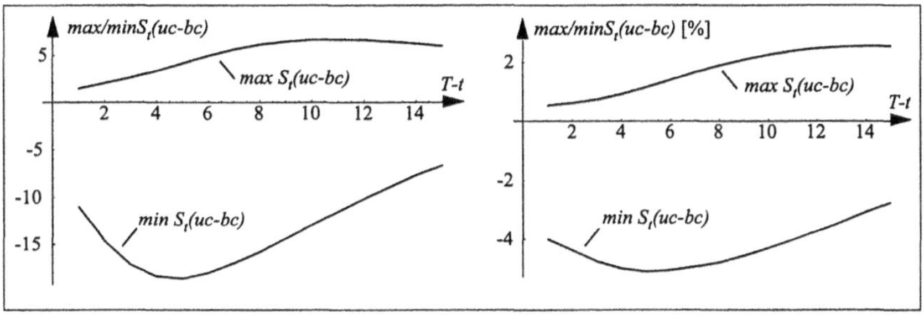

The stock value difference $\min S_t\,(uc - bc)$ before the drop in the block case is a negative function that decreases to a local minimum and then approaches zero when $T - t$ rises. We can see in figure 7.13 that the size of the difference of $\min S_t\,(uc - bc)$ is remarkable. It is more than four percent for maturities up to ten years with a value of 18 Euros or 5.1% at $T - t = 6$. Therefore, the absolute size of $\min S_t\,(uc - bc)$ is about twice as high as $\max S_t\,(uc - bc)$. Since the focus of the different conversion variants is the convertible bond value rather than the stock value, the three optimal strategies can result in higher differences for the stock values than for the convertible bond values.

The reason why $\min S_t\,(uc - bc)$ decreases first is due to the fact that this negative difference is shifted to the preceding conversion date and the deviating optimal conversion volumes in the unrestricted and block case result in an even lower difference. Then, for high maturities $T - t$, the debt value diminishes and therefore $\min S_t\,(uc - bc)$ approaches zero as in the case without debt.

We note that the distance between $\max S_t\,(uc - bc)$ and $\min S_t\,(uc - bc)$ indicates the magnitude of the jump of the stock value in the block case. The magnitude of the jump can be high and lies at 23 Euros or 6.5% at $T - t = 6$. Again, for high $T - t$, the magnitude of the jump approaches zero, because without debt the stock value exhibits no jump.

Figure 7.14: Differences between the Stock Values under Block and Monopolistic Conversion over Time to Maturity

The left diagram shows $\max S_t\,(mc - bc)$ *and* $\min S_t\,(mc - bc)$ *as a function of time to maturity* $T - t$. *The right diagram is the corresponding diagram of* $\max S_t\,(mc - bc)$ *and* $\min S_t\,(mc - bc)$ *as a percentage of the stock value* $S_t\left(V_t^-, r_t, 0, k_t^*\right)(mc)$ *under the monopolistic conversion. The parameter values are* $n = 100$, $m = 100$, $K_t = 0$, $F = 100$, $FD = 50{,}000$, $c = 5$, $\delta = 0.03$, $T = t_{N+1} = N$, $TD = N + 1$, $t = t_1 = 0$, $t_i = i - 1$, $r_0 = 0.05$, $\sigma = 0.5$, $\eta = 0.01097$, $\rho = -0.1$, $\kappa = 0.16643$, $\theta = 0.0639$.

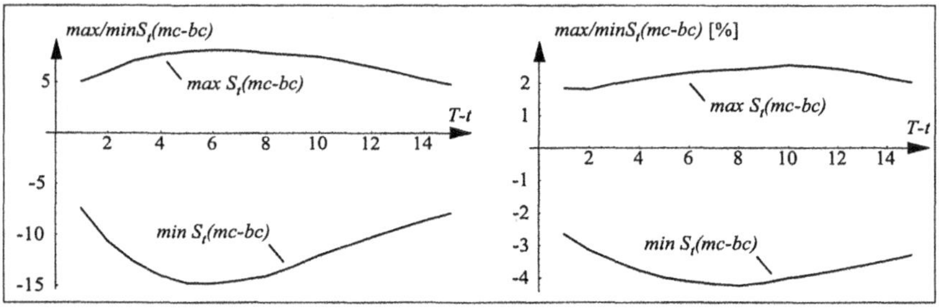

The behavior of $\max S_t\,(mc - bc)$ and $\min S_t\,(mc - bc)$ over time is similar to that of $\max S_t\,(uc - bc)$ and $\min S_t\,(uc - bc)$. According to figure 7.14, $\max S_t\,(mc - bc)$ and $\min S_t\,(mc - bc)$ are slightly higher. The reason is that the stock value in the monopolistic case at $\overline{V}_t\,(bc)$ for these maturities is higher than in the unrestricted case. This effect is because the monopolist, who has certain stock holdings after a conversion follows a strategy that hurts the debt holders rather than the stockholders compared to the unrestricted case. For large maturities, both $\max S_t\,(mc - bc)$ and $\min S_t\,(mc - bc)$ tend to the same limit, because the magnitude of the stock value drop in the block case approaches zero. In some cases, the stock value for large maturities in the monopolistic case is lower than in the block and unrestricted case such that the limits of $\max S_t\,(mc - bc)$ and $\min S_t\,(mc - bc)$ are strictly negative. This effect occurs if the monopolist can follow a more favorable strategy than the unrestricted conversion.

The difference $\max S_t\,(mc - uc)$ between the stock values in the monopolistic and the unrestricted case behaves qualitatively like the corresponding difference $\max W_t^{(2)}\,(mc - bc)$ of convertible bond values, because these two quantities only exist if the firm has additional debt outstanding; without additional debt the stock value under unrestricted conversion exceeds that under monopolistic conversion. Due to this analogy, $\max S_t\,(mc - uc)$ increases first and then declines with $T - t$. However, the stock value differences are greater than those of the convertible bond values. They are above one percent for all maturities

Figure 7.15: Differences between the Stock Values under Unrestricted and Monopolistic Conversion over Time to Maturity

The left diagram shows $\max S_t\,(mc-uc)$ *and* $\min S_t\,(mc-uc)$ *as a function of time to maturity* $T-t$. *The right diagram is the corresponding diagram of* $\max S_t\,(mc-uc)$ *and* $\min S_t\,(mc-uc)$ *as a percentage of the stock value* $S_t\,(V_t^-, r_t, 0, k_t^*)\,(mc)$ *under the unrestricted conversion. The parameter values are* $n=100$, $m=100$, $K_t=0$, $F=100$, $FD=50,000$; $c=5$, $\delta=0.03$, $T=t_{N+1}=N$, $TD=N+1$, $t=t_1=0$, $t_i=i-1$, $r_0=0.05$, $\sigma=0.5$, $\eta=0.01097$, $\rho=-0.1$, $\kappa=0.16643$, $\theta=0.0639$.

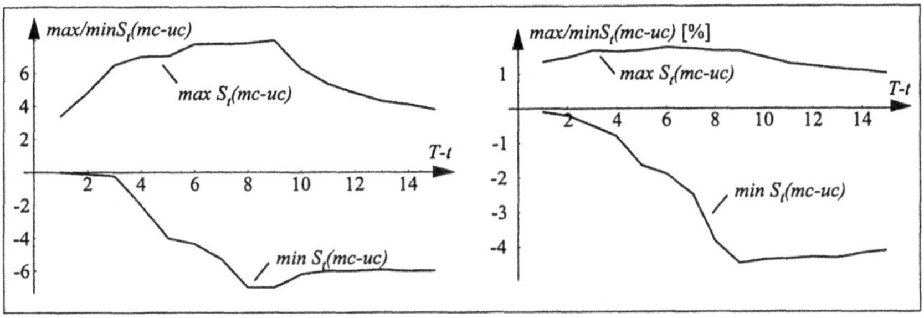

up to 15 years and have a maximum of eight Euros or 1.3% at $T-t=6$. For this maturity, the convertible bond difference is about half as high. Again, the reason for this shape is that the conversion volume in the monopolistic case initially lies below the one in the unrestricted case and the distance becomes stronger with $T-t$. Therefore, the stock value under monopolistic conversion benefits from the lower wealth transfer to the debt holders. When $T-t$ becomes huge, $\max S_t\,(mc-uc)$ diminishes because for a debt value equal to zero, the stock value cannot be higher under monopolistic conversion.

The other difference $\min S_t\,(mc-uc)$ tends to be a negative function of maturity that decreases first. According to figure 7.15, $\min S_t\,(mc-uc)$ can attain remarkable differences of up to -6 Euros or -4%. This shape occurs because in this example the distance between the two critical firm values $\underline{V}_t\,(0)\,(mc)$ and $\underline{V}_t\,(0)\,(uc)$ nearly increases with maturity which indicates that the optimal conversion volume in the monopolistic case exceeds that in the unrestricted case more sharply the higher the maturity. In several cases for $T-t\rightarrow\infty$, $\min S_t\,(mc-uc)$ has a negative limit. However, for $c=0$, the difference $\min S_t\,(mc-uc)$ tends to zero for $T-t\rightarrow\infty$, as $\max W_t\,(mc-uc)$ does.

Chapter 8

Conclusion

In this dissertation, we address two classical and closely related problems in corporate finance: the valuation of convertible bonds and the structure of optimal conversion strategies. In the literature convertible bonds are primarily considered as a portfolio of a straight bond and an American call option with the firm value as the underlying. Its arbitrage-free value is determined under the assumption of a block conversion, i.e. all convertible bond holders convert all their bonds simultaneously. Technically, the valuation problem is solved as a free boundary problem with a high contact condition where applicable.

Contrary to this literature, we follow Constantinides (1984), Emanuel (1983), and Spatt/Sterbenz (1988) and address the strategic character of the conversion problem. For this purpose, we not only consider block conversion but also allow for unrestricted conversion, which corresponds to perfect competition among the convertible bond holders, and monopolistic conversion, which is the strategy of one investor who holds all the outstanding convertible bonds. We extend the literature by allowing that the firm has issued not only stocks and convertible bonds but additionally ordinary debt. This extension has the important effect that a conversion results in a wealth transfer from the stockholders to the holders of the additional debt and convertible bonds.

These results are derived in a model framework in which trading takes place on continuous, complete, and frictionless markets without any information asymmetries. The evolution of the value of the considered firm follows a geometric Brownian motion, and the dynamics of the short rate are governed by a Vasicek process. The characteristics of the convertible bonds are chosen with regard to consistence to those traded in the German market. As a consequence of these characteristics, it is sufficient to assume a discrete set of conversion dates, namely the coupon dates plus a last one at maturity of the convertible bonds.

As a result of the consideration of different conversion strategies in the presence of additional debt, we see that optimal conversion strategies in equilibrium and the related value of a convertible bond can differ considerably from those obtained under the option-theoretical assumption of block conversion.

The block conversion assumption is not consistent with an equilibrium strategy resulting from competitively or monopolistically held convertible bonds, because a sequential conversion can take place under unrestricted and monopolistic conversion in equilibrium. In the presence of additional debt, even at maturity of the convertible bond a partial conversion can occur in contrast to the block case.

If no prior conversion has occurred, the monopolist converts even for lower firm values than the investors under unrestricted conversion who themselves start to convert for lower firm values than in the block case.[1] On the other hand, a complete conversion occurs in the block case for lower firm values than a complete unrestricted conversion and a complete unrestricted conversion takes place for lower firm values than in the monopolistic case.[2] The reason why the monopolist — at least for some firm values — converts less convertible bonds than the investors in the unrestricted case is to mitigate the wealth transfer to the debt holders. Without additional debt, the monopolist converts more bonds than under unrestricted conversion.[3]

The optimal conversion strategies for the different conversion variants result in a ranking for the convertible bond values when no prior conversion has occurred. The value of a convertible bond under monopolistic conversion is highest and lowest in the block case.[4] The maximum differences between the convertible bond values in the monopolistic and unrestricted case are about 1.2 percent and those between the unrestricted and the block case are 2.5 percent for the typical parameter set considered in this thesis. This result is a fundamental difference to that in the case without additional debt for which the convertible bond values under block and unrestricted conversion coincide.

The stock value under every particular conversion variant can be higher or lower than under a different conversion variant. As a consequence, corporate financing policies to prevent the monopolist from following non-block strategies, as proposed by Spatt/Sterbenz (1988), do not necessarily result in higher stock values. The reason is that the monopolist as a potential future stockholder might act in favor of the stockholders and at the cost

---

[1] This statement is consistent with all considered examples. However, the assertion concerning the unrestricted and block case could only be shown at the last premature conversion date, and the proof for the assertion concerning the monopolistic case requires no additional debt.

[2] The proof of this assertion at an arbitrary conversion date bases on the assumption that the optimal conversion volume in the unrestricted case increases in the firm value.

[3] We have proven this statement for the last premature conversion date.

[4] This property holds at an arbitrary point in time assuming that the optimal conversion volume in the unrestricted case increases with the firm value.

of the debt holders. However, these corporate policies, that force a block conversion to achieve a higher stock value than under the monopolistic strategy, are successful in the absence of additional debt.

The size of the differences between the stock values under the different conversion variants are even more striking and often approximately twice as high as the differences between the convertible bond values. The maximum stock value differences between monopolistic and unrestricted conversion and between unrestricted and block conversion are above four percent for the typical example in this thesis. Moreover, there is a puzzling property of the stock value concerning the block and monopolistic case. Under these two conversion variants, the stock value can decrease with the firm value in contrast to the convertible bond value and therefore a unique representation of the convertible bond value as a function of the stock value does not always exist. This non-uniqueness contrasts with the reduced-form models for the pricing of convertible bonds presented in section 2.3. These market based approaches, which use the stock value as the state variable, can only be consistent with our firm value model in two cases. Either conversions occur according to the unrestricted case, or a block conversion takes place but the considered firm does not have additional debt outstanding. However, these models are incapable of accounting for a monopolistic conversion.

These differences between the three conversion variants reveal that we cannot use the simpler block conversion to value convertible bonds in the unrestricted case if the debt value plays a distinct role. Only if the value of additional debt is neglectable or if the debt value is not sensitive for the conversion volume, i.e. the conversion decision hardly impacts the firm's probability of default, then the block conversion assumption can be justified for valuation purposes in the unrestricted case like in the case without debt. The monopolistic case is a special case that is not supposed to explain observable market prices when convertible bond holders act competitively but it rather demonstrates the potential value that can be achieved with the convertible bonds when the investors cooperate.

The results derived in this thesis leave room for extensions and further research. One natural but difficult extension is the oligopolistic case with its strategic interactions. Furthermore, we could allow for the convertible bond holders to have additional holdings of stocks or debt. In the unrestricted case, these additional holdings do not affect the conversion decision of a particular investor, because any investor cannot impact the values of the additionally held securities by her or his individual strategy. However, in the block and monopolistic case, a fundamentally different conversion strategy can be optimal if investors also account for the holdings of other securities. For example, in the block and monopolistic case, the optimal conversion volume is lower if the convertible bonds are held together with additional stocks, but it is higher if the convertible bonds are held with additional debt.

The wealth transfer between stock and debt holders, which is the core for many results in this thesis, is not only relevant for convertible bonds but also occurs in many other settings. We can apply the findings about the wealth transfer to examine e.g. the effects of a capital issue or the exercise of corporate warrants and employee stock options. Whenever a firm issues certain claims and changes its capital structure, a wealth transfer between the different groups of the former stakeholders must occur. However, the literature explains e.g. a drop of the stock value as a response to an equity increase by the result of a negative signal conveyed by the management to the market, even though wealth transfers are also in effect. Moreover, wealth transfers also play an important role for the determination of the optimal exercise strategies of corporate warrants or employee stock options. Although analogous arguments as presented in this thesis lead us to these strategies, the properties of the convertible bond strategies can deviate in certain aspects from those for corporate warrants or employee stock options.

Another possibility for further research is to check by an empirical study how good the equilibrium conversion strategies unrestricted or monopolistic conversion explain the real conversion behavior. We have seen in section 2.4 that the block conversion assumption is not suited to describe real conversions. However, to examine the empirical relevance of the two sophisticated strategies, unrestricted and monopolistic conversion, we might need a more extensive data set of empirical conversions than that used in section 2.4. As an alternative to these strategies, it is reasonable to regard certain frictions that the investors face to describe their conversion behavior. Similar as in Stanton (1995), who models the prepayment of mortgages, we can allow for heterogenous implicit and explicit transaction costs incurring with a conversion. As a result, the empirical conversion behavior can be described by a parametric model. Then, we can apply our firm value framework to determine convertible bond values resulting from the empirical conversion behavior, because our model is capable of accounting for such flexible conversion strategies.

Bibliography

[1] **Abhyankar, A., Dunning, A.,** 1999, "Wealth Effects of Convertible Bond and Convertible Preference Share Issues: An empirical Analysis of the UK Market," *Journal of Banking and Finance,* **23**, 1043–1065.

[2] **Ammann, M., Kind, A. H., Wilde, C.,** 2001, *The Pricing of Convertible Bonds,* Discussion Paper, University of St. Gallen.

[3] **Ammann, M., Kind, A. H., Wilde, C.,** 2003, "Are Convertible Bonds Underpriced? An Analysis of the French Market," *Journal of Banking and Finance,* **27**, 635–653.

[4] **Asquith, P.,** 1995, "Convertible Bonds are not called late," *Journal of Finance,* **50**, 1275–1289.

[5] **Asquith, P., Mullins jr., D. W.,** 1991, "Convertible Debt: Corporate Call Policy and Voluntary Conversion," *The Journal of Finance,* **46**, 1273–1289.

[6] **Bagella, M., Becchetti, L.,** 1998, "The optimal financing strategy of a high-tech firm: The role of warrants," *Journal of Economic Behavior and Organization,* **35**, 1–23.

[7] **Bank for International Settlements,** 2001, *The Changing Shape of Fixed Income Markets,* BIS Working Paper No. 104, Basel, Switzerland.

[8] **Bascha, A.,** 1998, *Venture Capital, Convertible Securities und die Durchsetzung optimaler Exitregeln,* Discussion Paper, Discussion Contribution No. 147, Eberhard-Karls-University Tübingen.

[9] **Bascha, A., Walz, U.,** 2000, "Hybride Finanzierungsinstrumente als Anreiz- und Kontrollmechanismen bei Venture Capital," *Finanzbetrieb,* **2**, 410–418.

[10] **Bascha, A., Walz, U.,** 2001, "Convertible Securities and optimal Exit Decisions in Venture Vapital Finance," *Journal of Corporate Finance,* **7**, 285–306.

[11] **Baskin, J.**, 1989, "An Empirical Investigation of the Pecking Order Hypothesis," *Financial Management,* **19**, 26–35.

[12] **Baxter, M., Rennie, A.**, 1996, *Financial Calculus*, Cambridge University Press, Cambridge.

[13] **Bechmann, K.**, 2000, "The Difference Between Out-Of-The-Money and In-The-Money Convertible Bond Calls," Working Paper, Copenhagen Business School.

[14] **Bell, M. G.**, 2000, *Venture Capital-Finanzierung durch Wandelpapiere: Eine theoriegeleitete Analyse*, Dissertation, Paderborn.

[15] **Bhabra, H. S., Lee, Y. W., Patel, A.**, 1997, "An empirical Examination of Calls of Convertible Bonds when they are out of the money," *Advances in Financial Planning and Forecasting,* **7**, 83–105.

[16] **Bhabra, H. S., Patel, A.**, 1996, "Convertible Bond Financing: Are Some Issuers Mimickers?," *Financial Management,* **25**, 67–77.

[17] **Billingsley, R. S., Smith, D. M.**, 1996, "Why do Firms issue Convertible Debt," *Financial Management,* **25**, 93–99.

[18] **Black, F., Cox, J. C.**, 1976, "Valuing Corporate Securities: Some Effects of Bond Indenture Provisions," *Journal of Finance,* **31**, 351–367.

[19] **Black, F., Scholes, M.**, 1973, "The Pricing of Options and Corporate Liabilities," *Journal of Political Economy,* **81**, 637–654.

[20] **Blonski, M.**, 1999, "Anonymous Games with Binary Actions," *Games and Economic Behavior,* **28**, 171–180.

[21] **Bohn, A.**, 2001, *Bewertung von Wandelanleihen*, Dissertation, Augsburg.

[22] **Brennan, M.J., Her, C.**, 1995, *Convertible Bonds: Test of a financial signalling model*, Working Paper, University of California, Los Angeles.

[23] **Brennan, M. J., Kraus, M.**, 1987, "Efficient Financing under Asymmetric Information," *Journal of Finance,* **42**, 1225–1243.

[24] **Brennan, M. J., Schwartz, E. S.**, 1977, "Convertible Bonds: Valuation and optimal Strategies for Call and Conversion," *Journal of Finance,* **32**, 1699–1715.

[25] **Brennan, M. J., Schwartz, E. S.**, 1980, "Analyzing Convertible Bonds," *Journal of Financial and Quantitative Analysis,* **15**, 907–929.

[26] **Brennan, M. J., Schwartz, E. S.**, 1988, "The Case for Convertibles," *Journal of Applied Corporate Finance,* **1**, 55–64.

[27] **Brigham, E. F.**, 1966, "An Analysis of Convertible Debentures: Theory and some empirical Evidence," *Journal of Finance,* **21**, 35–54.

[28] **Broman, K. L.**, 1963, "The Use of Convertible Subordinated Debentures by Industrial Firms 1949-59," *Quarterly Review of Economics and Business,* **3**, 65–75.

[29] **Bühler, W., Göppl, H., Möller, H. P.**, 1993, "Die deutsche Finanzdatenbank (DFDB)," *Zeitschrift für betriebswirtschaftliche Forschung: Sonderheft,* **31**, 287–331.

[30] **Bühler, W., Koziol, C.**, 2001, "Analyse optimaler Wandlungsstrategien," Working Paper, Mannheim University.

[31] **Bühler, W., Koziol, C.**, 2002, "Valuation of Convertible Bonds with Sequential Conversion," *Schmalenbach Business Review,* **54**, 302–334.

[32] **Butler, A. W.**, 2002, "Revisiting Optimal Call Policy for Convertibles," *Financial Analysts Journal,* **58**, 50–55.

[33] **Byrd, A. K., Moore, W. T.**, 1994, "Valuation Effects of Convertible Security Calls: An Update," *Quarterly Journal of Business and Economics,* **33**, 26–40.

[34] **Byrd, A. K., Moore, W.T.**, 1996, "On the Information Content of Calls of Convertible Securities," *The Journal of Business,* **69**, 89–101.

[35] **Calamos, J. P.**, 1998, *Convertible Securities: The latest Instruments, Portfolio Strategies, and Valuation Analysis*, McGraw-Hill, New York.

[36] **Carayannopoulos, P.**, 1996, "Valuing Convertible Bonds Under the Assumption of Stochastic Interest Rates: An Empirical Investigation," *Quarterly Journal of Business and Economics,* **35**, 17–31.

[37] **Chesney, M., Gibson-Asner, R.**, 2001, "Reducing Asset Substitution with Warrant and Convertible Debt Issues,", *Journal of Derivatives,* **8**, 75–87.

[38] **Constantinides, G. M.**, 1984, "Warrant Exercise and Bond Conversion in Competitive Markets," *Journal of Financial Economics,* **13**, 371–397.

[39] **Constantinides, G. M., Grundy, B. D.**, 1987, "Call and Conversion of Convertible Corporate Bonds: Theory and Evidence," Working Paper, University of Chicago.

[40] **Constantinides, G. M., Grundy, B. D.**, 1989, "Optimal Investment with Stock Repurchase and Financing as Signals," *Review of Financial Studies,* **2**, 445–465.

[41] **Constantinides, G. M., Rosenthal, R. W.**, 1984, "Strategic Analysis of the Competitive Exercise of Certain Financial Options," *Journal of Economic Theory,* **32**, 128–138.

[42] **Dann, L. Y., Mikkelson, W. H.**, 1984, "Convertible Debt Issuance, Capital Structure Change and Financing-Related Information: Some New Evidence," *Journal of Financial Economics,* **13**, 157–186.

[43] **Datta, S., Iskandar-Datta, M.**, 1996, "New Evidence on the Valuation Effects of Convertible Bond Calls," *Journal of Financial and Quantitative Analysis,* **31**, 295–307.

[44] **Davidson, W. N., Glascock, J. L., Schwarz, V.**, 1995, "Signaling with Convertible Debt," *The Journal of Financial and Quantitative Analysis,* **30**, 425–440.

[45] **D' Souza, P.**, 2000, "Convertible Securities as a Revelation Mechanism and Incentive Scheme in Venture Capital Finance," Working Paper, University of Munich.

[46] **Duffie, D., Singleton, K. J.**, 1999, "Modeling Term Structures of Defaultable Bonds," *The Review of Financial Studies,* **12**, 687–720.

[47] **Dunn, K. B., Eades, K. M.**, 1989, "Voluntary Conversion of Convertible Securities and the optimal Call Strategy," *Journal of Financial Economics,* **23**, 273–301.

[48] **Eckbo, B. E.**, 1986, "Valuation Effects of Corporate Debt Offerings," *Journal of Financial Economics,* **15**, 119–151.

[49] **Ederington, L. H., Goh, J. C.**, 2001, "Is a Convertible Bond Call Really Bad News?," *Journal of Business,* **74**, 459–475.

[50] **Emanuel, D. C.**, 1983, "Warrant Valuation and Exercise Strategy," *Journal of Financial Economics,* **12**, 211–235.

[51] **Fabozzi, F. J., Pollack, I. M.**, 1987, *The Handbook of Fixed Income Securities (2nd ed.)*, Dow Jones-Irwin, Homewood.

[52] **Fan, H., Sundaresan, S. M.**, 2000, "Debt valuation, Strategic debt service and optimal dividend policy," *Review of Financial Studies,* **13**, 1057–1099.

[53] **Fields, L. P., Mais, E. L.**, 1991, "The Valuation Effects of Private Placements of Convertible Debt," *Journal of Finance,* **46**, 1925–1932.

[54] **Fischer, E. O., Zechner, J.**, 1990, "Die Lösung des Risikoanreizproblems durch Ausgabe von Optionsanleihen," *Zeitschrift für betriebswirtschaftliche Forschung,* **42**, 334–342.

[55] **Gebhardt, G.**, 2002, "Announcement Effects of Financing Decisions by German Companies: Synthesis of an Empirical Research Program," *German Financial Markets and Institutions: Selected Studies – Schmalenbach Business Review, Special Edition,* **1**, 107–134.

[56] **Geske, R.**, 1977, "The Valuation of Corporate Liabilities as Compound Options," *Journal of Financial and Quantitative Analysis,* **12**, 143–153.

[57] **Goldman Sachs,** 1994, "Valuing Convertible Bonds as Derivatives," Quantitative Strategies Research Notes, Goldmann Sachs.

[58] **Gompers, P. A.**, 1997, "Ownership and Control in Entrepreneurial Firms: An Examination of Convertible Securities in Venture Capital Investment," Working Paper, Harvard Business School.

[59] **Green, R. C.**, 1984, "Investment Incentives, Debt, and Warrants," *Journal of Financial Economics,* **13**, 115–136.

[60] **Harris, M., Raviv, A.**, 1985, "A Sequential Signalling Model of Convertible Debt Call Policy," *Journal of Finance,* **40**, 1263–1281.

[61] **Herzog, H.**, 1992, "Aktienpreiseffekte von Options- und Wandelanleihensemissionen schweizerischer Gesellschaften," *Finanzmarkt und Portfolio Management,* **6**, 303–316.

[62] **Heubel, G.**, 1983, *Das Problem der Konversion von Wandelschuldverschreibungen aus der Sicht des Emittenten und des Anlegers*, Dissertation, Hamburg.

[63] **Hung, M. W., Wang, J. Y.**, 2002, "Pricing Convertible Bonds Subject to Default Risk,", *Journal of Derivatives,* **10**, 39–52.

[64] **Ingersoll, J. E.**, 1977a, "A Contingent-Claims Valuation of Convertible Securities," *Journal of Financial Economics,* **4**, 289–322.

[65] **Ingersoll, J. E.**, 1977b, "An Examination of Corporate Call Policies on Convertible Securities," *Journal of Finance,* **32**, 463–478.

[66] **Isagawa, N.**, 2000, "Convertible debt: An effective financial instrument to control managerial opportunism," *Review of Financial Economics,* **9**, 15–26.

[67] **Jalan, P., Barone-Adesi, G.**, 1995, "Equity financing and corporate convertible bond policy," *Journal of Banking and Finance,* **19**, 187–206.

[68] **Jensen, M. C., Meckling, W. H.**, 1976, "Theory of the Firm: Managerial Behavior, Agency Costs and Ownership Structure," *Journal of Financial Economics,* **3**, 305–360.

[69] **Kim, J., Ramaswamy, K., Sundaresan, S.**, 1993, "Does default Risk in Coupons affect the Valuation of Corporate Bonds? A contingent Claims Model," *Financial Management,* **22**, 117–131.

[70] **Kim, Y. C., Stulz, R. M.**, 1992, "Is There a Global Market for Convertible Bonds?," *The Journal of Business,* **65**, 75–91.

[71] **Kim, Y. O.**, 1990, "Informative Conversion Ratios: A Signalling Approach," *The Journal of Financial and Quantitative Analysis,* **25**, 229–243.

[72] **Kim, Y. O., Kallberg, J.**, 1998, "Convertible Calls and Corporate Taxes under Asymetric Information," *Journal of Banking and Finance,* **22**, 19–40.

[73] **King, R. D.**, 1986, "Convertible Bond Valuation: An Empirical Test," *The Journal of Financial Research,* **9**, 53–69.

[74] **King, R. D., Mauer, D. C.**, 2000, "Corporate Call Policy for Nonconvertible Bonds," *Journal of Business,* **73**, 403–444.

[75] **Koziol, C.**, 2002, "Optimal Exercise Strategies of Corporate Warrants: Block Exercise vs. Unrestricted Exercise," Working Paper, Mannheim University.

[76] **Koziol, C., Sauerbier, P.**, 2002, "Valuation of Bond Illiquidity: An Option-Theoretical Approach," Working Paper, Mannheim University.

[77] **Koziol, C., Sauerbier, P.**, 2003, "Pflichtwandelanleihen: Einsatzmotive, Aktienkursreaktion und Bewertung," Working Paper, Mannheim University.

[78] **Kruschwitz, L., Schöbel, R.**, 1985, "Die Bewertung von Options- und Wandelanleihen mit Hilfe der Optionspreistheorie," Technical University of Berlin, Discussion Paper 92.

[79] **Kwok, Y. K., Wu, L.**, 2000, "Effects of Callable Feature on Early Exercise Policy," *Review of Derivatives Research,* **4**, 189–211.

[80] **Leland, H.**, 1994, "Corporate Debt Value, Bond Covenants, and optimal Capital Structure," *Journal of Finance,* **49**, 1213–1252.

[81] **Leland, H.**, 1998, "Agency Costs, Risk Management, and Capital Structure," *Journal of Finance,* **53**, 1213–1243.

[82] **Leland, H., Toft, K. B.**, 1996, "Optimal Capital Structure, endogenous Bankruptcy, and the Term Structure of Credit Spreads," *Journal of Finance,* **51**, 987–1019.

[83] **Lewis, C. M., Rogalski, R. J., Seward, J. K.**, 1998a, "Agency Problems, Information Asymmetries, and Convertible Debt Security Design," *Journal of Financial Intermediation,* **7**, 32–59.

[84] **Lewis, C. M., Rogalski, R. J., Seward, J. K.**, 1998b, "Understanding the Design of Convertible Debt," *Journal of Applied Corporate Finance,* **11**, 45–53.

[85] **Lewis, C. M., Rogalski, R. J., Seward, J. K.**, 1999, "Is Convertible Debt a Substitute for Straight Debt or for Common Equity?," *Financial Management,* **28**, 5–27.

[86] **Lewis, C. M., Rogalski, R. J., Seward, J. K.**, 2002, "Risk Changes around Convertible Debt Offerings," *Journal of Corporate Finance,* **8**, 67–80.

[87] **Limratanamongkol, P.**, 1999, "Credit Risk and Liquidation Cost: Effects on Prices of Convertible Bonds, as well as Conversion and Call Strategies," Working Paper, Kenan-Flagler Business School, University of North Carolina.

[88] **Long, M. S., Sefcik, S. E.**, 1990, "Participation Financing: A Comparision of the Characteristics of Convertible Debt and Straight Bonds Issued in Conjunction with Warrants," *Financial Management,* **19**, 23–34.

[89] **Longstaff, F., Schwartz, E.**, 1995, "A simple Approach to valuing risky fixed and floating rate Debt," *Journal of Finance,* **50**, 789–819.

[90] **Mauer, D. C.**, 1993, "Optimal Bond Call Policies under Transaktion Costs," *The Journal of Financial Research,* **16**, 23–37.

[91] **Mayers, D.**, 1998, "Why Firms issue Convertible Bonds: The matching of financial and real Investment Options," *Journal of Financial Economics,* **47**, 83–102.

[92] **Mella-Barral, P.**, 1999, "The dynamics of default and debt reorganization," *Review of Financial Studies,* **12**, 535–578.

[93] **Merton, R. C.**, 1973, "Theory of Rational Option Pricing," *Bell Journal of Economics and Management Science,* **4**, 141–183.

[94] **Merton, R. C.,** 1974, "On the Pricing of Corporate Debt: The Risk Structure on Interest Rates," *Journal of Finance,* **29**, 449–470.

[95] **Mikkelson, W. H.,** 1981, "Convertible Calls and Security Returns," *Journal of Financial Economics,* **9**, 237–264.

[96] **Mikkelson, W. H., Partch, M. M.,** 1986, "Valuation Effects of Security Offerings and the Issuance Process," *Journal of Financial Economics,* **15**, 31–60.

[97] **Myers, S. C., Majluf, N. S.,** 1984, "Corporate Financing and Investment Decisions when Firms have Information that Investors do not have," *Journal of Financial Economics,* **13**, 187–221.

[98] **Nyborg, K. G.,** 1995, "Convertible Debt as delayed Equity: Forced versus voluntary Conversion ," *Journal of Financial Intermediation,* **4**, 358–395.

[99] **Nyborg, K. G.,** 1996, "The Use and Pricing of Convertible Bonds," *Applied Mathematical Finance,* **3**, 167–190.

[100] **Pilcher, C. J.,** 1955, *Raising Capital with Convertible Securities*, Ann Arbor, MI, University of Michigan Press.

[101] **Poensgen, O. H.,** 1965, "The Valuation of Convertible Bonds," *Industrial Management Review,* **7**, 77–93.

[102] **Reiß, A., Schöbel, R.,** 1999, "Die Bewertung von Options- und Wandelanleihen bei Konkursrisiko," *Wirtschaftswissenschaftliches Studium,* **28**, 131–135.

[103] **Ross, S. A., Westerfield, R. W.,** 1988, *Corporate Finance*, Times Mirror/Mosby College Publishing, St. Louis.

[104] **Ross, S. A., Westerfield, R. W., Jordan, B. D.,** 1991, *Fundamentals of Corporate Finance*, Irwin, Boston.

[105] **Schmeidler, D.,** 1973, "Equilibrium Points of Nonatomic Games," *Journal of Statistical Physics,* **7**, 295–300.

[106] **Schmidt, K. M.,** 2003, "Convertible Securities and Venture Capital Finance," *Journal of Finance,* **58**, 1139–1166.

[107] **Schmitt, A., Spaeter, S.,** 2001, *Improving the Prevention of Enviromental Risks with Convertible Bonds*, Working Paper, Universite de Lille.

[108] **Shimko, D. C., Tejima, N., van Deventer, D. R.,** 1993, "The Pricing of risky Debt when Interest Rates are stochastic," *Journal of Fixed Income,* **3**, 58–65.

[109] **Spatt, C. S., Sterbenz, F. P.**, 1988, "Warrant Exercise, Dividends, and Reinvestment Policy," *Journal of Finance,* **43**, 493–506.

[110] **Spatt, C. S., Sterbenz, F. P.**, 1993, "Incentive Conflicts, Bundling Claims, and the Interaction among Financial Claimants," *Journal of Finance,* **48**, 513–528.

[111] **Stanton, R.**, 1995, "Rational Prepayment and the Valuation of Mortgage-Backed Securities," *The Review of Financial Studies,* **8**, 677–708.

[112] **Stein, J.**, 1990, "Convertible Bonds as Backdoor Equity Financing," *Journal of Financial Economics,* **32**, 1525–1539.

[113] **Swoboda, P., Kamschal, M.**, 1979, "Die Bewertung deutscher Wandelanleihen und die Optimierung des Umwandlungstermins bei steigenden Zuzahlungen (unter Anwendung der Black-Scholes-Methode)," *Zeitschrift für betriebswirtschaftliche Forschung,* **43**, 295–321.

[114] **Takahashi, A., Kobayashi, T., Nakagawa, N.**, 2001, "Pricing Convertible Bonds with Default Risk," *Journal of Fixed Income,* **11**, 20–29.

[115] **Tsiveriotis, K., Fernandes, C.**, 1998, "Valuing Convertible Bonds with Credit Risk," *Journal of Fixed Income,* **8**, 95–102.

[116] **Uhrig-Homburg, M.**, 2001, *Fremdkapitalkosten, Bonitätsrisiken und optimale Kapitalstruktur*, Habilitation, Mannheim.

[117] **Uhlir, H.**, 1976, *Die Bewertung von Wandelanleihen – Modelle zur Prämienerklrung österreichischer Emissionen*, Wien.

[118] **Vasicek, O.**, 1977, "An Equilibrium Characterisation of the Term Structure," *Journal of Financial Economics,* **5**, 177–188.

[119] **Wachsmann, A.**, 2001, *Optimale Unternehmensfinanzierung*, Dissertation, Bielefeld.

[120] **Welcker, J.**, 1968a, *Wandelobligationen*, Dissertation, Bonn.

[121] **Welcker, J.**, 1968b, "Wandelobligationen," *Zeitschrift für betriebswirtschaftliche Forschung,* **20**, 798–838.

[122] **Wolf, O.**, 1999, "Wandelanleihen: Emissionsboom in Europa," *Die Bank,* **39**, 778–785.

[123] **Wolve, S., Daliakopoulos, S.**, 1999, "Equity Valuation Effects of the Issuance of Convertible Bonds: U.K. Evidence," *The Journal of Fixed Income,* **9**, 7–18.

[124] **Zhu, Y. I., Sun, Y.**, 1999, "The singularity-separating Method for two-factor Convertible Bonds," *Journal of Computational Finance,* **3**, 91–110.

Beiträge zur betriebswirtschaftlichen Forschung

Herausgegeben von

Prof. Dr. Sönke Albers, Kiel
Prof. Dr. Bernhard Pellens, Bochum
Prof. Dr. Dieter Sadowski, Trier
Prof. Dr. Martin Weber, Mannheim

Auswahl der erschienenen Bände:

Band 7 H. Albach
Wirtschaftlichkeitsrechnung bei unsicheren Erwartungen

Band 10 H. Hax
Vertikale Preisbindung in der Markenartikelindustrie

Band 14 D. Schneider
Die wirtschaftliche Nutzungsdauer von Anlagegütern

Band 40 B. Rudolph
Die Kreditgewährungsentscheidung der Banken

Band 43 A. Luhmer
Maschinelle Produktionsprozesse

Band 46 H. Simon
Preisstrategien für neue Produkte

Band 59 T. Hartmann-Wendels
Dividendenpolitik bei asymmetrischer Informationsverteilung

Band 61 R. Ewert
Rechnungslegung, Gläubigerschutz und Agencyprobleme

Band 65 W. Neus
Ökonomische Agency-Theorie und Kapitalgleichgewicht

Band 66 U. Backes-Gellner
Ökonomie der Hochschulforschung

Band 71 M. Steven
Produktion und Umweltschutz

Band 72 E. Terberger
Neo-institutionalistische Ansätze

Beiträge zur betriebswirtschaftlichen Forschung

Herausgegeben von

Prof. Dr. Sönke Albers, Kiel
Prof. Dr. Bernhard Pellens, Bochum
Prof. Dr. Dieter Sadowski, Trier
Prof. Dr. Martin Weber, Mannheim

Neuerscheinungen:

Band 95 H. Ernst
Erfolgsfaktoren neuer Produkte

Band 96 B. Pirchegger
Aktienkursabhängige Entlohnungssysteme und ihre Anreizwirkungen

Band 97 S. Neubauer
Multimarket Contact and Organizational Design

Band 98 T. Ehrmann
Restrukturierungszwänge und Unternehmenskontrolle

Band 99 M. J. Klumb
Organisationale Flexibilität und Marktstrukturen

Band 100 C. Watrin
Internationale Rechnungslegung und Regulierungstheorie

Band 101 S. Valcárcel
Theorie der Unternehmung und Corporate Governance

Band 102 D. Simons
Kosten und Nutzen von Aktienoptionsprogrammen

Band 103 A. Mohnen
Performancemessung und die Steuerung von Investitionsentscheidungen

Band 104 M. Spann
Virtuelle Börsen als Instrument zur Marktforschung

Band 105 P. Grundke
Modellierung und Bewertung von Kreditrisiken

Band 106 A. Walter
Technologietransfer zwischen Wissenschaft und Wirtschaft

Band 107 S. Gensler
Heterogenität in der Präferenzanalyse

Band 108 T. Pfeiffer
Corporate-Governance-Strukturen interner Märkte

Band 109 T. Mellewigt
Management von Strategischen Kooperationen

Band 110 C. Koziol
Valuation of Convertible Bonds when Investors Act Strategically

GPSR Compliance

The European Union's (EU) General Product Safety Regulation (GPSR) is a set of rules that requires consumer products to be safe and our obligations to ensure this.

If you have any concerns about our products, you can contact us on ProductSafety@springernature.com

In case Publisher is established outside the EU, the EU authorized representative is:

Springer Nature Customer Service Center GmbH
Europaplatz 3
69115 Heidelberg, Germany

Batch number: 10725993

Printed by Printforce, the Netherlands